# BEAR IT ALL

The Tanya Jean Story. An Inspiring
true story of Survival.

## Tanya Jean Steeves

**Williams House Publishing Inc**

*This book is dedicated to all of those who struggle with Narcissistic abuse.*

*Please know that you are not alone.*

*I was born to two parental parasites*
*They gave me a devil's fright*
*Got to watch their every move*
*Or trust me, you're bound to lose*

*Living a life of lies*
*Can't you see it in my eyes*
*Truths covered up are not an easy sell*
*In packaging straight from hell*

*In time, you will learn*
*Follow me, it's almost your turn*
*Promises of the moon and stars*
*Have left some lonely scars*

*This was my life it's true*
*And now, I'm telling you*
*For doing so makes me feel free*
*I will no longer bend the knee*

*You look but do you see*
*Are you looking at, or through me*
*Do you know that I am unwell*
*Your words make it so hard to tell*

*A push through your poison in a sharp turn*
*Has left in me a deep and dark ,lasting burn*

DW

# CONTENTS

# FOREWORD

I would like to make a special note of **Thanks** in this book, to all of the hardworking medical professionals out there, who give their *all* everyday!

Please know that your efforts and kindness are truly appreciated!

Love, Tanya Jean

# INTRODUCTION

Hello, it's me Tanya Jean and for most of my life, up until a few years ago, my past has followed me like a very dark shadow. It's the kind of dark shadow that usually only appears in nightmares.

My nightmares, however, were very real and very horrifying and I just wanted to run! I wanted to run far and very fast! But, there was no use, my dark shadows caught up to me at every turn.

This book tells my story, from my earliest childhood memories to the present day. My hope is that it will, in some way, be able to help those who have experienced, or are currently experiencing, similar situations or circumstances to the ones I have lived through.

This story is not for the faint of heart. So, if you can bring yourself to read it until the very end, maybe it can help you to save yourself, or someone that you love and care about, from the same torture and torment that I have endured.

I have always been an animal person. I have always felt a connection and found comfort in the presence of animals. Though it wasn't until recently, after doing a great deal of research, that I started to understand what this gift of mine really was. It was like I could hear them and understand how they felt or what they were trying to communicate.

It was with that in mind, some twenty-five years ago, when another "just for now job" fell through, that I decided to become a pet groomer. A perfect fit I thought. I would get to work with animals all day, everyday. What could be better for someone like me? I so loved working with the animals. Until one day, completely out of nowhere, I had a massive heart attack. It was the type of cardiac event commonly referred to as the "Widow maker". I had a 100% blockage and was in full cardiac arrest for approximately 35 minutes. I was forty-eight years old, at the time.

We were told by my medical team that less than 5% of individuals who experience an event such as mine survive. Add to that the "arm's length" list of complications that I had to overcome and it is truly a miracle that I am still here. It's a miracle that I am here and able to share my story with you. It is in writing this book that I find strength, comfort, healing and purpose. It has helped me to not feel so alone.

I thought my world was complicated before, and it was. However, it is amazing how an experience such as the one I am living, can change one's perspective in such a profound way. It certainly gave "complicated" a whole new meaning for me. This "arm's length" list of mine has opened up a whole new world for me. A world that I'm so looking forward to sharing with you.

Its been one hell of a journey! A journey I hope you will find interesting and enjoy following.

Maybe it will become something you would want to share with someone close to you. Or, maybe someone you know who is experiencing challenges and difficult times in their life, or with their own health. It is my hope that through sharing my experiences, we can help those who are struggling in their own life situation. Maybe they too, will come to see that they are not alone and that there is always hope... even in the darkest of times.

Please hear me when I say, you don't have to Bear It All... like I did.


With love,

Tanya Jean

# CHAPTER 1

*An Introduction to the Pack*

I was born into a pack of wolves. I was taught in the ways of the wolf, but never allowed into the den.

◆ ◆ ◆

My mother gave birth to me in the early morning hours of March 21, 1969, at the Moncton Hospital in New Brunswick, Canada. I was the second of two children born into a young struggling family. A new family for two young adult parents, little more than teenagers themselves, for whom life was about to take some challenging turns.

My father was a young and driven entrepreneur focusing on his business first and foremost. My mother was a young woman who tried to focus on her family, while juggling the responsibilities of two kids, a job and a mostly absentee husband. They were a typical baby boomer generation young family, who's first child's birthday is slightly less than nine months after their wedding anniversary. When I was born my mother told me, as soon as I was old enough to understand, that my father was too tired to come to the hospital to see me, that day. In fact, she told anyone and everyone who would listen. She told them all about just how difficult that was on and for her. She has told the story over and over again, which I think this may have set the tone for some of the upcoming challenges that I would have to face in my life time. I had two parents who clearly were not, nor would they ever be, the source of connection, strength or encouragement that I would hope for.

I did not realize until much later on how it was all truly going affect me, growing up. I didn't realize how difficult it was going to make my life and how much of it would leave a permanent stain, on what would later become a very sad and lonely childhood. Not to mention that how it contributed to a huge lack of self-esteem and self-doubt. Which has snowballed into a complete avalanche of twisted shit! I don't blame my young parents for being uneducated in the ways of supportive parenting. In fact, I'm sure they did what they thought was best. The fact remains, however, that what was best for them and what would have been best for me, seemed to be at polar opposite ends of the spectrum.

Let me paint a picture of who I saw my father to be. He was always busy. Busy, busy, busy. Or at least, those were the words that always came out of his mouth. It didn't matter who he was talking to, it was always the same. He was busy, busy. He was the best. He always had the best and, of course, his ways were the best. He was constantly wheeling and dealing, as the old saying goes. At absolutely anything that would make him another dollar. After all, as I saw it, that was his one true love, *money*. If he wasn't working at making a dollar, he was working on one of his many hobbies or socializing with people who could, in one way or another, potentially help him to get his next dollar. It was all part of his obsessive quest for success and becoming successful, as he saw it.

His parents, who had also become parents at a young age, lived in a home just down the road from the one I grew up in. It was there that they had four children, two girls and two boys. As their young family life presented many challenges, I believe they tried to carry on with the religious family examples that had been set for them, during their upbringing. The greater the challenges became, the more forcefully they enforced and imposed their religious beliefs and ways on their children. The greatest of those challenges came as the loss of my father's older brother. He was struck and killed by a large truck on the very road they lived on, right in front of their home. Unfortunately, my father was there and watching when this accident took place. I believe that when a person witnesses such a horrible event, it softens parts of their inner self and hardens their outer self. This tragedy was a defining moment for my father and the rest of his family. It was a moment that would have an everlasting negative effect for them all. I don't think that his parents ever found a way to cope with the tragic loss of their son, or a way to move forward in life, with their remaining children.

My father was four years older than my mother. Once he graduated from high school, he went to business college and played, what was then considered professional hockey, for the Prince Edward Island team. He was always quite an intelligent individual, especially with numbers. As it was told to me, a local business man took an interest in him and helped him get started in the world of business. I'm still not sure exactly what that meant or what type of help he was truly been given. But regardless, it seemed that he was on his way. All of which led to many endeavours. There was a car dealership, a junk yard, a construction business, a motel and likely many other businesses that I will probably never know about.

He started a maple sugar camp, where he produced and

marketed all natural maple products for many decades. He was a sports enthusiast and loved the outdoors. He also loved to drive stock cars, which he seemed to be quite good at. With all of these interests, he was "always busy". It was his truest statement. I think that back then, as well as at the time of this writing, he just needed to keep busy all of the time. I believe it was a way to quiet his demons, in an effort to keep them at bay. A conscience really can have a loud voice at times.

It seemed to me, that this approach to life left no time for sharing in my growth or interests. My birthday usually fell right in the middle of his sugar making work. So, it was very rare that I ever him on my birthday. Unless of course, I went to the camp to see him, after he had missed my party. When I was growing up, he was usually gone in the morning before I got up and he didn't come home until after I was in bed. If I did see him, it was because I heard him first. He liked to socialize and drink, a lot. He saw it as "networking" and a way to further his success. The problem with that, however, was that he and my mother would always argue and fight when he came home, thoroughly sauced. My mother was young and she didn't trust him. He was a real ladies' man and he liked to flirt, with anyone who would show him even the slightest bit of attention. She was always very suspicious of him because he did cheat on her when she was still in high school. A wonderful environment for an innocent and creative little girl to grow up in, don't you think?

My father *was* very successful overall. Or, at least that is what he would have us all believe. I'm really not sure anyone, besides him, knows or knew the real truth. He seemed to master anything he ever tried. Well at least that's the way it seemed. Appearance was everything in our home. You never, ever let anyone from the outside know or see what was really happening and the way things really were!

He had determination and drive. In my opinion, the only thing that he ever failed at was being a father to me. I'm not sure if it was that he couldn't relate to me or that he saw some of himself in me. Maybe the reflection he saw, when he looked at me, was a constant reminder of what was truly within him. Of course, me being a girl didn't really help things either. I tried to show him that I loved all of the same things he did, but it never seemed to matter. He rejected me at every turn. He used to call me "pussy cat" in my younger years. Oh wait, did I mention that he absolutely hated cats? In his opinion, it was my mother's responsibility to look after and raise me, the little girl. He did however show interest in my brother. The golden, name carrying boy. The boy who showed great promise as an athlete. He was intelligent, he got good grades and he had an aptitude for numbers. Just like his father. He portrayed the image of a perfect son, from a perfect family. The social elites embraced him instantly.

As I mentioned earlier, my father was a real ladies' man. The phone would ring at our house at all hours of the day and night. When someone picked it up, there would always be a slight pause and then the person on the other end would hang up, without saying a word. This was ongoing, for a very long time. My mother was convinced it was "another woman" and I believe she was right. In fact, I think there was probably several of them. Our phone number was changed more times than I can recall, because of this. I understand that people fall in and out of love. I think my parents loved each other but I don't think they were ever really "in love" with one another and there is a really big difference between the two.

They were married after finding out my mother was pregnant with my brother. My father came from a religious family and had to do what was expected of him, so they got married. Two years later, I came along, another mistake. Or at least, that's the way it was put to me.

When it came to the issue of "other women", my parents

talked, well they argued. Okay, they yelled about it, all the time and there were little ears that were always listening. I heard a lot, and a good portion of it was true. I'm sure this must sound like I'm dumping on my father and to some degree I am, but he deserves it. That said, he was only human and everyone makes mistakes. I believe he had a lot of issues that he never dealt with and it resulted in a never ending cycle of hurt and betrayal. He was a truly unhappy man. I used to see it in his eyes. I believe he had some regrets, but not enough to ever make him change his ways. The only thing my father loved more than himself, was his money. He was willing to protect it with all his might, until the bitter end. The one thing he didn't seem to realize was that you're brought into the world with nothing and you will leave it in the same manner. You can only leave your mark. It is sad to me that he has left so much hurt and torment in his wake.

He seemed to have a few close friends, a sister and a few nieces and nephews who appeared to care for him. But really, it was hard to know who was sincere and who wasn't. Remember in that world, appearance is everything. He eventually got re-married. To a woman who appeared to care. Exactly what she cared about, however, I'm not certain! She would have you believe that she is a good christian woman. However, the fact remains that she and my father were together for years before my parents got divorced. What some folks will do, "in the name of the Lord" never ceases to amaze me.

My father either got sloppy or finally just wanted someone to catch him, I'm still not sure which it was. One day, I received a call from a friend who worked at a local hotel in Moncton. She told me that she believed my father had checked in under a false name and that he just reversed his license plate numbers on the registration card. She felt positive that she had recognized both him and his handwriting. But, since it had been years since she had seen him, she asked if I would consider stopping by to confirm her suspicions. I agreed and said that I would be right over. Sure enough, it was him and his hand writing but I was unable to catch them in the room. I believe that he recognized my friend and had most likely moved on to another place.

Armed with this information, I confronted him. I told him that if he didn't tell my mother, I would. He denied it completely! Even with the documented proof, he denied it. So, of course he couldn't tell her because he maintained that he had done nothing wrong. As for me, I made the mistake of telling my Grandmother. My mother's mother, with whom I was very close. I was not looking forward to telling my mother and I just didn't have anyone else to confide in. As it turned out, she got to my mother before I did. I think that Grammy was trying to spare me the burden of delivering that kind of news. I was young and she believed that this information should not come from me. Now, years later, I agree. That type of family involvement was no place for a young daughter. Especially one who was considered a mistake child. Little did Grammy know however, that little tidbit of information barely scratched the surface of the things that I had been involved in. Things that I should never been involved in or exposed to. Remember now, appearance was everything, in our house!

As the story was told to me, my father met a young woman many years before, during his early high school years. She was quite a bit younger than him, but there was an instant attraction between them both. Because of her age, it would have been frowned upon (that's how they used to say "illegal", I guess) for either of them to act on their attraction and have any kind of relationship, at the time. Apparently, she used to go to the race track to watch my father race his stock car. She must have sat at the other end of the grand stands from where we, his family, were sitting. As the years passed, they continued to see each other at social functions, from time to time. Eventually, she got married and gave birth to a daughter. As more time passed, her marriage started to crumble and my parent's marriage had been rocky right from the start. Though I am not sure of all the particulars, one thing is certain, they found their way back to one another and started having an affair. It went on for years.

In fact, my father and his younger model bought a house together before he and my mother were separated. I remember my mother blocking her in the driveway of their new home with her vehicle so that she couldn't drive away, one time. The younger model chose the high road. Or, maybe it was the chicken path, I'm not sure which. At any rate, she decided to stay in the car, which was probably her safest bet. Honestly, as angry as my mother was, I probably would have stayed in the car too. She went on to scream and yell at them both, for some time and put on quite a display for all of their new neighbours to hear and see. What a lasting impression that must have made on their neighbourhood appearance.

Once again, I was right there in the middle of the whole ugly affair. The craziness between my parents, that I witnessed, heard and even got involved in at times, has left an imprint on my young mind which, at times, still haunts me today. It all led to some serious trust issues for me, especially with adults. After all, if your parents carry on like that, all other adults must be the same, right? My young mind determined that adults were not safe! "You can't trust them to look out for you.". "You will have to protect yourself.", I thought.

After the dust settled, my father and his new family all lived together in their happy little home, on their new street, in their happy little neighbourhood. From all appearances, he was more of a father to the younger model's daughter than he ever was to me. Which was something that I was sad about for a very long time. That said, I'm sure he was no picnic at their house either. However, the younger model would have never stood for the same type of abusive behaviour toward her daughter, that I received at his hands and I think he knew that. Maybe that was part of the attraction?

This was not the only story of adultery committed by my father, but it was the one that started the divorce ball rolling. Well, I guess maybe that was a result of my involvement. My mother seems content to allow me to believe that is how she feels about it, at least. I mean she put up with and allowed everything leading up to it. Why didn't or couldn't she tell someone or ask for help? Perhaps she just applied her "put up and shut up", "the pay off will be worth it" beliefs and approach to life to that as well. Maybe she was scared. Maybe she just couldn't or wouldn't see it. Or, maybe it was the old "he needs to have his fun, but at least I'll be looked after" mindset. Which she saw and heard from some of his friend's wives. I really don't know. Whatever it was, I just never saw the appeal!

There are several people who would say that my father was a great friend to them. They would say that he helped them through some of the most difficult times in their life. They would talk about how good he was to them. Well, maybe he was, to them. Or, maybe that is just how it appeared. At times, I used to wish that he had been there for me, but he wasn't. We fought all the time. His repeated critical and rejecting remarks eventually made me extremely angry and bitter. He and my mother arguing all the time really got to me. So, I started to fight back and tried to defend my mother. At least she was somewhat present in my life. Or, so I thought at the time. My father was then, and remained mostly a stranger to me. It was easier to be angry then it was to try and cope with feeling so hurt all the time. All the years of clearly being a disappointment to him and as a result being rejected, forced me to find a way to protect my young self. The tools I found most satisfying, in my broken state, were anger and rage.

I so desperately wanted a loving relationship with my father, but it never happened. Finally, all the years of begging and pleading for some positive attention turned into indifference. He simply wanted nothing to do with me, and eventually I wanted nothing to do with him. Even in planning a family vacation, he would usually include another family, or some friends. I think it was so he wouldn't have to be alone with us. I think the only one in our family that he really wanted to spend any time with, was my brother. His prized son! When we did go on a trip that was just our family, it was torture! My parents fought constantly and the trip was usually cut short. Or, he would just disappear for hours at a time. He was late for everything, if he ever showed up at all. I spent a great deal of my young life sitting around and waiting for him. Maybe that's why I am so strict when it comes to punctuality today.

I remember asking my father for help with my homework once. His reply was, "This is so simple. I can't believe you don't understand it!" He made it very clear, in that moment, just how stupid he thought I was. Which, I eventually started to believe. When I got to high school, I really struggled with low self-esteem issues. Wonder where that started?! Then suddenly, I met a young man. He was someone that both of my parents absolutely hated. "We have a keeper!" I thought. This brought forth even more disgust and disapproval for me and my choices, from my father. He made his disappointment very clear! He called me every bad name or thing he could think of in his drunken rage and he had quite a repertoire, when he got going. Wow, could he curse! I was kicked out of the house and disowned more times than I can recall. My new found relationship with this individual ended up being very abusive and very toxic! But, at the same time, it was very normal to me in the life that I had known up until that point.

The relationship elements that my young mind had recorded were lying, mistrust, yelling, fighting, violence and more yelling. Oh, and did I mention there was yelling? All the time!

It just never stopped. It was all just part of everyday life for me. The more my father showed his dislike for my newfound love, the more I wanted to keep him around. Not to mention that he showed, what seemed like, a genuine interest in me, at first. This was something that I longed for but had never known, up until that point. My relationship with my grandparents, my mother's parents, was the only relationship model that I had ever seen that, to me, seemed to work and they were old in my eyes. So, I guess I figured that this new relationship model and the things I saw and lived, were just the way things were done now. After all, that's the way my parents did it. That's what I saw and heard. That's what was normal to me. This "normal", nightmare of a relationship lasted for 6 very long years. But, I'll talk more about that later.

As I mentioned earlier, my father had his hands in many different business endeavours. At one point he bought a motel, which he had only planned to own, on paper, for a matter of hours. Well the deal fell apart and it turned into 12 long years. Eventually, my mother was talked into quitting her nursing job at the hospital to work at the motel. It was then expected that I too would help out, and so I started out by cleaning rooms. Sometime after that, I ended up managing the place for a little while, after they finally got divorced.

It was the last couple of years that he owned the place, before it was sold. I was just the right candidate then. When he had no one else to turn too. The motel was for sale for 12 years and I knew that one day, it would eventually sell and that I would be out of a job. When I graduated from high school he took every opportunity to remind me of this and pushed me to take some type of college program. I showed an interest in his construction business but he would not even entertain the thought of having me there. "That's hard work! It's no place for a girl." he said.

For as long as I can remember, I had a real knack for sketching.

I loved to draw, do crafts and make things. I also loved to sing and often thought I would love to learn how to play the guitar. Although I felt that my art and my creativity was where I truly excelled. I felt that I was good enough to maybe even pursue it as a career. So, I went to high school with the intention of working on my portfolio and going to art college after I graduated. However, once I got to high school things seem to get worse with my life at home. Though I really didn't think that was possible at the time, it seems that it was. My father just wanted to be as far away from my mother and I as he could get, and so the fighting got worse. I know you're thinking "how could it possibly?", well me too. I'm going to put it this way, they were both "over achievers" in the art of battle!

At that point, my brother had gone off to university and in doing so had escaped having to deal with all of the day to day craziness, as I struggled to find a way to cope with it all. (As I said day to day, but it was all day and all night.) It seemed that my father could see no promise, potential, or maybe no "return on investment", in encouraging me to pursue my passion of being an artist and really going for it. He was anything but encouraging and so eventually, I gave up. I knew that if he did not agree with it, there would not be any kind of help from them. "You do it my way or you're completely on your own". Up until this point in my life, I had been convinced, or should I say brainwashed into believing that my sole purpose in life was to care for and look after others. All others. Before myself. "How could I possibly do this all on my own?", I thought. There's just no way. I couldn't see the opportunities or the possibilities that were in front of me, then. Besides, if I was to go away to art college, who then would look after my mother? "She'll have no one to care for her and will be all alone." Those were my thoughts, or, maybe they were the thoughts that had been programmed in to me, at that time. As a result of it all, my portfolio was never finished.

In the days before I started going to high school, while my brother was still living at home, you could feel the tension that filled our house, from the sidewalk. As I am sure you might have guessed already, there were a number of household chores that I was responsible for. One of my chores was to always look after doing the dishes. Yes, by myself and yes, always. I was putting the dishes away while my brother and I were arguing about something. In an attempt to make a point, futile as it was, I slammed the drawer where the utensils were kept. This of course made a mess of and mixed up everything in the drawer. Now, you may be starting to get the idea, or have begun to form a picture, that my father was a controlling neat freak, to put it bluntly. He wanted things done his way period, or, believe me, there would be consequences. On this particular day, while my mother was working, he had come home early. I believe it might have even been on a weekend. At any rate, it was a rare occurrence, for sure. He came in the house and said that he was hungry. I told him that I had prepared some food and put the leftovers on a plate, in the fridge. He was drunk and when he opened the drawer to see the mess of cutlery and utensils all mixed up, it triggered his rage. He came flying down the hallway to my room, jumped on top of me, on my bed and started swinging. I will never forget how heavy he felt on top of me and how powerless I felt. After he finished hitting me and had rid himself of his rage and frustrations, he left the room. Unfortunately for me, this was not the first time that my young body and soul had endured the wrath of his rage. It was however, the first time that he got the upper hand. I waited until I heard him go downstairs and then I quietly went to my brother's room looking for some help. All my brother would say was that I should have known better. He was always out for himself and never got involved where I was concerned. I went back to my room, all bloody and with a black eye, crawled out the window and ran off to a friend's house. Where I stayed until I knew that my mother was home.

After graduating high school I moved in to a place with my boyfriend. You remember "the keeper" from earlier. Well you guessed it! It was against their wishes. I told them I wanted to take a year to think about my next move. The real reason I left was because things there were always just so tense and unpleasant. I had been living with this constant feeling of fear from a very young and innocent age and just wanted a break from it all. As time went on however, I could see that my mother was not dealing with things very well on her own. So I decided, or was convinced, I still can't decide which, that I should move back home. When it finally became clear that they were actually going to get a divorce, I moved back in. I thought what I was seeing, was that my mother was becoming drained, both mentally and physically, and needed my help. My father was making things completely unbearable when he was there. One night, we had a big blow up and I was kicked out and told to leave, again. I gladly went back to my boyfriend, for a short while. Just as long as it took for my mother to get her lawyer to get a court order to have my father legally removed from the house.

As he was moving out, I was moving back in. Can you just imagine the scene? Being damned to the bowels of hell by your "father", for trying to help and protect your mother. Young girl self-esteem building course 101 right there. Thanks "Dad"! I think he moved to his motel. Well, his stuff was there at least. Although, it was rare for him to actually spend the night there. Now, he was free to do all the *socializing* he wanted and had no one to bitch at him back home. I wonder if he was happy?

Okay, so that's my father! Let's introduce the rest of the pack now.

It's time that I describe to you how I saw my mother and the parts she played in this crazy story. My mother was the first of four girls. I think Grammy and Grampy gave up on having a boy after the fourth girl. They were kind people who enjoyed living a simple life. At times, I think that they struggled financially with raising four girls. My mother's father was a brilliant man. Even though formal schooling beyond the sixth grade was not for him, he could fix and/or build anything. He had very strong mechanical reasoning skills and brilliant natural problem abilities. He was a very kind man and had a big heart, which people would sometimes take advantage of when it came to getting paid for his services. As I'm sure you can imagine, at times, this could make it hard to make ends meet. He could fix or build anything, but a dollar would only stretch so far.

My grandmother was a nurse who worked very hard and loved her occupation. She definitely made for that line of work. She was well liked by all who had the pleasure to make her acquaintance. To this day, I still meet people who say that she was the most kind, hard working nurse they ever knew. Her love for her work really came through in the care she provided to her patients.

My mother found life to be a bit of struggle, as I think a lot of young women who grew up in her era, did. She grew up in a home with very modest means and six very healthy appetites. So, when a young and handsome, hardworking entrepreneur took an interest in her, when she was attending high school, she fell hard. She was a beautiful young woman but was self-conscience about her clothes and her appearance. I think that when she fell for my father, she saw an opportunity for a new and exciting life. Her leaving the nest would also help my grandparents financially, to some degree. Any doubts that she may have had about her relationship with my father, would have to be put aside when she realized that she was late and nine months later they had a baby boy. At that time and in that neighbourhood, or maybe I should say in that church, marriage was the only option. It was a choice that seemed to have been made for them. So, she moved out of her parents house and, as she often put it, into my father's house. In fact, at the time of this writing, she still resides there. She has never lived anywhere else.

After high school, she took a nursing course and started working at the Moncton Hospital. Where she worked until she could no longer keep up with working at both the hospital and the motel my father had bought. She said that my father had pushed her to quit her nursing career so she could work at the motel for him. It was a decision that she would later come to regret.

She felt that she was very close with her family. So much so, that they were basically her everything. She was shy but did have a few friends. Of course they were mostly the wives of my father's friends, so she never really felt any close connection with any of them. As a result, she poured everything into her family, it was all she knew. This of course, can make for a very unhealthy and unbalanced way of life, at times. She didn't have any hobbies to speak of. I'm not sure if it was a lack of interest or lack of time, as she saw it. Her whole life was based around her work and looking after her family.

As time went on in their relationship, my mother grew very suspicious of my father's whereabouts during his dealings and meetings. She grew more and more angry at the fact that he was never home. When he was home, there was usually a fight, or he just went to bed and paid no attention to her. She grew very tired of the endless list of excuses and him not spending time with her and their family. Eventually, she started to hear rumours of his extracurricular activities and managed to confirm her suspicions a couple of times. Or, so she thought. Of course, he would just flat out deny any involvement with anyone. He was very skilled at turning things around on her and would accuse her of being crazy and making up stories. Appearance is everything remember?

I think she was hopeful that if she just gave him more time, he would eventually get tired of his ways and see that our family was what he really wanted. That day never came, which made her very angry and very bitter. She felt like she had sacrificed so much and received nothing in return. There's the "return on investment" decision making platform again. Are you familiar with the concept?

She would antagonize him when he was home and so I think he just stayed away as much as possible. She was always picking fights and when she did, things would escalate quickly. They both needed to be right and they both needed to win, and sometimes things got physical. Really physical!

In her defence, I think she was frustrated and so very hurt. However, it all started to affect my brother and I, well me more so than him. He hated confrontation and worked hard to avoid it. I, on the other hand, would try to get in between them. This strained my relationship with them both, in different ways. My mother, still and to this day, claims that she does not have much, if any memory of these events. Her statement is always, "I must have blocked that out". She "blocked" that stuff out, but, she remembers every single material thing that she ever gave me? Maybe she did, in fact "block it out", I don't know. Perhaps it was a coping mechanism for her? Or, maybe it all had something to do with that "N" word, but we'll get into that a little later on.

In my eyes, my mother always showed favouritism toward my brother, her first born. She says that is not the case, but it sure felt that way to me. Actions speak louder than words, remember? To this day, any and all of his "words of wisdom" and advice are taken as gospel in her ears. I believe it is because she sees so much of what she could have had, through her window into his life and doesn't want that window to be closed. The resemblance between him and my father is uncanny. He reminds her of him, in everything he says and does. She would sometimes ask my opinion, though I'm still not sure why. She has never really listened to a word that I have said or trusted that my involvement could, somehow be of benefit to her. Even though, I was frequently be the one trying to get in between them, to help defend and protect her, when things got physical. Did I mention that things would often get physical? Oh yes, right I did tell you that. I'm sorry, being in a coma has made me forgetful at times. (More on that later. Stay tuned.) I always seemed to get way more than my share of the blame whenever something went wrong. I guess it was easy to blame me. After all, I was born and I was a girl. Maybe it was the strain of another child who was, how is it we say that in today's world? An unplanned surprise? Yes, that's it, an unplanned surprise. She knew my father didn't like me and I think, in part, she blamed me for some of their troubles. After all, if given the opportunity, she will still tell the story of how my father was too tired to come to the hospital and see me on the night I was born. She will tell her listeners all about how hurt she was and how much she cried. I wonder if it was as upsetting to experience it, as it has been to hear about it and watch her tell the story, to anyone who will listen, ever since? It seems that maybe it would be, to a second born, unplanned surprise, artistic girl, doesn't it? Oh wait, I know this one. Yep, it has been. It definitely has been!

Some days it seemed to me, that for my mother, I was to blame for all of her troubles. It felt like everything fell on, or was laid at my feet. It's like I was her only friend. I was the only thing she could control, in her life. Because that's what friends are for right? So, depending on what she wanted, or needed, I would be her friend, or her servant, or sometimes just someone else she had to look after. It seemed that she really didn't like for me to have any friends of my own. That would take away from the attention and time that I could give to her. Other than me, she mostly relied and depended on her parents and one sister. It was devastating for her when her marriage fell apart. Or, should I say erupted. Yes, I think erupted is a better description of what happened to her marriage. At times, I was not certain she would survive the experience. Any guesses on where I was to be found then? Yes, that is right. I was right back smack dab in the middle of the whole hot lava storm. I moved back home, again. I picked up some gloves, taped up my knuckles and got back in the ring. Over the years, she met and had some other companions and fumbled through trying to carry on living her life. Though I really don't think she will ever come to terms with, or get over, the loss of her one and only. Her first and only love. I'm just not sure exactly what it was about him that she loved so much?

I think the next most difficult thing she had to deal with was the death of my grandmother, her mother. This tragic loss left with it a tonne of obligation and responsibility for her. Obligation to and a sense of responsibility in helping her father. Helping him adjust and live life without his "Jean". He loved, adored and relied on her so completely. The process of working through all of this seemed to put a great deal of strain on her and her relationship with her closest sister. Their relationship certainly evolved, or maybe broke down would be a better term to use. As a result, her other best friend, her closest sister, pushed her away. Which seemed to be something that she could not understand. Then, or at any point since. It has added to her distrust and feelings of hurt. Her losing this close relationship with her sister seemed to put her on a one way express lane to clinging to a relationship with me. After all, I'm usually the one who is there when things go side ways. This focused clinging left a path of chaos and destruction through the state of my mental health like a tornado through a trailer park.

My mother has a habit of trying to hold onto her relationships so hard that she ends up smothering most people. I don't think she has ever really learned how to be in a normal relationship. To her it has to be all or nothing. Sometimes I wonder if she feels that she learned all she needed to learn about relationships on the playground. Though I don't know what it was like to be on the playgrounds she grew up on. Did she ever have an opportunity to learn? I really don't think so. As the years have gone and continue to go by, she has never gotten the professional help and support that she needed. She did go to see someone once, for one session, but said she did not care for the individual and that it didn't help anyway. I have even offered to go with her, on more than one occasion, but she refuses. Well, she sees no point to it. "She is fine!", she says. From all of this, I have learned, a most difficult lesson. You cannot help someone who does not want to be helped.

My brother, the first born. The one who could do no wrong in either of my parents eyes. The epitome of the "golden child", was mostly absent in my life. Now, I'm sure he had his challenges, being brought up by two narcissistic parents, both of whom were constantly competing for the "Alpha" position in their relationship. However, the thing is, I never saw him struggle, at all. Quite the opposite in fact. It seemed to me that my brother got everything he needed and/or ever wanted. He never had to do any chores except maybe mow the lawn, once in a while. That said, it was amazing to me just how quickly he figured out that if he complained about it, just long enough, he would be excused from having to do that too. The things he was given and the treatment he received from our parents was much different from what I received. Don't get me wrong, if I *needed* something, some "thing", they would provide it. Most days however, the unconditional, lovingly safe environment, filled with encouragement and positive energy store, was closed! Maybe if there had been Sunday shopping back then, I would have had better luck!

I could never really understand why he received such special treatment, until sometime in my twenties. It was then that I learned the definition of a narcissist. I also learned that they can travel in packs. Just like wolves. Unfortunately, for me at least, the treatment he received turned him into one too. He too, became a wolf. Through his observation of them, my parents taught my brother how to treat me, which was very poorly, in my opinion. Well it's not like he is going to say it, is he? He would constantly tease me, pick on me, physically abuse me and then push me away, whenever I went looking for some brotherly compassion.

As the years went on, his ego grew and his position in the pack advanced. My father's endless praise coupled with him being awarded a spot at the head of the family business table has really sharpened his pack skills. My brother feels very entitled and has made a lot of friends. Some of them may even still like him? I have found myself face to face with many of them over the years. Of course, the ones I met were all members of his ex-fan club. Some of them have even judged me before getting to know me, because of his behaviour. Guilt by association, I guess. My brother has never stuck up for me, quite the opposite, in fact. In the process, however, he helped to teach me a very valuable lesson. Which is that the only person you can *always* count on to stick up for you, is **you**! For that lesson, I am truly grateful! It has served me well and made me strong! Oh and by the way, *my* fan club has never lost a member! And we have regular meetings... lots of them.

I really couldn't say which one my parents spoiled him more. Maybe that too, was a competition between them. I was never able to find the sign up sheet for being the recipient for those competition spoils. Never saw it. I mean, I really should have found it, while I was fulfilling my servant duties. Well, they called them my chores. In any case, where was I? Oh yes, my brother. Stupid coma. (Keep reading, I'll get there.) He has always been very good at sports. Hockey, golf, wrestling, football, and later on, beer drinking, were some of his favourites. He was a typical jock. My parents sent him to university to get an education so that he could eventually take over the family construction business. The way I saw it, he never wanted for anything. I do remember that he got a part-time job at a fast food joint near our home once. Well, I'm not sure how many consecutive days of showing up it takes, to call it job now, but he had a uniform and a hair net for a little while. He hated it so much that he approached our father for a summer job, while he was completing his university education. Maybe he did hate having someone always telling him what to do. Now let me tell you, I could *relate* to **that!** But as far as I could tell, working for our father would not, in anyway, lessen the instances of having someone tell you what to do! That was his only job outside of the family business. Maybe all of the instruction from his father was bearable because he knew what the outcome was going to be, eventually. I guess he could see himself at the head of the table. A good way to sustain the life of ease and abundance that he had become accustomed too. He would be his own boss and do very well taking over a successfully established business. Or would he? I wonder if it really was mostly ease and abundance? It certainly does look like it from a distance. A far distance. Back. Waayyy back. Oh, but wait, appearance is everything in the world of abundance, isn't it?

Even though the business was well known, he still required assistance from our father and, on the odd occasion, from our mother too. It's amazing the things that you can come to know just by listening. I have always felt that my brother was very, what I like to call, book smart. His leadership skills and his ability to direct and motivate people may have lacked a little, however. Or, at least in the environment of the construction business he was to take over. It was always unclear to me how he aligned his priorities. They never seemed to line up with the patterns that were beat into me, both figuratively and physically. My brother had one failed marriage but managed to meet someone else with whom he is very happy. They make a lovely couple and have two boys. It seems that my brother has everything he ever wanted. A life of ease and abundance, a family with a big house on a hill, a successful business and so much more. I truly hope that he is happy with the path he chose.

I think that for a very long time, I grieved over not having a close sibling relationship in my life. I always felt that I had a lot to give and that I would be quite good at it. Being close with someone and sharing our happy and positive life experiences as we grew, in the wolf pack hunting grounds, together. Really, most of all, I just didn't want to be all alone. I could accept what our family was, I just didn't want to feel so alone all the time. I still don't completely understand why our parents would pit us against one another the way they did. It seems that we never really stood a chance. I really wish things had been different.

So that's a bit about the den I was brought home too. Think of this chapter as the marque sign on the front of the theatre. Want to see the rest of the film? Open the door and take another step inside, if you dare. Can you *bear* a little more? Can you *bear* to go on? It is going to get gruesome. It is okay though, I made it through. You're sure to be just fine.

# CHAPTER 2

## *First Living Nightmare*

From the very beginning, life for an innocent young soul, who was born into a family like mine was a struggle. It has been a long and twisted, pot hole filled, muddy, crappy, bumpy, rough road of a struggle. Some of my earliest childhood memories are of times that were like living in a real life horror film. Most of the time, it seemed like nightmares and dreams that maybe I would wake up from. I can remember waking up to my parents screaming at one another and asking myself, "Wait, am I awake?", "Is this a dream?". At times, I couldn't tell.. I can remember hearing slapping noises and furniture being thrown around. I can still hear my father yelling so loud that it would drown out my mother's cries for help. She was young and so desperate to have him change into the man she wanted. A family man who loved and cared about her more than anything. She wanted to be his one true love. She wanted to be the most important thing there was to him.

I remember one night, in particular, that I was woken up by my mother. She was sitting on the side of my bed, sobbing and crying. She told me that she was leaving and that I would have to stay behind. What? You're leaving? You're leaving me with him? Really?? I was devastated of course! My young mind could hardly grasp the concept. I was only 4 or 5 years old at the time and was not even in school yet. This was absolutely terrifying news and literally scared me to the point of feeling sick to my stomach. The mean man I knew as my Father was going to be my only parent now? How could this happen? Please wake. Please wake up, I thought... This can't be real? You can't leave me alone with him?? Please mother, don't leave me here??

I can still see it as plain as day. The room was black except for my mother's silhouette sitting on the edge of my bed rubbing my arm to wake me. My father was standing in the doorway leaning against the door casing. The room had just a slight bit of light coming through the curtains from the street light at the end of the driveway. The room felt cold to me, but not in the sense of temperature. It was a cold  and haunting feeling that chilled me to the bone. My face was soaked from my tears streaming uncontrollably. I was panicking!! I was never sure what I would wake up to when I went to bed! I was terrified all of the time!!

I begged her not to leave me or to take me with her. She said she couldn't. Then my father appeared in the doorway saying "You're not going anywhere!" He motioned to her to come out of the room as I jumped out of bed and ran to her side. Now, looking back, I realize that it was her way of getting his attention. As I clung to her and he dragged me back to my bed, he told me to go back to sleep and that she was not going anywhere. I kept getting out of bed that night and sneaking down the hall to check that she was still there. One time, I asked for glass of water. Then I told them I had to go to the bathroom. Anything my young mind could think of to keep my eye on her. How could I survive here without her, I thought? I didn't sleep a wink from that point on. Finally the sun came up, my father got up, got ready and went to work just as he always did. My mother acted like nothing had happened at all. How could this be, I thought??  My whole life has just been turned upside down and they just resumed regularly scheduled programming? Regularly scheduled programming for this dysfunctional family horror show I had been born into, that is.

Even as I write these words, I can feel the emotional scar, that the experience left behind. I am so very disappointed in her for doing that to me. I was just a child! A little girl who would *never* forget that moment. My mother, the only person who even seemed to care about me or my well being, was leaving... and leaving me with *him*! This experience haunted me for a very long time! At the time, I could not understand why she didn't wake my brother to tell him of her plan. Why did she only come to my room? Only to my bedside and not my brother's? After all, he is the only one that this crazy man you call my father likes, remember?

In thinking about it today, I totally understand why she did what she did. She didn't want to upset her precious boy for nothing. I don't think she had any real intentions of leaving that night. She was just trying to get my father's attention, and she did. At my expense! I have been plagued with nightmares ever since that night, which was the beginning of my childhood.

What happens now? Who can I trust? Who can I go to for help? Who will love and protect me? Is there somewhere safe for me? So many hard questions for a 4 year old mind to process. Oh, I almost forgot to mention, I got my annual Christmas card from my team of therapists, in the mail this morning. Such a wonderful picture they all took together this year. Oh yes, now where was I.

In spite of, or maybe because of, all the craziness in my childhood home I was always looking for friendly companionship. I was lonely and longing for some positive interaction with others. Any kind of interaction. Our home was located right beside a busy neighbourhood convenience store and I would play in the front yard, near the side walk, and talk to anyone who would talk to me. I would try to make friends with anyone who seemed friendly. My mother seemed to try to squelch my thirst for social contact. I believe that she tried to keep me isolated as much as she could. I think she was fearful of people finding out what was really happening in our home. She always seemed to want to keep me close, after that night, which was quite confusing for me. You were going to leave me behind, not that long ago? Was it guilt, perhaps? Or, maybe it was to satisfy her own need for the presence of another person. Was I her source of companionship and control? I don't believe she wanted me to have friends. If I did, it would mean that I would have less time to spend on or with her. You know, someone to do the important things she needed to have done. Things that were just for her. Special, pampering things, like doing all of her nails for her. Something that she insisted I do for her on a regular basis. I mean after all, boys hockey equipment and custom made golf clubs were expensive in those days! I was free and of course she deserved to be pampered with everything she put up with and all!

She said she was busy enough trying to meet my brother's needs, with his friends and his sporting activities. "She didn't want to have to lug, another child back and forth to play dates and things.". How inconvenient that would have been for her. It was just better for her, if *she* was my friend. It was better and easier, for *her*. This way, she could decide what we did and when we did it. She could decide what I liked and what I didn't like. You get the picture?

So basically, I had to tag along and hang out with my mother, while my brother played on sports teams and have outings with his friends. My mother tried to encourage him to let me join in with him and his friends, but he would have no part of it. Her life situation would have just been so much easier for her, if she had only had two *boys*. On the odd occasion, if I was sneaky, I would try to worm my way into his circle. It was always short lived though. As soon as he saw me coming, he would start to pick on me or push me away. So, I would just go on my way and find something else to do. It really wasn't fun anyway and it was never really worth the effort. I was just lonely... After that, I would usually go crying to my mother, who would give me a cookie and put me in front of the television. That was a friend I was always allowed to have. We became best buds, me and the television! It was one small way that I could escape into a world other than the one I lived in. Even if it was only for short periods of time. It was *something* and it made me feel happy. I liked that! Feeling happy.

For as long as I can remember, my mother would always take me visiting with her. We would mostly visit my Grandparents, her mother and father, and if not them, we would frequently visit her sister and her kids. Sometimes we would visit her aunt, which was her mother's sister, until she became very ill with cancer. I loved going to my grandparents house for visits. They lived in a neighbourhood where there were some other kids my age. I loved it there and was able to quickly make some friends. I had made some friends of my very own.

We also used to spend a fair bit of time at my Aunt's house. She and my mother were very close and seemed like they were best of friends, as well as sisters. They had two children, a girl and a boy, who were quite a bit younger than I was. But that didn't really matter to me then, I was so desperate for companionship, I tried to relate to and play with them as best I could.

When I finally got old enough to leave our yard on my own, I met the young girl next door, who was also much younger than me. She was a very pleasant and shy young girl, who only spoke French and I only spoke English. At that point in my life though, language was not going to keep me from having a friend of my own. Especially one that lived right next door. Her parents were always very nice to me and were very welcoming each time I would visit. It seemed that we were only summer time friends, but I didn't care. I would take all the friendship time I could get, if she was home, we were together. She did learn to speak a little bit of English which I really appreciated because I had no opportunity to learn French, at home or school. This friendship only lasted for a couple of years, however. She eventually went to a French school, when she was old enough, and made a new group of friends there. Throughout the years, as neighbours, we would see each other in passing and were always very friendly to one another. We just simply grew apart. I was always very thankful for her friendship in a very confusing time in my life.

When I would visit my grandparents, it was an opportunity to spend time with my new friends on the crescent beside their home. There was one boy in particular that I really seemed to get along with well. His family was always very welcoming to my visits and almost always permitted him to come out to play. We really seemed to hit it off, smashingly, I would say. We both had very good imaginations and frequently played a game that we made up together. It was a detective game. We would find a piece of "evidence" in among the dusty, rarely used items stored in my grandparents attic or in and around my grandfather's work shop. We would make up an entire story about the item. How it got to be there, when or why it was left behind, and so on. It was so very much fun! We would play it for hours. When I was finally old enough and had the option to ride my bike to my grandparents house after school, I would go as often as I could. Just so that we could hang out together and play our favourite game. Sometimes, if I was lucky, my grandparents would invite me stay for supper. I liked that because we could play later and Grammy always made the best suppers. After supper, I would ride my bike home or my mother would come and pick me up. When my grandparents decided to sell their home and move to the country, I lost contact with my friend. We had a good friendship for quite a few years and I really missed him.

I remember one time, when it seemed like my mother had finally had enough of my father's crap and his lies, she decided to take my brother and I and go live at my grandparents, for a little while. I thought that it was great and would have happily stayed there, forever. My grandparents were so very good to me, I spent a lot of time with them both growing up. Grampy was like a big kid and loved to play with me. It was a kind of attention and genuine interest in me, that I craved. My grandmother would show me things in the kitchen, like how to make bread. She was a fantastic cook and her bread was absolutely the best! I still make my own version of her scratch bread recipe, on a regular basis for my husband and I. As it turned out though, this arrangement would not last very long. Which was sad because I believe that the time we did spend there was probably the best period in my entire childhood. I was living somewhere where I had friends, next door. My grandparents were always there, and for me, the best part was that there was no waking up in the middle of the night to the sounds of fighting, screaming and yelling. There was always so much yelling at our house.

My father came from a religious family who did not believe in divorce and I believe he felt pressure from them to reconcile with my mother. What would people say about them, if he didn't? How would that look to the folks at the country club or the church?? So, it wasn't very long before he started coming around, asking my mother to come back. She always said that it was because Grammy and Grampy couldn't afford for us to stay there. But, I know that wasn't *really* the reason why she took us back there, to the house of horrors. It was because my brother kept crying to her and pleading with her to go back home. Back to his Dad. Some years later, she finally did admit that it was because of my brother that she decided to take us back there. Thank you to a vintage box of sweet red wine for that confession! I believe she was under some pressure from my grandparents to go back as well. It was advice given to her, based on the appearance they were shown. I wonder what advice they might have given had they known the truth? That can be the trouble with keeping up appearances. No one ever really knows the truth about what is *really* happening. I don't believe they would have pushed the issue, if she had told them what was really going on. We could have just stayed for a little while. Maybe just until we got back on our feet. Hell, I would have gotten a job, or maybe two, as long as I didn't have to go back *there*. Anywhere but there.

From that point on, when things got tough at home, or tougher than normal, I was either sent to or just went to my grandparents house. This was my steady reprieve from the insanity. That is until they moved to the country.

When it was time to start getting ready to go to school, I thought to myself this is going to be great! I'll make lots of new friends. What fun this is going to be! As it turned out, I met many new young people my age. Some of them were kind and sort of became friends and some of them were just mean and did not. "Oh great!!", I thought. "There's mean people here too?". I guess the confines of my childhood home is not the only place where I'm going to be picked on, ridiculed and bullied. I was a chubby girl at that age. Remember my best friend from earlier? The television and the constant supply of cookies my mother would give me? I'm sure some of you have heard stories about what can happen to young chubby girls on the school yard? They tend to be easy targets for bullies and get picked on, a lot. A few more mean people picking on the chubby young girl, just so that they had someone who felt worse than they did. I guess it must have made them feel better about themselves, somehow? At least that's the way it happened on the school yard I attended. It never made sense to me. I'm not sure how the *war on bullying* is going in the school system these days?

I think it was at that point, or maybe even a little earlier perhaps, that I started to learn how to become or transform into whomever or whatever the bullies, seemed to be less likely to pick on or target, in any situation. Anything I could do to lessen my constant state of discomfort. Not only was this a daily reality at home, but now I had to try and avoid this crap at school too? Suddenly, time spent with my television, my stuffed animals, who all loved me and a bowl of cookies, alone in my room, didn't seem so bad. I was six years old.

There was one larger than average size kid that I recall, in particular. He had bright red hair and freckles that I can still see, vividly. Everyone was afraid of him. He was very intimidating. He picked on me for quite a while. I thought that maybe if I went home and told my brother about him, maybe he would stick up for me and make him stop. So I tried it, but it didn't work, he never did. Maybe he was afraid of him too, I'm not sure. He never said a word about it. That is until one day, I took his bike out for a ride, without asking of course. Wouldn't you know it, along my travels, I ran into this big kid with the red hair and freckles and a couple of his buddies. They beat me up and took the bike. After the beating was over, I gathered my things and hobble home to tell my brother what had happened. He was furious! He called a couple of his friends and they all went to get the bike back and teach those kids a lesson on bullying. You're thinking, "that's so nice of him to stick up for you like that!". Well nope! That's not what happened. The thing I came to realize was that, he only did it cause they took *his* bike. Not because I got beat up. "Well that backfired!", I thought. So the next day, I went back to school and to my surprise the red headed boy came to me and said he was sorry for what he had done. Not because he and his friends had beat me up and took the bike, but because I had such a jerk for a brother. He said that, if he had known, he would never have picked on me in the first place. We became and remained friends after that, until he moved away. The small school house I attended, with just four class rooms was only two blocks away from our home. I spent my first four years of school there. As it turned out, I would attend three more different schools before reaching junior high. Each one of them with a new group of potential friends and bullies, new staff and teachers to get to know. Numerous new situations to learn how to adapt and adjust too.

Remember earlier, when I told you that I was starting to get pretty good at becoming whomever or whatever the people or situation required? Well, all of this adapting and adjusting that I had been doing really honed this new skill set of mine. It became an instinctual self-preservation mechanism that I had somehow managed to put into place, somewhere around the age of 4 years old. This mechanism had now started to become a group of protective personalities that I could summon quicker and quicker everyday. I got better at entering and reading a room while adapting and adjusting to it before I got to the chair waiting for me on the other side... Can you feel the spirit of a small child resorting to such measures? It's okay if you don't show me love or even like me. But please, just don't pick on me so much? I don't know what to do. I'm just a child and the only things I know, are the things I've watched *you* do. *You*, the people who brought me home from the hospital. I just need time to learn what you want? I'll keep trying. But please, just don't pick on me so much.

Before I get too far into my school years, I would like to touch on church. It was *so* much fun! Can you feel the sarcasm? As I said before, both sides of my family came from religion following backgrounds. My grandfather, on my mother's side, was not much of one for going to church. He preferred nature to pulpits and pews and I am thankful that he shared his love for nature and the outdoors with me, from the very beginning. Being present in and appreciating all of nature's beauty is such an important part of how I try to maintain balance in my life, now. Both of my Grandmothers and my Grandfather on my father's side, were faithful believers and followers, who attended weekly worship. I was brought up going to Sunday school in a United Baptist church. Following our weekly Sunday school class, I was often required to attend the weekly church service right after. It was there, that I first met a young girl the same age as me. In fact, our birthdays were only a month apart and her home was only five streets away from ours. We quickly became friends and have maintained an on again, off again friendship that had lasted most of our lives. She was an energetic and active young girl who was always on the go. She attended and participated in all sorts of things, like youth group and pioneer girls. Soon after we met, I too started to attend and participate in a lot of the same activities and functions. We had so much fun together! Had I finally found the friendship that I had so desperately been looking for? There were many other kids that lived on her street and they all seemed to be a really good group of friends. They welcomed me and encouraged me to join in with them. I very much liked becoming part of a group of people who enjoyed having me around! It was a place where we could all just act silly, be loud or laugh and be ourselves. It was somewhere safe for me. It was somewhere that I could be, just a little bit, of what I felt inside. Just a little bit of what felt natural to me. It was a place where I didn't have to be so vigilant and constantly have my newly developed adapt and adjust survival skills ready to go, at the blink of an eye.

Both her mother and her grandmother were teachers and we ended up attending classes with both of them over the years. There were even times when we were in some of the same classes with them, at the same time. As the years went by and we drifted in and out of each others lives on a regular basis, I always remained very fond of her. She was very energetic and truly fun to hang out with. Just being with her helped me to forget what my home life was like. Even if it was, just for a little while. She always made me laugh and she had, what I thought, was a wonderful family. Her parents and older brother seemed to really be good to her and really care about her. The picture I saw of her life was exactly what I thought I had always wanted. She was close with her family and it seemed like a very safe and loving environment, to me. Over time, we stayed in touch even though at times we attended different schools. I think that maintaining some childhood bonds, ones that are developed at such a young age can be comforting. They can leave within you a desire to check in every so often. A desire to make the effort and take the time to reconnect, once in a while.

She was very popular and always had a lot of friends. Her energy was magnetic and I was always excited to reconnect with her after some time had passed, to hear of the adventures she had been on and the people she had met or became close too. She would tell stories of the adventures she had been on , with people from all walks of life. I believe listen to her was a way for me to escape my own life situation. It was like I could step right inside of the television now and become part of the story. It all started to motivate me to step out on my own, and I soon started my own journey. I started my own book of adventures. It seemed to me that people were so drawn to her because she was so full of energy and wanted to experience all that was good and fun in life. It seemed that she lived for the joyful things in life and tried to leave the sadness behind. Which was exactly what I wanted, and after getting a glimpse of it, through her eyes, I did just that. I came to believe that it was something worth striving for. I had seen how it could be. I had seen what life could really be like. I had experienced what it felt like to be in the presence of that energy. What it *could* be like to become part of the story. This must be what everyone wants to do? Isn't it? Live for the joyful things in life and leave the sadness behind? Sadness will come. Accept it, embrace it and then move on. Focus your forward attention to the joyful things in your life. Whatever that may be for you. Have you ever thought about it? What is it for you? Now of course this while always showing empathy and respect for nature and all living things. Be kind to plants, animals and people!

I consider her to be my oldest friend. She was the only constant in my life for many, many years and for that, I **Thank her**! She was there on my first day of school and we even ended up in the same class. Before that, we were in Sunday school together. Considering we are now both in our 50's, that is a long time. Although I have not seen her in a few years, I know she will never change. If we were to reconnect again, it would be like no time had lapsed. I hope she is well!

Another person that I considered a friend was one of my first cousins. She is the daughter of the sister who was once my mother's best and closest friend. Although she was quite a few years younger, I think we were able to relate and played quite well together. It was kind of like she was a younger sister. Or, at least that's how I about it. Now that said, we would sometimes fight, like sisters do, but it was rare. I have always been thankful to have had her in my life. She was and still is very soft spoken and extremely kind, and in my eyes, she has always maintained that same kind, positive energy that I remember.

One of the things that we used to like to do together was colour and draw. I loved to draw and remember being quite good at drawing certain cartoon figures, freehand. I would just refer to and look at the pictures that I had or had seen and could draw from what my eyes saw. Some of the drawings we did, were really good! I remember this one time, I had just completed a drawing that I was particularly proud of and, being such a proud young artist in the making, I wanted to share our accomplishments with our mothers. I wanted to show them what a good job we did. Look Mother? I found something I'm really good at. It's something that makes me happy! Do you see? Look? Can you see?

When I showed them what we had done, all in one day. My mother's chosen words of encouragement and uplifting support were, wait for it, "you must have traced that!". "I can't do that!". "You must have traced it!" "You couldn't have done that all on your own!" "Don't lie to me!". "You must have traced it!!". Did I mention that my team of therapists send me a Christmas card every year?

What a blow to a young person's self-esteem. Now, after having done the work on myself to improve my life situation, I realize that she did this because of her narcissistic tendencies. That is why she would always say things like that. Things I found to be hurtful. Very hurtful, at times! She just couldn't let me have it. She couldn't praise me for being better at something than she was. Or, demonstrate and show promise or talent, above hers, in any special way.

She has done that over and over again my entire life.  It has always had to be about her. Eventually, once some of my work started to get published, she couldn't deny it anymore. My mother had to admit that I had some talent. I wonder if that was uncomfortable and difficult for her? Well okay, you got me. I kind of hope that it was. Her comments then became anchored to the fact that I was *her* daughter and that it was *her* talents as a mother that gave me my talents. One year, I created and served a particularly delicious hors d'oeuvre at a family holiday function. When the guests would compliment my creation, she would say, "well now, how did I raise such a smart cook?". Ho Ho freakin' Ho Mother! For those of you who can relate, please know that the things that the narcissists in your life do, have absolutely nothing to do with you. You are merely a pawn, a resource, or an obstacle, in them getting what they need or want. You are perfect just the way you are! Don't listen to them.

At one point, my friend from Sunday school and I decided to join the church youth choir together. I absolutely loved to sing! Singing just made me feel so good! It doesn't matter if you have a real "Queen of Soul" set of pipes, or not. If singing makes you happy, sing and sing loud! Some time after joining the choir, our Christmas concert debut was upon us and we were so very excited! We sang our little hearts out!! It was great and so much fun! We had a great performance! That said, I still remember the feeling of "the wind coming out my sails" and my excitement fading, after hearing my mother's critical and negative review. Her comments hurt for a while. Quite a while actually. But, its okay though. Its okay because, she couldn't carry a tune in a bucket and I now sing lead with a band from time to time! It wasn't long after that though, that I chose to quit the youth choir.

A few years later, I became interested in singing again, but mostly I wanted a guitar. I saved my money and bought my very own guitar. It wasn't a great quality instrument but it was a guitar and to me that's all that mattered. I was so excited! I had a Guitar! My mother used to say that she would pay for piano lessons, if I wanted, but not guitar. This was usually followed by a story of her woes and how much she always wanted to take piano lessons, but nobody would ever give her what she wanted. Well how about that? But, that's not at all what I was talking about, or what I even wanted. I wanted to learn how to play the guitar. I bought a guitar, not a piano! There was never any offerings for guitar lessons. In fact, she would make me go outside or down to the basement, with my guitar when I was trying to learn. It's not so much that there was no monetary support. I could have done that by myself, eventually. It's not that there was no encouragement, I was used to having to encourage myself. It's that the critical or negative comments, and most times both, is all that there ever was. I was just tired of it, and eventually, I put the guitar aside. I would still sing to the radio in my room or outside, but never where anyone could hear me. I had come to fear the criticism and negativity, it always made me feel so bad about myself.

When I reached junior high school, I met another young girl who shared my love for singing. She loved to sing and had a beautiful voice and had encouraged me to sing with her at a school assembly. We practised every chance we got and I was so excited to get up in front of everyone and sing my heart out. I thought we blew it out of the park! I was so happy and filled with adrenaline after our performance, that I was just bouncing from energy and excitement! Eventually, and after some hesitation, I went over to the grand stands, where my mother was sitting. Her only comment to me was that, all she could hear was me singing too loudly and how she thought that all I had done was just overpower the other poor little girl. Well that took the wind right out of my sails! Again!! After that, I wouldn't sing in front of anyone, unless I was making fun of myself, before someone else had a chance too. That was until I met Derek, my love, my best friend and my soul mate. It was his encouragement that got me to sing in front of others again. I absolutely love to sing! It fills me with joy! I will touch more on this later.

When I got to junior high school, it looked that the coming years would be full of opportunities for me. As I mentioned before, I really liked to sketch and found myself to be quite creative. My new school had a good art program and fortunately for me, I met an art teacher who thought I showed great promise. He took a real interest in my work and was very encouraging, which was something I was not accustomed too, but found quite enjoyable. I learned as much as I could from him, I was like a sponge. I absorbed his teachings and his techniques thoroughly.

In applying my new skills, I created some pieces that I thought were really good. Some of them were even chosen to be published in our local newspaper, which I thought was a big deal! Wow! My work was going to be in the newspaper! Some of you may have to do a web search for "what is a newspaper?", I suppose. But trust me, it was a big deal then! I was very proud of my accomplishment and thought that maybe, I had found my calling. Remember I mentioned earlier, how drawing made me feel full and so good about myself? To be naturally good at something that makes you feel so good. That *is* what a calling is? Isn't it??

I seized every opportunity I could, to soak up as much energy, technique and knowledge from my new teacher, as possible. The fundamentals I learned in those classes gave me a good basis and starting point for doing well in my High School Art program. It was a real thing then! High School Arts programs! Really, I was in one. Do they still do that?

I thought that I would very much like to go to art college, after graduating from High School. So I said, "I would like to go to Art school, please?". Yes, that is what I would like to do. That is my passion! I've found it! Are you all as happy as I am? Hello? Is anyone there??

My family was far from encouraging. Far! Really far, from it! I mean after all, the only other person in my immediate family who knew anything about or could appreciate Art, was my Uncle. His name was Art! Hahaha. Well not really, but you get the point. These people were semi-professional hockey playing, golf loving, important and successful, country club going individuals. "You want to be an Artist?" No, "I **am** Artist.". "It's not something that you become. It's just something that you **are**.". Kind of like being a "jerk". You know, some people were born a jerk and just grew bigger. They replied. "You can't be an Artist!!" "None of us are Artistic!" "If we can't do it, you certainly can't!" "You'll never be *successful* being an Artist." "Besides artists only make money after they're dead." "You better take some business courses." "So you can be successful, like me!"

It ended up that I believed them. I didn't want to believe them, but I did. Even though there was a part of me that knew I could do it. I felt very passionate about it. Maybe if I just tried to do it? I mean what did you do when people said you couldn't be a successful at whatever it is that you are, father? It seems to me that you said, "Oh yeah?" "You just watch me!" "I'll show you all!" Well, I am an Artist and no matter how hard you try, you'll never beat it out of me, father.

I gave a professionally made copy of my favourite piece, which was one of the two pieces that were published, to my Grandparents. They were always very encouraging toward my abilities. They framed it and hung it on the wall in their home. Right there, for everyone too see! I was so proud that they liked it enough to show everyone who came to visit. "Look." they would say, "Our grand daughter did that!" "It was in the newspaper!". Trust me it was a big deal back then! I think that when my mother saw that, she must have figured she would look bad, if she didn't do the same with the original. Because, it was just shortly after that she framed it and hung it on the wall at our house. My teen aged heart always felt so heavy and so very discouraged. It seemed that nothing I did or ever tried to do was good enough for them! I mean I really liked the things I did and tried! I had never known things that made me feel that good and I thought they would be happy for me. Happy that I was happy? Well for a little while at least. Why didn't they want me to be happy? I'm not completely sure when it was, that I started to believe that other people had to be happy with me, before I could be happy with me. Whether it was what I was doing, how I was acting or being, how loud I was, it just didn't seem matter, they were never happy. Eventually, I started to believe that if they weren't happy with me, then I shouldn't be either. Have any of you ever felt this way? Where did it come from for you? I read somewhere that the first step to being present and happy is to, "free yourself from the good opinion of other people.". I now agree with this, fully and completely! This is the first step. Please take it.

As I mentioned earlier, life was all about appearances in my family. There were always so many secrets and lies. How was I to figure out for myself, what was right and what was wrong? Thank goodness for Grammy and Grampy. They were good people, not perfect, but I believe that they always meant well. Especially, where I was concerned. They were my constant. I tried to use their example as my compass. However, by this time I was a teenage girl and I needed to push the boundaries from time to time. Sometimes just because I could. I was filled with frustration and maybe even resentment, for my family, I just wanted to be loved and recognized as an equal member. Not just someone to do household chores and clean up after the "Lords and Ladies". Sometimes I would act out just to see if anyone really even cared about what happened to me. I discovered that most of the time, they were only concerned when my actions, and/or the consequences of my actions disrupted their carefully crafted appearances, in some way. How inconvenient that must have been for them! I mean really. Those poor, busy and important people! How dare I?

Starting my junior high school years at a new school seemed like a good opportunity for me to meet a lot of new people my own age and maybe find the companionship that I so desperately craved. I made a few friends, some of whom came and went, as is typical of young school mate relationships. Some were more memorable than others, of course. In getting out on my own, I was starting to feel more independent. I was starting to feel like I might have a chance at a real, normal life. Or, what I thought a happy and "normal" life could be. I got a glimpse of the lives of the kids I met and formed friendships with throughout my school years. Some of the window views into their lives that I saw, were very exciting! Some of them were very scary... The exciting ones gave me hope. The scary ones reminded me to be quiet and unseen when I went home.

For awhile, it seemed that my mother was so wrapped up in trying to keep her marriage together, that she really wasn't all that concerned about the things that I had going on. You see my parents travelled a lot in those days. My brother and I were either left with caretakers, usually our grandparents, or depending on the allure and timing of the trip, we were just left home on our own. Perhaps the distance and/or duration of the trip had something to do with it. I'm really not sure. We must have proved to be responsible enough to maintain the proper appearances, thought. Well that, or they just really wanted to go, regardless. I think that my father made the absolute most out of crafting and creating ways for their trips to be "of benefit to his business", somehow. In fact, he was so good at it, he could have made a career out it! Or wait, did he?? Maybe that was his passion? Maybe he too was an artist? Just with a different stroke of the pen, as it were. I always got the feeling, that what he really wanted was to just leave and never come back. A decision I would have supported! Fully and completely! It's okay, I will be fine. Really! I won't miss you! Bye bye! Please don't write. Just go.

Unfortunately however, he always came back. I mean really how long could he stay in the public eye with my mother constantly nagging at his heals? She was always just complaining about something. It was a real gift. She could always find something, or even creating something to complain about. I think maybe it depended on how little attention she felt she was getting that day, that would set her off. I can certainly see how it would. I was told that when they would travel together, he would just up and disappear. Apparently, he would leave her on her own for hours and hours at a time. She, unlike his younger model second wife, was nowhere near as naturally gifted in dealing with, or maybe even manipulating the manipulator to correct some of this type of behaviour. Maybe he thought he deserved this time, free from complaining. You know a little "me time!". I would say, from the little bit of travelling experience I had with them, that even if he had spent every moment with her, she still would not have been happy.

I could never understand why she looked at things this way. I mean she was doing it. She was living the life she said she had always dreamed of. The Dinners out. The Events. The regular trips. They went to places like Japan and Hawaii, among others. They had at least one an annual trip to Florida. Maybe she just didn't or couldn't understand the rules of that way of life? What does it *really* take to live that life. Go to those places and do those things? After all, there is always another Alpha wolf to learn from or maybe even, eventually, challenge someday. Especially, if you have your sights set on being at the head of the pack and I believe that is where my father's sights were set. How courageous of him. That is courage, isn't it?

I really liked it when they would go on a trip and leave us home. After all, we were in school and they said they didn't want us to miss any time. They were so very concerned about the quality of our education. They were Parents of the year candidates, for days. When they did decide to travel, in the name of quality education, I found that for a little while at least, the only person I had to deal with was my brother. He seemed to be a bit more respectful when they weren't home. We would have a disagreement now and then, but for the most part, things were better between us when they were gone. It seemed to me that my mother was constantly encouraging him to pick at me. Then when I reacted, she would laugh, which only encouraged him more. Or, she would act like he wasn't doing anything wrong at all and ignore the situation and then just walk away. All of which made me see *red*. Now just in case you haven't sensed it yet. I can have a bit of a temper! In fact, the words hot headed come up in sentences referring to me on a regular basis. It's one of the survival skills I had to learn at a very young age. And it can be Savage!

I can remember getting ready for bed one night, when I was very young. Without me knowing it, my brother had crawled under my bed. He knew at that time, that I was very fearful of what could possibly be hiding under my bed at night. I mean the rest of the house was filled with monsters, there could be one under my bed too. As I was taking off my clothes and putting my night dress on, he reached out and grabbed my ankle from under the bed. It scared me so bad that I let out a chilling scream and actually wet myself a little. My mother came running down the hall to my room to see what was happening. As she got there, he was crawling out from under the bed and laughing hysterically. As soon as she saw us, she seemed to know what he had done and immediately joined in his hysterics. My little feelings were horrifically stomped on and hurt. I was terrified and nobody cared!! The monsters in my house were very real!

For years after that, I would have to run and jump to get on my bed. I would never stand next to it. I had already been having nightmares about things hiding under my bed for some time and now this. After a while, my fear was mildly soothed by the safety of a night light. At least this way, I thought I would able to see any possible threats before they got to me. Maybe I shouldn't have shared my nightmares with my mother or went to her for comfort? There was never any apology or consequences for his actions. She never scolded him at all. She just laughed, while I cried.

I can recall another incident between us, in our teen aged years. We were fighting over the use of the telephone. A common teen sibling argument in those days. Especially because in those days the one or two telephones in the house were connected to the wall with wires. There were no cell phones back then. Every phone had a cord. This argument escalated to the point where he grabbed the receiver from my hand and hit me in the face with it. The hit broke my nose. As I was running to the bathroom, trying to contain the bloody mess, which I was going to have to clean up. My mother came in to see what all the commotion is about. I told her what happened and you guessed it, her immediate response, hysterical laughter. Which again, just encouraged his behaviour. He got another laugh and had no consequences. I can't remember him ever getting punished or having consequences for any of his actions. He was then and still is her golden child and can do no wrong. Unless of course, it is something that concerns her. She does not like that! Not at all! It seemed that where I was concerned, however, he was smart and very rarely did anything to upset the apple cart to the point where he would have to suffer the consequences. Although, I don't know what the hell he would have had to do, to get to that point. I'm glad we didn't have to find out, really. For the most part, the arguing between my brother and I seemed to only be when our parents were home. So when they were away travelling, it was like a little vacation for me too.

For the duration of my junior high school years and the early part of my high school years, I escaped the craziness of my home life by sneaking out of the house at night to meet up with my friends. If we were lucky enough for someone to have a car, we would all pool our money for gas and could end up in all sorts of places, doing all sorts of things. If there was no car, we would just walk around the city, all night long. They wouldn't miss me. I mean really, my door had been locked at night, from the outside, in the hall way, for years by this point. So I couldn't get out at night.

We would hang out in the coolest places. We would meet up in the grave yard next to our house and scare the crap out of each other, for instance. One of our other favourite places was a vacant lot that had grown up into a field close to where we all lived. Years later, there was a school built on that piece of ground and kids are probably still raising hell there. We would have shopping cart races in the parking lots of different department stores. I think that maybe *we* are the reason they don't leave the carts outside anymore. Lol.

My absolute favourite game was when my friends and I would pick a random subdivision and then pick two houses side by side that had a lot of lawn ornaments. Then, we would switch the ornaments from one yard to the other and then wait until morning to see their reactions when they came out to get the paper with their morning coffee. Even the home owners would laugh most of the time. We never broke or stole anything. We just switched their yards up. I found this to be the funniest and most entertaining of the midnight madness games we would play. That game was only for those nights when we could stay out all night and into the next morning. I have to say that those damn lawn and garden statues were a lot heavier than they looked.

You can picture it can't you? I wonder how many of you will scan the yard tomorrow morning when you grab the paper? Oh wait, do they still print the news on paper?

I sometimes miss those days. I'm glad I have those pleasant memories.

# CHAPTER 3

### *Shattered Rose Coloured Glasses*

Okay, so we've made it to my teen years and how I have recently gotten a glimpse of what life can look like, through a different set of lenses. There really are homes where people get along and show love and respect to one another, I've seen it. They don't scream and yell all the time. They aren't physically and verbally abusive toward one anther. Not one of them has thrown a TV through the wall yet! This is really something!! I'm in disbelief.

As I continued to get more than just a glimpse of what life could really be like and spent more time in these environments, my sense of independence continued to grow, as did my new found friendships. My desire to feel more of the magnetic energy that I had felt with my friend and the group of friends she introduced me to, really started to strengthen. It was right around this time that she introduced me to another one of her friends. He lived on the same street as her and her family, just a few doors down. The three of us became very close. In fact, we quickly became nearly inseparable. He was a year older than us, but that didn't seem to matter. For the most part, we were always together. It even got to the point where, even if she wasn't around, he and I would meet up and just hang out. Or, we would tour the city in his family's Lincoln town car. Which he often got to use, to drive us all around. To have become part of this group was really something for me and I was very grateful! Those "Town Car" nights were something that I really looked forward to. In addition, I am thankful that there were no social media platforms, where pictures could be posted in those days... I mean really! Nobody else needed to see those pictures!! Those memories are reserved strictly for attendees only! Lol.

I think it was him who taught me the true meaning of friendship and what that can feel like. Or to put it another way, it was the bond that grew between us that was my first experience with what I had always dreamed a true friendship could be. He was very loyal and I was extremely happy to have finally found someone who seemed to truly care about *me*. It was a type of relationship that I was unfamiliar with at the time. It was something that I always thought I wanted and something I thought I would be very good at. I was willing to give my all to a relationship like that, if I got the feeling that it was safe and that someone would reciprocate. By this point, I already knew a fair bit about what it felt like to *not* have a genuine friend. Someone who cared about me and my feelings. Someone who cared about my wants needs. My likes and my dislikes. Someone with whom I could just be myself. Someone who's energy I didn't have to try to read or adapt and adjust to at every moment... I could just relax and be me when I was with him. We quickly became the best of friends and remained very close for about 6 years. This was the case throughout junior high and for most of our time in high school together. Unfortunately, we started to grow apart in our later years of high school, though. I think maybe part of the reason for this was because he was going to be graduating and heading to University, at least a year before I would. At the time, I felt that us living in different cities would make it really difficult to maintain the closeness of our relationship. I didn't want to accept this change. I didn't like the thoughts of it at all and, as a result, I was the one who started to pull away first. I think that I was just so hurt by the thought of losing my best friend to the distance of his move, that it was just easier to blame it on growing apart. Maybe this was becoming a well developed technique of mine? Another self-developed tool in my self-preservation arsenal. I could see the hurt coming and I had learned that the best way to avoid, or minimize its effects was to have as much of it as possible be on my terms. My approach had become to get ahead of it, or them, quickly before it or they got to me first! I knew he would be moving to another city to start a new chapter in his life and that I would, once again, be on my own. It was another situation that was beyond my control. But, I could control the flow of this hurt and the disappointment that came along with it. So that's just what I did, I started to create distance between us and control the flow of it all.

Alternately and from a different perspective, something closer to the lenses that I look through today, it could simply have been that we were just growing into two new and different individuals. Individuals who needed to live and experience some of the other new and exciting things that life now had to offer. It was time for us to carve out our own, separate new paths in new circles. It was time for us to create and have new and different friendships and relationships. So, I started to build walls between us and put obstacles in place that would quickly allow me to begin to seek out others my own age. I was starting over again and was, once again, in search of companionship or, maybe even a new friendship, if I was lucky.

So I looked around and tried to find a place to fit in. I tried to find somewhere that I could belong. I discovered, however, that I quite simply was not made for most of the usual spots where most high school kids found their place. Those groups and their ways just weren't for me. I didn't fit in, at all! I think that I just got to the point where I didn't care who I had for friends just as long as I had some people around me. I just wanted to have a group of people that I could call my friends. This way, even though I may still be lonely, at least I wouldn't be alone.

As I continued my search, I eventually found a spot. I found a group that was easy to fit into. Well, at least it seemed that way at first. I think it was at that point, that I started to learn about what a code of ethics and a moral compass was. This of course, was other than the examples I had observed from my immediate family. You see loneliness was something I already had a really good understanding of and I was in no hurry to revisit what that felt like. My search lead me to a group of people who made me feel like family, or what I had hoped that would feel like, at least. We were a group of young people that came from a wide variety of backgrounds, but we all had one thing in common. We were all looking for a sense of belonging. We were all looking for somewhere to fit in. We were looking for a group to be part of. A place where loyalty was something that was just understood, it was the price of admission, as it were. Respect, on the other hand. Respect had to be earned and was not distributed evenly just for showing up.

Unlike in today's world, you did not get a trophy just for being present... I felt right at home. I could be fiercely loyal and I had no problem with having to earn respect. A "cake walk" compared to where I came from. When it came to being different and displaying one's individual uniqueness, this new group I had found were all over achievers, relative to the day and age. My elders would refer to them as being "rebellious" and "racy". Whatever the hell that meant? We wore tight jeans and leather jackets. Or, sometimes what we affectionately called, "Albert County dinner jackets", which were basically plaid and flannel jackets, commonly worn by trades people and country folk in those days. They were warm, very comfortable and best of all, they were very different from any urban fashion trends, at the time. Especially at the Country Club my parents frequented, I absolutely loved them! I had one in every colour. We also wore steel toed, leather work boots. Which finished off the ensemble quite nicely, I think. Basically, we wore anything that was different and maybe somehow, in doing so, showed others that we were not to be pushed around. There were a lot of us and we were proud to be different. Being part of a group like that, was something that really appealed to me. I had always been very different from all of the people that I live with and it seemed like everyone in this new group could relate to that. Given that most of us had come from similar backgrounds. I felt that I was protected in being part of the group. They looked out for me and, in return, I did what I could to prove my worth and earn their respect. Whether it was offering to give someone a drive, having someone's back in a tense situation, or just offering a smoke to someone who could really use one, we were there for each other.

As time progressed and my place in this new group became much more solid and constant. I began to meet others who all seemed to be looking for the same things I was looking for. Eventually, I met a new someone through this group that I kind of liked. He was the type of individual who had his own ways of doing things. Some of which I was unfamiliar with and had never known. Some of them, I had always known and was far too familiar with. I fell for his handsome looks and his rebellious ways. He let me believe that he *saw* things in me. Things that I so desperately wanted someone, anyone to see. He was very good at hiding what he *truly saw* when he looked at me. What *I* saw, was that he truly understood and cared for me. Finally, I thought, someone who gets me! It felt like such a relief! Well, for a while at least... Once things progressed to a certain level of comfort, on his part, he became very abusive, very quickly. Overnight, this dream I was living with my new found love had turned into a nightmare. A living nightmare!

Well, actually it was another living nightmare. I had jumped from one very bad situation at home into an equally, or maybe even worse situation with him. Where did I get the idea that this was "normal"? This was just the way it was done, right? I mean that is what I saw and heard.. That's how things were at home. That's where I came from.

He had just been released from a drug rehab centre and his first stop was one of the apartments where I had started hanging out. This place was a busy spot as there were always people coming and going, stopping by to check in. We were all very loyal and all getting or needing something a little different from being part of our group.

Our group was our chosen family, at the time. I think a lot of us were just trying to survive some very confusing times. We were trying to figure out where we belonged and where we fit in. We were trying to figure out just who the hell we were and what the hell we wanted in life. I so wanted to be cared for and appreciated. Not looked after, I could do that myself, thank you very much! I just wanted to be cared for. I wanted to be cared about. I wanted to matter to someone. I wanted to be part of something, one day. I wanted what I think everyone wants, to be loved, appreciated and respected.

One night when I arrived at this place, in hopes of finding some friendly faces, there he was. As soon as I walked through the door, I could feel his eyes on me. I *thought* he saw what I wanted him to see when he looked at me. His gift was making me *think* that is what he saw. However, that *wasn't* what he saw. Not at all.. Our eyes met when I looked into the kitchen. My first thought was, I wonder who he is and does he have a girlfriend. As the night went on, I got answers for both of my questions. Soon after, we started dating and at first I thought I was oh so lucky. I had finally found someone that I could relate to. Someone who really and truly cared for *me*. Well, as it turns out, I was wrong. Very wrong! In fact, I really want to tell you about just *how* wrong I was. Maybe in doing so, it will prevent someone else from having to try to live through similar circumstances. Maybe they will recognize the signs and patterns and be able to avoid putting themselves in, or staying in such a position.

He was a master at his craft and a very good actor. Wait, he sounds just like someone else I knew, at that point. He sounds just like my father. He wanted or needed someone to control. Someone to do his bidding. Someone who would do what they were told, when they were told. Oh and most importantly, someone who would not ask questions or bitch about doing it. Just do it! Yes, he was just like my father. Well I had been in training for this position and this role since before I could wipe my own ass! I think he was looking for someone who would make his life easier. He needed money, I could earn money. It certainly **appeared** that my family had money. I guess sometimes it's easy to forget just how far the *appearance* we craft and present, really can project. Maybe one forgets just who sees and hears the way we appear to look and the things we appear to do. He needed to make connections with people for jobs and opportunities. I could make introductions. He needed to smooth things over with his family. I could and would talk to them. I was good at adapting and adjusting to the room on the fly, remember? He saw that in me, *instantly*! He needed to vent his frustrations and his anger. I was a punching bag. I think you are probably starting to develop a clear picture, aren't you?

He had a gift when it came to playing on my emotions. He was very good at it. He used me. I was just a tool to anchor his life for awhile. He never truly loved me. It all just happened so quickly. I didn't even realize what was happening at first. He "love bombed" me and I had very little experience with, or in, positive relationships. Experiences and interactions with other people that made me feel good were a very rare thing for me. I mean my home life and family relationships had not set the bar very high. By the time I realized what was happening, it was too late. I was in it and I was in it all the way! I was into something that *appeared* to be the exact opposite of what it really was. It was just like being out on a business dinner with my family. I bought into it all. The charm and charisma, the gestures of kindest and "love". The special treatment and affectionate words. I bought it all! Except that this time, I was now experiencing a new level of relationship affection and intimacy. A new level of connection that I quickly realized would be much harder to break free or pull away from, than what I was used to. It was the same type of collision course, with a much bigger impact and far more residual damage. A much bigger impact and more residual damage to *me*. I allowed myself to be fooled by the *appearance* of something that would turn out to be the exact opposite of what it truly was. It was a living nightmare dressed up as the life of my dreams.

This charismatic and handsome young man placed me way up high on a pedestal. He talked of all the opportunity and promise in the world. I mean he really sold it. He too, was very good with words and appearances. For his way in, he chose to tell me of the hardships and troubles with his home life and you guessed it. I fell for it. I fell for it and I fell for him. I too, saw myself as someone who came from an abusive family and home. I thought to myself, this is perfect! We can relate to each other in this way, we have something common. We come from similar backgrounds and we are going to be able to help each other heal and move forward with our lives. We are going to be able to build a life together. We are going to have something that is meaningful. A relationship that is filled with love, respect and happiness. It wasn't long, however, before there were several cracks in those "rose coloured glasses" of mine. I was going to say that it was because I was "young and foolish". But that wasn't really it. I just really wanted to believe it was possible for *me* to have something that I wanted. Something that I wanted, so very much! Some place safe. Some place where I can just be me and be loved for it. I thought to myself, this is finally it. This is my time! All of my years of suffering are going to be rewarded. He is going to take me away from my abusive home and parents and we will live life happily ever after, together.

Do you see what I did there? I don't even realize it sometimes. But I *still* make those references every once in awhile. Something I adopted from my mother's "living the good life" manual. Simply put, it is the practice of continually monitoring every single "investment" one makes. These are investments made, in the form of giving of time or gifts of material items. Or, maybe even an investment made in putting up with unacceptable abusive behaviours, like *infidelity*, for example. It's a book I wish I had never even heard of let alone read and been hit with.

You see, the principle is that doing or giving any or even all of the above can be acceptable. It can be acceptable as long as the rate of "pay off" or "return on investment" is deemed acceptable or better than the initial investment. I know what you are thinking. But wait, there's more, it's a convenience based, moving scale with no real valuation rules or guidelines. Actually, come to think of it, it would appear that none of the "pay offs" or "returns on investment" she has ever received, have been deemed anything other than **unacceptable**. Apparently, it's *not* really the thought that counts after all.

It was all too good to be true and it wasn't long before things started to go sideways and he started showing a lot of anger toward me. I thought maybe it was just the frustration of trying to cut back on the drugs, trying to keep a job and that he wasn't getting along with his family. My thought was that if I loved and supported him enough, it would all just work itself out. I mean really, who was I kidding? I knew the signs and red flags for this kind of thing, right? The signs and red flags were everywhere. They were everywhere I looked, but I couldn't see them. I couldn't see, what I didn't want to see. How could this be? He really means it, right? He loves me, doesn't he? The view from my glasses changed so much, as the lenses began to scratch and then crack. Eventually the lenses were so damaged and broken, that I had to take my glasses off. My shattered rose coloured glasses.

Looking back now, I made a lot of mistakes and "being young" was no excuse. I just wanted a win so bad that I decided to ignore a lot of what was happening. I "turned a blind eye". Can you guess where I got that one?? Well, it is on the title of chapter one in my mother's "living the good life" manual. "Turn a blind eye.", "it's ok as long everything appears to be good on the outside!".

The first time we got in a really heated argument he gave me a black eye. At this time, I was still in contact with my parents and they hated him from the first time they met him. I wonder what reflection they saw when they looked at him? I didn't want to give them any ammunition, so I lied about my eye. I told them we were play fighting and I fell and hit the corner of the coffee table. I wonder what they would have done if I had told them the truth? Or do I? He knew it was hard to hide a black eye so next time he made sure the injuries were easier to cover up. He lied to me about everything. I think he knew that I wanted to make it work so badly, that I would just believe whatever he told me to be true. Then eventually, the lies started to catch up with him. After we got our own place and we were living together it was harder for him to keep his secrets. My friends tried to tell me what kind of person he really was. But I wouldn't hear it. The last thing I wanted to hear was how badly I had messed up. I did not want to admit that I had made a mistake in getting involved with him. Not to myself and certainly not to my parents! You can't even imagine what kind of fall out that would have had. How they would have used it to their advantage, where I was concerned. Over and over and over again. I just couldn't do it!

After moving in together, his anger and frustration continued to build. He wanted me there but just wanted me to do as I was told, when I was told. Anyone who knows me would say that I can't keep my mouth shut and so I asked a lot of questions. All of which were met with rage and it never turned out well for me.

One particular day, after a fight, he left the apartment and didn't come home until the next day. I asked where he had been and he said he was giving a friend a tattoo. This was his latest endeavour to make some extra cash. I found out a couple of days later that the tattoo he was working on was of a unicorn and was being placed on a young woman's inner thigh. This news made me extremely angry! I knew this young woman and she had been chasing him for some time. She was looking for any excuse to steal him away. In hindsight, I wish she would have succeeded. I really wish I would have let her win.

It was a couple of months later, but the truth that he *had* slept with her that night, after giving her the tattoo, eventually came out. A friend of his, who apparently hated to see him hurt me, told me of his "romp in the hay" with little miss unicorn. I was devastated! But, apparently not enough to leave him. After all, I would have to admit that I had made a mistake. I would have to admit that I made a bad choice in moving in with him. So, I decided to keep up appearances and stick it out. He assured me it wouldn't happen again and that he would make it up to me. He claimed I drove him to it because of our argument that night. I just wanted to forget about it and move forward, and so I tried.

It seemed that he was trying harder and things had improved and were better, for all of a couple of days. Until his next bout of rage set in, that is. This was usually brought on by him not having enough money to support his drug habit. The whole thing was an ongoing pattern and a living nightmare that lasted for six long years. The fights progressively got worse and more frequent, even after I gave him money or something of some value, that he could pawn or sell. As it was, I was pretty well paying for everything, he was draining me. He was draining me of my energy, my money, my possessions and my will to live.

Our friends were starting to turn on him as they watched what he was putting me through. They started putting distance between themselves and us. They too were getting frustrated with him, as he was making deals that never seemed to pan out the way they were supposed to. One of my friends, who had been born into a well known family business, made a deal with him. As it turned out, the deal did not go as it had originally been planned and agreed upon. Everyone knew not to play games with this particular family, but he just couldn't resist the temptation. It was a huge mistake on his part because he got picked up shortly after and was taken to a place that people rarely returned from in the same shape and on the same night. It was a place known only by a chosen few. He told me that, as they are driving he was pretty sure he knew where they were going, and he thought that was going be it.

Once they arrived and the vehicle came to a stop, the three of them got out, my friend, his second in command and my ex. The beating started immediately and didn't stop for what seemed like hours, he later told me. At which point, I think we both realized what had just taken place. They were trying to put a scare into him and give him an unforgettable warning. At the end of the beating, my friend told him the only reason he was going home was because of the respect that he had for me and that if he ever screwed him again, there would be no second chance.

After this, he decided not to make any more deals with them.

Which I thought was wise considering he never kept his word. On the other hand however, my friend *always* kept his! I was thankful that he made that decision. I think that his actions would have eventually blown back on me and I had worked too hard to earn my spot and the respect I had, to lose it in that way.

This was not the only troubling incident that he got himself into. Over the six years we were together, I mostly slept with one eye open. I was never truly relaxed and certainly never slept soundly. Mostly because if he wasn't angry and frustrated, it was usually because he had or *was* making someone angry, in some way. I just never knew how his actions or the deals he made would or could blow back on me and my standing in the group.

I remember one time, before we moved in together, when his roommates had some things stolen from their rooms. It took a little while, but eventually they found out that he had taken the items and pawned them to buy drugs. I had no idea, until the toughest one of them decided to try and teach him a lesson by beating the hell out of him. He was no slouch but this roommate was massive and very well muscled. After that happened, I told him that he should have come to me first and I would have done my best to get him the money he needed. The people he stole from in this group, were very loyal individuals and they never forgot that betrayal. After that, he was kicked out of the apartment, which is what led to us moving in together. I chose not to see that incident as a red flag, although I knew better. I was blinded from the flash of his "love bomb". I thought that he just needed someone to teach him their ways. I thought that he was like me. He just needed a chance to prove himself. Well, that's what I thought at the time, at least.

I was later told, that the only reason all of those people put up with his behaviour was because of me and my good standing with them. Thinking about this now makes me sad. The fact that I was so blinded and that my friends had put up with that type of behaviour is upsetting to me now. Unfortunately, it is one of my big regrets in life. He did not deserve their loyalty. On the other hand though, it also makes me feel proud that they respected and thought enough of me that they chose to hold back.

I understand now why I put up with all the lies and abuse. It is because this type of environment was normal to me, it's what I knew. It's what I lived, from day one, when I was brought home from the hospital. I was going towards something that was familiar to me.

In the house I lived in when I was growing up, my feelings did not matter. The rage that my father had shown by being physically, verbally and emotionally abusive towards both my mother and I, was just a segue for me. He showed a great deal of anger and disdain for us both, which I just thought was normal. Well, it was normal for me. My mother would tell me after one of his "episodes", "you know he loves you, right?". What a message to send an impressionable young person. You mean that was "love"?? Really? Quite an example you set mother! She thought she was helping, I suppose. Okay, so let me get this straight. What you are saying is that when my father would just go crazy and throw the television against or through the wall and chase you down the hallway screaming at you, that was love? Or, when he came home drunk and became enraged and lashed out or beat me because the utensils were all messed up from closing the drawer too hard, while my brother was picking on and arguing with me, that was love?? That particular time he showed his love by coming into my room, jumping on top of me, on my own bed and beating me bloody. I was black and blue and had a black eye! I got the message loud and clear that time. I know mother, it was "love"!!

So my ex was a good choice then, right? He showed lots

of "love" mother. He must have really loved me, because he thought it was okay to drag me up the stairs by the hair on my head and beat me, just because I was trying to get away from him. He was in one of his moods and I wanted to leave to avoid a fight. He, on the other hand, wanted me to stay so he could get his frustrations out and provide another one of his lessons in obedience.

I reached the last straw with him when my parents had started the process of separating and their divorce proceedings had finally begun. I had moved back home to try and help my mother. She seemed to be struggling mentally and I thought it might be better if she was not alone. He didn't like that my attention was focused on something other than him, which made it really hard to try and help my mother. Once I moved back home and started to put a little distance between us, I started to see things more clearly and realized that I had been living in a nightmare. I started sleeping better at night and my mind was able to start the process of letting go and trying to move forward with my life.

We continued our relationship for a few months, after I moved back in with my mother. During which time, things got so bad that my mother had to get a court order to keep my father out of the house because of an incident between him and I. We got in a huge fight one night when he came home drunk, again. As things escalated and one thing led to another, I ended up pushing him down the basement stairs. I think the only reason why he didn't get seriously injured was because he was so loaded drunk. Once again, he called me a "no good, rotten, ungrateful, little whore", who he said he was ashamed to admit was his daughter. I was "written out of the will" and "totally disowned" in his eyes. This was not the first time that these words had been said by him but it would be the last time. He said as long as he still lived in that house, that I was not welcome and I needed to take my "mutt" and leave, and so I did. I went straight back to my ex and his craziness, for about a month or so. Just until my mother was able to legally have my father removed from the house. The day he moved out, I moved back in smiling as I passed him in the hallway.

I started to feel like I wanted a real life. I started to feel like I deserved more. Hell, if my mother could do it, I certainly could. My ex did not like this new sense of independence I was feeling, at all. I broke off our engagement and told him that I simply wasn't ready for marriage. I came up with an exit plan and actually got out of the situation quite well, or so I thought at the time.

Later that night, he found my car parked outside of a friends apartment. I was only in the apartment building for about a half hour and when I came out all the windows in my car had been broken out. My poor dog Bear was still in the back seat with glass all over her! I felt so bad for her. She must have been terrified! I was totally surprised that she didn't jump out and run in fear, I probably would have. She was my sidekick though, she probably knew to stay in the car. I think she knew that I would be along to save her. Or, maybe she was trying to protect the car. It was like our second home, after all. We spent a lot of time going for drives together. It was one of our favourite past times. After that incident, she stayed home or went inside with me, wherever I went. It was a hard way to learn a lesson, but we got it.

Then a couple of nights later he bumped my car on the rear bumper with his car, all the way up the local boulevard in our town. He just kept ramming my car with his trying to drive me off the road. The next visit from him would be the last. He showed up at my mother's house one night, uninvited. I decided to go outside as mother wasn't doing very well that day and I wanted to spare her the drama. I should have just called the police right away. I had filed an official complaint after the window breaking and bumper ramming incidents.

When I went out to talk to him, he grabbed me and slammed me up against the garage door so hard that the noise was heard by one of our neighbours. I could see her peeking out her window trying to see what was going on. I think that was the saving grace because he saw she was witnessing his actions. He threatened to kill me that night and I really believe he meant it. He might have gone through with it, but my mother flicked the light on at the back door and with the neighbour watching, he didn't dare. Then my mother screamed out the door that she was calling the police, so he left.

I knew I had to do something or he would follow through with his promise. So, I decided to contact a well respected friend, and called in a favour. He said he was happy that I reached out to him and that he would be glad to help. I basically told him what had happened and what was continuing to happen and that I just needed it to stop. I didn't want to know the particulars of what he would do to make this happen. My only request was that I wanted him to go away and leave me alone, but still wanted him to be able to live his life.

After about a week or so, my friend reached out and told me, quite bluntly, that he would never bother me again. I found out later that my friend roughed him up some and put the fear of God into him. It was just enough encouragement for him to finally leave me be. I was finally able to start to move on with my life, though I still kept a constant watch over my shoulder. I will admit that it took years for me to finally feel at ease while being out in public again.

My life in that world was always exciting and I truly felt a sense of belonging, just not with my ex. It had come to the point where I could not continue to be part of that world anymore because of him. The chances of running into him were just too great! The last thing I needed was for that door to be opened again. My friends in that world understood and wanted me to be able to move on. They gave me their blessing to leave it all behind and encouraged me to build a new life for myself. Which was exactly what I started to do. I still saw some of them from time to time, in passing or at the grocery store or maybe a local bar. It was really nice to be able to give them a friendly nod and know that all is well.

I did see my ex one more time after that. It was when I was on a date with my new boyfriend, who is now my husband. We were at a local club when I saw someone from my past. He came to me very discretely at the bar and leaned in and he told me that my ex was there. Then he told me not to be concerned however, they were watching out for me and my new friend. I decided it would be good to clear the air with my ex, seeing as I was in a safe zone. I could feel his eyes on me and eventually I got up the courage, I told my guardians what I was up to and took him outside.

I basically told him that I forgave him and didn't want any trouble. I had moved on and hoped that he had as well. I wished him a long and happy life but there was no longer a place for him in my life. He reacted with a comment that he had been moving on even before we split and that he had a child with another woman. He had gotten her pregnant while we were still together, which was no surprise to me. Regardless, we left the conversation on good terms, wished each other well and have not spoken since. I think he may have just been happy that I didn't have him maimed or worse. All that being said, I consider myself very lucky. It all could have turned out much worse for me.

I had met my ex when I was in high school and all of the craziness with him made it hard for me to focus on what I needed and wanted. His needs and wants clouded what I really should have been focusing on, which was me and my future. I ended up spending an extra year in high school because the requirements to graduate were changed during what was supposed to have been my graduating year. As it turned out,

I was missing one course credit and would not be able to graduate with my peers. So, I had to return the following year for one morning class in order to graduate and get my diploma. Honestly, at that point, I really wasn't sure what I was going to do anyway and so it bought me another year to try and figure it out.

My plan when I entered high school was to build a portfolio and apply to a well known art college in Nova Scotia. It was a dream of mine and I think that attending that school could have opened many doors for me and my future. Unfortunately, with all the problems with my ex and my parents, I did not get my portfolio completed. My ex would not have let me go anyway. His control over me was very strong. My parents said I could have gone but I could tell by their lack of encouragement and the doubt in their tone that they had no real faith in my abilities. My mother would have never wanted me to leave our city and my father would not have wanted to offer any financial help. He said he would have helped but I truly believe it would have ended up being all on my own steam. He never followed through with anything he ever told me. Looking back, I should have never listened to any of them and followed my heart. I could have done it all on my own! Look at what I had already done and accomplished. Look at what I had already lived through.

On the other side of that coin, if I had gone I might never have met the love of my life, Derek. I also would have never found one of the best friends of my life, my Irish Wolfhound, Bear.

Bear was a kind and beautiful soul. I found her as a puppy one day, in a tiny pet store, as I was walking through the mall close to where I lived at the time. This little pet store, which I visited frequently, had just gotten a litter of puppies who were in need of some forever homes. The store didn't normally sell or place puppies and kittens unless someone was just looking to find homes for them. I have never been a fan of buying a puppy or kitten from pet stores but they assured me that it was a mistake litter and only charged me a small fee to cover the costs they had incurred while housing them. I spent more on the accessories than the sweet lovable little puppy.

I was really missing having a dog, as we always had a dog in the house when I was growing up. I just couldn't resist her cute little face looking up at me. She was sitting quietly by herself while the rest of the pups were playing and rough housing. I called her Bear, which was short for Teddy Bear. She was so cute and looked just like a little teddy bear and was just as cuddly. She could not have been more than six or seven weeks old when she came to live with me and my ex. At the time, I thought we would make an awesome little family so I scooped her up and brought her home. She was very intelligent and caught on to things very quickly. I couldn't believe that it only took three days for her to become fully house trained. She was very eager to please and I was very happy with her. We bonded and she had me wrapped around her little paw so very quickly. I knew right away that she would be the most loyal friend I ever had and that we would have a good long life together.

I took her everywhere with me. We were inseparable, I even took her to work with me. At the time, I was working at the motel that my father owned. She was a great friend and companion on those long and lonely night shifts working on the front desk. She was quiet and very well behaved. She just wanted to be with me and her contentment in that really showed. She grew very quickly. As some of you may know, Irish Wolfhounds are a very large breed. She certainly would make those people with a late night check in think twice about giving me a hard time. Although she was not one bit aggressive, just the look of her was enough to make a drunken jerk "back off". They didn't know she was a lover not a fighter! She never had to be tied and never wandered off. She was content to just lay around within view of me or sometimes follow me from room to room in case I dropped a treat out of my pocket.

There were some regular visitors to the motel who got to know and love her, as well. People would remember her and often ask about her if they didn't see her right away. In some cases, if they had their doors open and spoke to her as she sauntered on by, she would pop in for a visit and maybe a little snack and then be on her way again. Sometimes after my shifts, I would have to take a walk only to find her snuggling up with someone, getting attention and enjoying the tasty morsels they were sharing.

As soon as I was able to acquire a car, Bear quickly became a fan of letting her wispy, long flowing hair blow in the breeze of the open car window. I can remember several occasions when I allowed her to sit in the front seat, that people would mistake her long flowing hair for a person, from behind. As they drove up along side of us and looked at a stop light, they would be so surprised to see her sitting up in the seat with her long, wet and hairy nose. Most often, it would be men thinking they were going to get a glance at a pretty lady and hoping for a closer look. The surprised double take on their faces when they saw her, was priceless. I could almost see Bear smiling, it was just that funny! Once they realized they were mistaken and saw me laughing, the other motorists would always get a good chuckle too.

Bear was a hero, she saved me on many occasions. In the times when I thought that my life was pointless and that things would never be worth the effort, she would come to me. All she had to do was look at me with those beautiful eyes and my heart felt full again. I would remind myself that if I ended my life, there would be no one to look after and take care of her. Not to mention the fact that she made me feel like all the suffering and hardship that I endured was worth it to have a friend like her. The good times we had together were my saving grace.

I loved Bear like she was a part of me and I guess she was. She was part of my heart. A part of my heart that would be forever broken when it was time to let her go. I protected her from any form of danger, as best I could. I would put myself in between her and harm in any and every situation possible. But, in the end, when she was diagnosed with cancer, it was not something that I could protect her from. Our Vet told us that she had a tumour that had attached itself to her liver. Derek and I tried to keep her as comfortable as possible in her last days. The one Sunday night, the tumour basically burst inside her and I could tell, from my training with animals, that she was bleeding internally. I knew we had to get her to the clinic as soon as possible.

I will never forget watching Derek lifting her up into the back of our mini van. It was a dark and cold night and as he started to close the door and I remember telling him that I wanted ride in the back with her. I didn't want to leave her side as she would not have left mine, if the roles had been reversed. She laid her head in my lap and I held her on what seemed like the longest ride of our lives. As we pulled up to building, the vet on call that night was right there waiting for us. We rushed Bear in and put her on the cold metal table. I was holding her head as I asked if there was anything that could be done for her. The vet's response was that the most kind thing we could do for her at that point was to relieve her pain and not let her suffer any longer.

As the vet was saying the words Bear looked up at me with those loving eyes, asking me to let her go. I could feel her pain but at the same time I didn't want to let her go. Our friendship was the purest thing I had ever felt. She had been the only constant in my life for a very long time. I was so lonely before she came along. She filled my need to love and to be loved. I loved her like she was my child. How does one say goodbye to their child forever? How would I go on without her? What kind of friend would I be to let her suffer, even after she asked me to let her go?

Somehow, I found the strength and said my good bye, as did Derek, to my sweet loving Teddy Bear. As Bear closed her eyes I could feel peace for her but my pain was very real and almost unbearable. I don't think I have ever been the same since that night. She left a lasting impression on me that will never be forgotten. I think of her every day and I am grateful for having her in my life, for as long I did. She died just about two months shy of her fourteenth birthday. Which is very old for a dog as large as she was. By the time she passed away, my life with Derek had become something that was going to be long term and was something real. He loved her almost as much as I did. She lived long enough to see us get married and I believe that she knew that I was finally in good hands and that she could go to her resting place without any worry for me. As hard as it was to say goodbye, I could see in her eyes that she had become a very tired old girl and I knew that it was time to let her go.

Bear had changed my life and made my world a much better place. She was the reason I decided to become a dog groomer. She will never be forgotten and I am sure I will see her again in the afterlife. She is patiently waiting for me in the car. Waiting to go for a drive and get a snack. But most of all, she is waiting for a big hug and kiss. After knowing, loving and living with her, there is a piece of my heart that will never be the same again since her passing. I miss you old friend! So very much!

Bear was the first of many cherished pets and beloved animal companions that I chose to have and care for in my life. Growing up, our family had a golden lab mix named Candy. It doesn't seem right to not mention her. She was a great family dog. She, like Bear, was also a very loving friend and had a kind heart. She was sixteen years of age when my parents had her put to sleep. It broke my heart to see her go. She had been my only friend and ally in that house and I really wasn't sure how I would be able to cope without her. At the time, I too was almost sixteen years old and often wondered what would happen to me once my sixteenth birthday came around?

Shortly after that, my parents decided to get another dog. It was on my sixteenth birthday. They said the dog would be my birthday present. So, happy birthday to me, my mother picked out the breed. Which was a cocker spaniel. But then as an added birthday bonus, they said I could name her. That was of course as long as my mother approved, as she would have the final say. I picked and suggested several great names. But Elizabeth or Libby for short, the one that was on the very bottom of my list, was the one she picked. The one I liked the least. I guess you can probably see where this is going, right? The dog was always meant to be my mother's dog. My birthday was just the excuse she needed to get what it was that *she* wanted. More family love!

Mother quickly got attached to Libby and it was clear that she had no intention of letting me keep my birthday present. I asked to take her with me when I moved out of the house knowing full well what the answer would be. I had to ask though, just to confirm what I already knew. It was her wants and her needs first, again! Or still? Both, again and still? I'm not sure.

The sad reality of Libby's short life was that my mother basically fed her to death. She fed her unhealthy quantities of take out food, on a regular basis. It eventually got to the point where if you had her in the car with you, she would go crazy if she saw the MacDonald's golden arches. It was completely ridiculous. I remember right around that time Burger King had a special on, which they called "the two for". You could purchase two burgers and two fries for an extremely low price. Mother would get this special and eat one burger and one fry and would give the other burger and fry to the dog and she did this on a regular basis. Libby was five years old when she died alone at the vet clinic. Her back and hips went due to obesity. Mother had a trip planned to Prince Edward Island at the time, so she just took the dog to the vet and went on her trip. Libby passed away while my mother was gone and for some reason, I only came to find out how all of this took place, some time later. Happy Birthday Tanya! Oh, and remember, we "love you"!

I remember at one point in my first year of high school, that the fighting between the three of us, mother, father and myself had gotten bad to the point where we had a major blow up. I'm not even sure what it was all about, that particular time, it could have been anything. But, I do remember it to be one of the worst. My father was so angry with me fighting back that he said he just wanted me gone. I gave him his wish and called my friend who lived just down the road from us, who was a little older than me. She lived with her adopted parents and her adopted older brother. Their parents were quite a bit older than the parents of most the other kids our age. They were an older English couple with thick English accents, who were extremely pleasant and polite. I used to love talking with them. I very much enjoyed their polite and pleasant ways and their wonderful accent. Everyone in the home I grew up in was always so rude and mean. So this polite and pleasant English couple was a breath of fresh air for me. They always greeted me with such kindness and I always felt very safe and welcome in their home. Something I wasn't really used to. Safe, or welcome!

I envied my friend because her parents seemed so loving and caring toward their children, especially if I was comparing them to the way I was treated at home. When I called her, I was very upset and told her about the big fight with my parents and how my father just wanted me to leave. Without hesitation, she told me to start walking toward her house with an overnight bag and she would me meet me halfway.

I was so relieved! I had somewhere to go even if it was only for one night! When we met up along the road, she immediately hugged me and said her parents would be happy to have me stay with them. Which I thought she meant, just for the night. When we made it back to her house it was like we had a slumber party in her basement, where we usually hung out. Her parents were always very good about giving her privacy especially when having friends over. I recall that we stayed up most of the night listening to music and talking. Finally, we fell asleep in the early part of the morning. Thank goodness we didn't have school the next day!

When we did finally wake up and made our way up to the kitchen, breakfast had been prepared and was waiting for us. Her parents had already eaten and were sitting in the living room in their favourite chairs reading, as they did a lot. We had a great day together. I recall getting upset around supper time thinking I would have to leave and go back home. I wouldn't dream of overstaying my welcome. Especially after my visit had been on such short notice. As I got up and was preparing to go, I thanked them for everything, told them just how grateful I was and started to tell my friend that I would see her at school. She responded saying, "you can't go home". As we walked to get my belongings, I told her that I would find somewhere to go. I thought maybe I would call my grandparents, as I had done before, on many occasions. The problem with that plan, however, was that they were now living in the house they were building in the country. They were no longer close by in our neighbourhood anymore, which posed a problem for getting back and forth to school. Besides, I really didn't want to get into the whole story of why I was needing a place to stay, with them, again. My parents used to ship me off to them a lot when I was younger. But this time, I would have to tell them the real reason why I was needing a place to stay. I hated to tell them anything about the fighting because it would always upset them. So, I simply told my kind friend that I would figure something out and not to worry.

As I grabbed my bag and started toward the door, I heard her Mother's voice call out to me. She asked me to come into the living room where both of my friend's parents were sitting. She said that my friend had told them that I was having some problems at home and they wanted me to feel free to stay with them, for as long as I needed, if I would like. She said that, of course, there were some rules that I would have to follow, but I was welcome as long as I complied. She said that they had a spare room right beside my friend's room and that it was mine for as long as I needed or wanted it.

I was so pleasantly surprised and extremely happy to agree to the terms and rules that were set out for me. Was this my chance for a real family life? I loved her parents and they were very kind and generous toward me, with anything that I needed. I think they just always wanted to have a house full of kids and weren't able to have them on their own, which is why they adopted my friend and her older brother. They seemed like they were comfortable financially and able to help me. They were willing to give me a chance and I was more than willing to help out and earn my keep.

When I finally did called my mother, a few days later to let her know where I was, she didn't seem to be surprised at my news. We had been hanging out a lot and their home was relatively close. Of course she wanted me to come back home, but I refused. She didn't argue the point at the time, knowing how my father felt about me. Three weeks went by and I was very happy living in my new surroundings. I was becoming part of the family. I was doing my chores and my homework and having actual conversations with adults who listened and participated. They were lovely people and I grew very fond of them! Unfortunately, it wasn't too much longer before my friend's brother started to get himself into some trouble which started to add stress for their parents. I could feel that the tension building and that something may soon have to change. During these three weeks, I had hardly talked to my mother at all. But, when I did she would tell me that my father had calmed down. I did not want to go back but also did not want to burden my friend's parents considering the troubles they were having with their son. I thought long and hard about going back home and my friend and her parents tried to convince me to stay. But in the end, I decided to go back.

I had hoped that things would be different and that maybe they had missed me so much that I would finally have the loving family I had always dreamed of. Things were better for a little while but just like always, the fighting started again. I wished for the longest time that I hadn't made the decision to go back. I was happy and felt loved at the house down the road, I wish I would have stayed. I had made my decision, however, and would have to try and figure out a way to live with it, again, for just a little longer. I hoped that I would make it this time.

# CHAPTER 4

*Born with an artist's Heart*

I was born with an artist's heart. Up to this point in my life, however, I am the only one who really saw, felt or knew this. I can't really explain how I knew it, I just did. It was just something that always felt natural to me. It was something that always made me feel good.

Once I graduated from high school, I decided to take a year off from school to work and think about what my next move was. With all of the chaos in my life up until that point, I felt like I could benefit from a little time to think about what *I* wanted to do. A little time to think about which direction *I* could see my life going, before I committed to the next phase of my education. Once my year was up, my parents were relentless. They insisted that they thought I needed to have something to "fall back on", as they put it. Over and over again, my mother would remind me of this, daily. As if I had forgotten the previous two thousand and twenty-four times she had "just mentioned it". I was living this life after all and I was very aware of everything that had and was happening in it. They insisted that I needed some sort of secondary education, something more than just a high school diploma.

After finally graduating from high school, I had moved into a place with my ex, "Mr. Right". I think that a lot of my hesitation in deciding to go back to school was that if I did, I would not be able to keep up financially, with having my own place. This left only one option and that was to move back to house of horrors, while I went to school and I absolutely dreaded the thought of doing so. I was out! How could I go back to that place? How could I go back to the house of horrors, again?? In the end, I decided that I would try it. After all, it would only be for a year. Right? Wouldn't it? Yeah, that's it, just one year.

My dream was to go to art college and that's what *I* really wanted to do. I didn't just want something to "fall back on"! I didn't want to just settle for life's "plan B"! I wanted to live my passion, all day and everyday! *That* was the next step that I would choose, if it were just up to me. If I had chosen this however, it would have been the very first time in my life that I would make a decision that was based solely on what I wanted. The number one lesson that had been drilled, nagged and literally beaten into me up until this point in my life, was that the wants and needs of others were to come before my own. ALWAYS! Besides, how could I possibly even apply? During my time in high school, when I was supposed to be working on my portfolio, I was looking after others. Just like I was trained to do. Even if I would have had a portfolio ready to submit, I did not have the means. I would have had to ask for help from my parents and *if* that help had come, it would have come with a price. A very high price! Maybe not in the form of actual interest dollars, but certainly in other forms. After all, if I was to ask for, or get something that could have somehow taken away from what another family member could have had, or wanted, it would never have be forgotten. I would constantly be reminded of how someone else had to sacrifice or do without so that I could have this or do that. The repeated attempts to extract feelings of guilt and shame from me, after the fact, were simply relentless. They just never stopped! Even today, as I'm writing these words, it still happens. They never miss an opportunity to remind me of something they gave, or something they did, or something they did without, so I could have or do something. It was just not worth it!! Some things cost too much, even if they are "free"! I was very lost at the time and I think I was longing for some sort of guidance. I'm not even exactly sure what type of guidance I was looking for. Mostly, I think I was just wanting to have someone in my life to say "Yes, follow your dreams!", "I can see you have a real talent and passion for this.", "Follow your heart!", "You can do it!" It's a lot to ask for I know. But, it sure would have been nice at that time.

So, in the end, my parents both decided that the best course of action was for me to enrol in a local business college secretarial program. My father said he wanted me to go to the same college that he attended after high school. He had connections there you see, and of course, he knew the owners and some of the staff. Probably from one of his "males only" social clubs or some crazy circle jerk that he regularly attended. So, as a result, this was going to be a much cheaper alternative for him, than art college. Besides which, art college? "Nobody ever got rich, going to art college". Then at least, if he had to talk about me with his cronies, he could tell them that he sent me to school and he gave me this wonderful opportunity. As an added bonus, he would be able to seize every possible opportunity to talk about, and of course, remind me of what *he* had done for me. Maybe I thought that if I agreed to go, there was a slight chance that he would then show some sort of fondness or respect toward me. Maybe he would even *act* proud of me. Or, maybe I was just tired of listening to them go on and on about how they were right and that I just needed to do what they were suggesting. Yeah, maybe it was that! So, in the end I decided to apply and wouldn't you know it, I was accepted.

All of a sudden, there I was, a high school art major who had her sights set on having a perfectly prepared portfolio and attending the best art college in the area after high school, enrolled in business college. I was ill prepared, to say the least. My high school course selections most certainly did not prepare me for such a program. I'm just not wired that way and had no real foundation of knowledge for the courses and the material in a program of that type, which I felt put me at a real disadvantage. But, I was there and wanted to try to do my best. So, I studied and worked hard and I did manage to graduate.

In the end, I did well in all of my courses except accounting. Wait, wait I know what you're thinking. I was as surprised as you are. I mean really? An art major who didn't do well in the accounting program? Come on?? This was something that the faculty and staff were quite surprised by, I'm sure. After all, my father excelled in accounting. Which of course, made perfect sense to me. There was *nothing* he loved more than counting his money!

In a frustrated moment of weakness, I asked him for help with my accounting course, once. It didn't go well! He quickly got frustrated with me and told me that "you either get it or you don't and that I didn't", he then walked away and left me to figure it out on my own. I know, I know, Art major. He must have had some money to count that day. So, I went for some extra help after class and I did manage to pass the course. But the grade was the lowest of all of my courses. Surprised?

Remember that show of fondness I was hoping for earlier on? You know from enrolling in the same college as him. Well, it didn't come. There was no improvement in our relationship at all. Damn it, fooled again!!

I realize now why my parents wanted me to take some sort of secondary education, it wasn't to benefit me in my life. It was engineered to make them look like they were wonderful parents. You know, for sending their lost daughter to a wonderfully prestigious local business college. After all, we did have the *appearance* of having the perfect family with two successful and obedient children to uphold and for the whole world to see! Maybe they just really needed people to know how much *they* had done for us.

Maybe they thought that people would hold them in high regard for trying to give me a "successful" future? This was certainly not what I truly wanted, but it did seem to make them feel better about themselves. Maybe it soothed their conscience, or, maybe it stroked their egos? I'm not really sure which. After all, how could they send my brother to University and then have to tell their friends at the club that their daughter didn't have any secondary education? How would that look? Well, at least to the people who knew I existed. I actually got invited to a "club" function one time, where, when I was introduced to people they said, "really, I thought your brother was an only child?". Many years have passed in my life and I still meet people who have known my father very well for years, who have told me that they never knew he had a daughter. "He only ever talked about his son.", they would say. Maybe he was embarrassed of me and my artistic ways? Or, maybe he didn't like the reflection he saw when he looked at me? Either way, it really doesn't matter anymore. I like me!

Once I graduated, I did use some of my newly acquired business skills, for a little while. I applied for a job at a local transportation firm and got a position at one of their departmental mini reception areas, in the head office building. In addition to my reception duties, I also had some regular daily tasks provided by one of their many claims departments. Yay, more accounting! One question though. Just why did they have so many claims departments anyway?

I think that maybe I got this job because I went in for an interview right after I had all four of my wisdom teeth pulled out. I like to believe that I showed them my persistence in doing whatever it took to get the job and that I would work hard even through difficult situations. Maybe this proved that I was worthy of the job and would be a good employee. Plus, I looked pitiful. I could barely even talk through the interview. I think the man who interviewed me, who later became my supervisor, just really felt sorry for me. I was black and blue and swollen to the point that it looked like I had no neck. My chin and shoulders looked like they were connected with no separation. What a sight!

I had to have my wisdom teeth taken out, at the dentist's office, just before the interview. This, of course, was not his preferred approach. He did not want to perform the procedure in such a way, considering the extensive work that had to be done. He wanted to book an appointment for me at the hospital so he could put me under sedation and do things properly. As it turned out, he actually had to break pieces of my jaw bone in order to get the teeth out.

All of that considered however, I had to insist that he do the procedure in his office with just the freezing and as soon as possible. It was something that I had to have done and it had to be right away, as my father was taking me off of his insurance plan and would not wait so that I could have had the procedure done properly, at the hospital. Without insurance, of course, I could not have afforded to have it done. So, freezing in the office chair it was. I guess father won that round.

This new office job of mine was not something that I was particularly fond of. All repetitive, mundane and routine tasks, with very little physical activity or even movement. It was not something I was used to or really even enjoyed all that much. But, it was a job and a pay check, which I needed. So I stayed and thought that it was alright, for now. Well, alright, for now, ended up being a little over two years. In the end, however, I am glad I took the local college secretarial course and got the office job at the transportation firm, because it was those choices and decisions that lead to me meeting the love of my life.

I was still seeing the ex I talked about earlier, when I accepted my office job. But it wasn't long after that my world took another huge turn. In a matter of a year and a half I moved back home, again, to help my mother because her and my father were finally getting divorced. Which was my fault and my doing, depending on who you ask. In addition, my ex and I had also recently separated. I know it seems like a lot of chaos and moving in and out of the family home but really, my whole life had been like that. So, I guess it all just seemed somewhat normal to me, at the time.

I had a friend who worked in the same building where my new office job was, in a different department. He was fun individual who loved to play jokes and goof off. He was always trying to find an excuse to tour around the building looking busy. He worked in the mail room downstairs, which gave him lots of time and opportunity to tour around and entertain himself. One day he came to my area and introduced me to a new and handsome young man who had just started working in the department next to his. This new employee's name was Derek and although I did not know it at the time, he would become my future husband.

As part of his job, Derek used to deliver supplies around the building and when he got the chance, he would come and visit with me. I looked forward to his friendly smile and our fun conversations. As we slowly got to know each other, I discovered that his sense of humour really meshed well with mine and we quickly became friends.

We both travelled on the same stretch of highway to the office building where we worked and I can remember trying to time it so that my morning drive was at about the same time as his. He was a creature of habit, just like me and so I would try to catch up to him on the highway. If I saw him, I would pull up beside him and try to get his attention. At which point, I would smile and wave and then pass him and speed off. In doing so, we would reach the parking lot at about the same time and I could be sure that we could walk in together. He was quite shy and I don't think he even knew what I was attempting to do. I liked him and really wanted to spend more time with him.

We shared a love for music and so we easily connected in this way. When he told me about a band he was playing in, as a drummer, I was intrigued and very much wanted to hear them play. So, I told him about a bar that I liked, where they held regular Saturday evening jam sessions. I encouraged him to bring his band mates by some night, knowing that I could get them a spot in the evening, as I was a regular there and knew the owner and staff very well. This bar was always looking for new talent and from what he had told me about their type of music, I knew they would fit right in. So they showed up to play one night and they were a hit. It was a really fun night for everyone in attendance!

Then all of a sudden, Derek just stopped coming to work. It took a little digging on my part, but I managed to find out that their band had a gig at a club downtown, as the house band for a regular weekly jam night. So, I went to check it out one Monday night and I had a great time. The lead singer of the band spotted me smiling in the crowd and at break time came over to talk to me. Once again, I had freshly boarded the single train and I really couldn't tell if Derek was even interested in me. So, one thing lead to another and I thought why not play the field a little. I'll get to know this singer a little bit and see where it goes. He and I dated for a bit but I quickly realized that we were not compatible, long term. I broke it off and thought that it was probably best if I made myself scarce for awhile.

Then one day, when I was out running errands, I remembered that I was getting low on dog food. I used to buy a premium brand that you could only purchase at the vet clinic or one other specialty store, at the time. It just so happened that the specialty store was one of the store's that Derek's Dad managed. I remembered him telling me that his Dad's store carried the food I was feeding to my Bear and that he worked there occasionally. So I thought I would go see if I could get the food, and maybe Derek would be there. Or, maybe his Dad could tell me what he had been up to. With this plan, I decided to pay a visit.

His Dad was at the cash register when I went into the store and was the one who waited on me. As he was processing my purchase, I asked him if maybe, by chance, Derek was around? He said yes of course and that he would get him to bring the dog food out to my car for me, as he smiled widely. I knew it was his Dad because of the similarity in their facial features. So, Derek comes out to my car with the dog food and one really nice conversation lead to him finally asking me out on a date. Did I mention, finally? Anyone who knows me would tell you that subtlety is not what I'm most known for. I thought I was making myself and my intentions very clear. But, why didn't he get it? Well as it turns out, that was just his way. I am thankful that we took our time in getting to know each other, however. Because, you see that is how and where our life's journey together began.

We quickly became inseparable. I went to all of his gigs and we mostly always stayed together. We were either at his place or mine when it was time to get some sleep. Which we rarely did in those days. It was so much fun to be living that life! We were surrounded by music and people who loved it just as much as we did. It was one of the best times of my life and I wouldn't change one second of it!

When Derek and I started dating, I was living at home with mother. She and my father had just signed their divorce papers and she was having a really tough time with it. She seemed to like Derek and didn't seem to mind him sleeping over. I think she was just happy to have us there and have some activity in the house again. Once things finally did get going (insert eye roll here), they seemed to move quickly between Derek and I. Not long after, we decided to get our own place together. We stayed at my mother's just briefly before we got our own place, with Bear of course. Bear and I came as a package deal and it was non-negotiable. Derek and I didn't have a lot in those days. We were starting out and our life was based around the band and music. But we had each other and Bear and we made it work. We both worked hard and managed to have fun. Well, that was probably the thing we had the most of, fun!

Derek always made sure we had what we needed. I can remember that our first place, which was a mobile home, wasn't very well insulated. In fact, if it hadn't been for Derek's gig money to pay for oil, I think we would had frozen to death. We only stayed there for one winter, after finding out that our neighbours were stealing oil from our tank for most of the winter, we decided to move on. All of our charitable donations had to go to our own causes, in those early days of adulthood and musician life.

We lived in many places in the early part of our lives together. The first place that we bought was a mini home, which we later sold to his aunt, who wanted to move back home from Ontario. She wanted to be closer to her remaining family, after she retired. For a short time, we also lived in the superintendent apartment at my father's motel. These accommodations, came along with the Manager's position and the deal was that we would help people check in late at night, if someone was looking for a room. I also worked my regular day shifts and Derek helped out in every way imaginable when he was around. I liked it there because it was something familiar. Bear and I had started our life together there. But, like a lot of good things in my life, it too had a shelf life. My father was working hard on a deal to sell the place. So I knew that it was just a matter of time before I would be starting over, again.

We were still staying at the motel when my grandmother passed away. At the same time, my father was in the process of finalizing a deal to sell the motel buildings. Which the new owners would then move to their location in Nova Scotia. Then all he would have to do, was sell the land so it could be developed. Which he eventually did which meant that I was out of a job. It took some time for them to work out the details but it all worked out for him in the end. As most things seem to do, for him. He thought it would work out and happen rather quickly, so he decided to let me go immediately.

I started my search for new work with my father. Maybe, I thought? So I asked him if I could work with him and my brother in the family construction business. He refused and told me that there was no work for me there. Then a day or two later he hired his girlfriend, you remember the younger model from earlier, to do his secretarial and office work. "But wait, I thought, I went to your college and took the secretarial program to prepare me for office work just like you suggested. I could... oh never mind. Probably too damn much accounting anyway!". I was rather disappointed at the time, but was not surprised at all. He really did me a favour, when I think about it now though. That really was no place for me!

At that point, Derek and I were making plans to move to the country with my Grampy. Two weeks before my Grandmother passed away, in a one on one conversation, she asked me if I would consider moving in with and helping Grampy, should anything ever happen to her. To which I replied, "of course, but let's not talk about that right now.", "You're going to be fine!", I said. I guess maybe she knew something that I did not.

So that was exactly what we did. I took some time to just be there with and for Grampy, which gave us time to grieve together and gave me a chance to think about my next move. I needed a change in my career habits and this gave me a little time to think about it. It was at that point, I decided I would learn some new skills and develop a new career for myself. I decided I would become a dog groomer. It was something that I could eventually do for myself, which really appealed to me. I loved animals, I could be creative and I would be my own boss. I felt that I would be really good at it and it would be a great fit for me!

So I signed up for the three month course and I graduated at the top of my class. I absolutely loved it!
I was so excited! I can still remember Grampy and Derek building my very first grooming table out in the workshop. We even turned part of Grampy's basement into a make shift shop for me. I used the tub in the downstairs bathroom and started to groom some friends and neighbours dogs in the room across the hall. This helped me to get some practise and develop my newly acquired skills. After a few months, when it seemed that Grampy was going to be okay on his own, we moved back to town. I had just graduated and decided that I wanted to work with another experienced groomer until I felt really comfortable to groom on my own. My search for work lead me to a groomer in Amherst, NS, which was about an hour away from where we lived, at the time. This woman had been in the business for over thirty years and at that time had a pet shop and grooming shop all in one, in the town. I thought it would be a great opportunity for me, as I could learn a lot from working with someone who had that type of experience. I was sure that I would see and learn all sorts of things that I had not encountered in my three month course.

I called her up and she asked me to come to her shop and groom a dog for her, as this would be my interview. It was basically to see if I had any skills and the right temperament for the trade. I was very honest with her and told her that I was fresh out of school, but was willing to work hard and prove my worth. On the day I showed up for my test grooming, the shop was full of dogs. They were absolutely everywhere. It was easy to see by the number of the dogs, that she was extremely busy and really in need of some qualified help.

The test dog she gave me was one of her show dogs. No pressure though! At the time, she was breeding and showing miniature poodles from her home base in Parrsboro, NS, where she also had a boarding kennel. She was a very busy woman and to me, she seemed very driven and determined so I thought we would get along just fine. She was a single woman who was mostly married to her work and was totally devoted to her dogs. I was nervous to groom her show dog. What if I make a mistake, I thought? My want for the job and the experience it would bring helped me to quickly overcome my fear and get to work, however. I knew I could learn a lot from this woman and I needed to show her that I had skills.

She told me that she had no use for the school I had graduated from. She said that she had interviewed several people who had graduated from there and they were all useless. She did say however, that she was desperate and in dire need of some qualified help. So, she was going to give me a shot and hoped that I wouldn't disappoint her. She was a very gruff woman that never pulled any punches, with anyone, employees or customers. She was not long telling people what she thought of any situation. She spoke her mind, always! I saw it as a quality that I very much admired. As we worked together and got to know each other, I really did take a liking to her.

So back to interview day, I got started with the poodle, who was named Celine. Yes, I even remember the dog's name. She wanted me to show her my scissoring skills, which made me even more nervous because scissoring is a technique that can require a lot of practice to get right. I felt that I was naturally good at it and hoped that she would see some promise in my development.

I really took my time and spent almost two hours scissoring Celine. I wanted to make sure that I did the best job I could possibly do. In addition to scissoring, she also wanted me to shave her face and feet. These were all things that we were shown in school but did not get a lot of time to practice, so I was a little nervous. But just the same, I suppressed my nerves and gave it my best go. In the end, Celine looked pretty damn good, if I do say so myself. She was pleased and very shocked with the job I had done. She instantly offered me the job, which I accepted. For the rest of the day, she introduced me as her fantastic new groomer, to anyone that came through the door. I think my head got a little swollen that day, I was so proud of what I had accomplished!!

I drove there in the morning three days a week, worked the whole day grooming as many dogs as I could possibly do and then drove back home. It was really hard work, but I enjoyed every minute of it. She showed me so much more than I could have ever imagined or would have ever learned by just striking out on my own, fresh out of school. While we worked, she would tell me stories of when she took her grooming course. She was taught by an "old German lady", as she described it, who was extremely strict in her teaching methods. I found listening to her stories to be very intriguing. She told me of a time when her instructor told her that the dog on the table in front of her, needed to be shaved. So, she went to work on shaving the dog. When the instructor came back, she was shocked. My new teacher had shaved the dog alright. She shaved everything. The head, the face, the feet and even the tail. She cackled as she told me the story and I couldn't help but laugh too. Although I did feel a little sorry for the dog and the owner. One thing is for certain though, the hair would grow back. It would take some time, but it would grow back. The instructor cracked my new teacher on the knuckles with her wooden pointer and called her an idiot. Her instruction was to shave the dog, but not every square inch. Maybe the instructions were lacking a little? You do have to give my new teacher points for being thorough, however.

She had a very hardy laugh, which I found very contagious and she always told her stories with such enthusiasm. I thought we got along really well and were able to groom a lot of dogs together. I was right in thinking she could teach me a thing or two. She was a fountain of information and I absorbed all that I could and was thankful for the opportunity to do so. I worked with her for almost two years and then one day she told me that her vet, who was located in Truro, Nova Scotia was loosing her groomer. She asked me if I would be interested in going with her for a couple of Saturdays, just before Christmas, to groom some of their regular client's dogs. She told me that if I met her here in Amherst, early in the morning, she would drive to Truro and back. I'm thankful for the enthusiasm and energy I had back then. Because, to work a full day grooming and add to that, a total of four and a half hours driving time, made it a very large day. She told me that we would be well compensated for our efforts and, for me, some extra pay around Christmas time was always welcomed. I agreed to go and give it a try. I think on our biggest day, we did thirty six dogs. I could hardly believe it and I was there! I would rough them out and bathe them and then she would finish them. We used the cage dryers for some of them, which helped a lot, on such a large day. Personally, I have never been a real fan of cage drying, but at that time, in Nova Scotia, it seemed to have some popularity. The days were long and I didn't get home until late in the evening but, in the end, we managed to help her vet through a tough spot. We were able to accommodate and provide appointments for all of her grooming clients who were needing to have their dogs looking and smelling good for Santa.

The Truro Vet Clinic was an extremely pleasant and friendly

environment to work in. The staff were all around my age or younger, except for the owner, and they were all very kind and friendly. I was glad that I agreed to help them out. After the holidays, my teacher asked me how I liked it in Truro. I had a sneaking suspicion that I knew what was coming next, by the way she asked me. She told me that the owner of the clinic said she couldn't find anyone to replace her previous groomer and had asked if I would be interested in the position. Flattered by the offer, I told her that I would have to think about it and get back to her. It was a long way to travel for work and I wanted to discuss it with Derek first. Of course I wanted the position, but just wasn't sure how I could make it work. So, I discussed it with Derek and he said he would support whatever decision I made. A few days later, Derek came home and told me that a store manager position had just become available at the Stewiacke location, in the company that he worked for. Stewiacke was only a twenty minute drive from Truro, maybe this could work, I thought. I guess it was meant to be, because a couple of days later Derek was offered the branch manager position.

Both of us following a new path? At the same time? It was so exciting! We decided to go for it. We packed up our shit and moved two and a half hours away from our home town. What an incredible opportunity for both of us!!

We both learned and experienced so very much on this new adventure of ours. Come on, turn the page, I'll tell you all about it.

# CHAPTER 5

## *My Grammy, My Angel*

R ight after my parents got divorced, and maybe even before the ink was dry on the documents, my brother just had to get married, to his first wife. You know, just to get all the family, old and new of course, together for a grand celebration. You guessed it, everyone was there for the world to see and be captured in pictures. You know, for those who couldn't make it to the big event. After this celebration of love and public display of new relationships, I encouraged my mother to get out more. Maybe make some new friends or join a group of some sort. Meet some new people and get some physical activity.

She decided to join a curling club and try her hand at the sport. While there, she met a few ladies and started to get out on her own some. She started to become a little more independent and social, which was good for her. She had always been shy when it came to meeting new people, so it was a huge deal for her. Eventually, she started to go out on a few dates and I actually thought she had a real shot at making a new and happy life for herself. The first couple of occasions were just a casual sort of thing. There were no real expectations of any kind. I think, they were more just to get used to dating again. After all, it had been a very long time since she had gone on a date with anyone, other than my father. The first couple of men she went out with didn't really seem like they would last or that there was much compatibility. But, I suppose that's the way this sort of thing happens. It sometimes takes a few tries before one finds something that feels right. Then she met a very nice, handsome man through her friends at the curling club.

They started dating and seemed to hit it off quite nicely. The best part of it all, for me, was that I really liked him. He was good to her, friendly with me and seemed to be a very positive, hardworking man. It seemed that he was close with his parents and siblings and saw value and meaning in that, which we both liked. It seemed that they got along well and enjoyed getting out and doing things together. They made time for family, but they also had their own hobbies and interests. Things seemed to be fairly well balanced for them both.

Eventually, after what seemed like a short amount of time, they were getting along so well that he decided to sell his house and move in with her. I was so happy for her! Finally, I thought, she has someone to treat her well and dote on her, the way she likes. Though I thought they would be together the rest of their lives, their relationship only lasted about 10 years.

Unfortunately, after my grandmother died from a massive heart attack when she was 70, their relationship started to unravel. Not only was my mother heartbroken from loosing her mother, but she now found herself with the added responsibility of getting her parents financial affairs in order. Grampy found himself alone and could not understand the trouble he was in. All of this eventually put extra strain on my mother and her relationship at home. My grandfather only had a grade 6 education and though he was extremely smart when it came to fixing and building things, he found money matters to be a challenge. So my mother and her closest sister got to work and tried to make a plan for him. It seemed that it was a very stressful time for everyone. My grandmother had basically been "robbing Peter to pay Paul" as the old saying goes, for some time and chose to keep their situation a private matter. In my opinion, if we knew the truth of it all, I think that the stress of their situation largely contributed to the heart attack that took her life.

My grandmother was well known for falling asleep on the couch while watching television in the evening, after Grampy had gone to bed. Maybe she enjoyed a little alone time with the remote control? One night he woke up to find that she was not in bed beside him. When he went out to the living room to wake her and bring her to bed, she would not wake up. She had suffered a massive heart attack at some point and died at home on their couch. It was a huge shock to us all! Especially poor Grampy!

She was and had been his whole world, since they were very young. They had been a part of each other's daily lives for over half a century. He was lost! She lovingly did everything for him. Right down  to pouring his coffee and cutting up his orange every morning for breakfast. They were true soul mates and his heart was broken.

As I briefly mentioned earlier, just two weeks before her death while we were there for one of our regular and frequent Sunday afternoon visits, she asked me if I would consider moving in the help Grampy, should something happen to her. "Of course I would", I said. But I really didn't even want to think about such a thing. "Let's talk about something else?", I pleaded. I recall Derek and I discussing the conversation on the drive home that night. I was truly upset and remember telling him that I wanted her to live forever. I cried as I told him that I didn't know what I would do if anything happened to either of them.

So, all of sudden, in the blink of an eye, Grammy was gone and

Grampy was alone. I told my mother about the conversation that Grammy and I had and asked her what she thought about what she had asked of me. My mother said that she must have known her death was near. She told me that she had bought just enough of her medication to last her until that point. She also told me that she had been eating her nitro pills like they were candy for some time. I could hardly believe what I was hearing.

My mother discussed the idea of Derek and I moving down to the country with Grampy with her Sisters and then with him, to get his thoughts. Everyone agreed, including Derek, and a plan was put into motion for us to try it. Grampy seemed to love having us there. There was constant activity in the house again and we stayed for about six months to get him over the initial hurtle. He had since met a nice woman who looked a lot like Grammy. She was no where near the cook, but she was good company for him. I think he was one of those individuals who was never meant to be alone. He enjoyed his time with his new friend, but still missed Grammy very much. I think he found a way to live out the rest of his days with some companionship, but felt and held onto his belief that he would see Grammy again some day.

After we moved out, things started to get more difficult for my mother and her sisters. They were not happy with the way Grampy was carrying on with his new friend. I won't get into the details of it all, but I will say that it put a real strain on his relationship with his daughters. Which added stress to my mother's situation and eventually, started to put a strain on her relationship with her companion. It strained it to a point that they eventually broke up and went their separate ways. Which is always difficult thing, isn't it?

I was very saddened by this because I had let myself become attached to him. He had become a positive male role model in my life. This was something that I had always wanted but had never experienced until he came into our lives. I thought he was very good to us all, my mother as well as Derek and I. He treated us like his family. We were close and it was hard to let him go. He had been like a father to me in many ways. He encouraged me to do things for myself. Things that were of benefit to me and our time together was always positive and fun. If I went to him looking for advice, he would make time for me and was always there if I needed help, in any way. We loved each other and, to me, it felt the way I thought being in a real family should feel! Then, all of a sudden, it was gone too! I figured my mother would not approve of me keeping in touch with him so I started trying to let him go.

When he was moving out and trying to move on with his life, he left Derek and I a note. Which I kept and still have today. It basically said that he did not want us to become strangers and hoped that we would still have some sort of contact. The next time I saw him was at my Grandfather's funeral a few years later. As soon as I saw him, I gave him a great big hug and told him that I loved and missed him.

Eventually, Derek told me that he had found out where he lived and as it turned out, it wasn't very far from where we live, now. He asked me if I would like to go pay him a visit. I didn't want to go for the longest time because I figured it would become a big thing with my mother. Either I would have to listen to her go on about it. Or, I would have to try to keep if from her so that I wouldn't have to listen to her go on about it. I figured where she was concerned, those where my only two options. That had been the case with everything else. Why not this too, I thought? As time went on and the years passed, I thought about going several times but continued to hesitate, so as not to upset mother. Finally, I decided I didn't care anymore and told her that I was going to reach out to him. To which, and much to my surprise, she replied that it didn't matter to her. I think there are times when she wishes she hadn't taken that approach, but she won't go back on what she said now. I now call him my Papa and we are in regular contact which makes me happy. He has a wonderful partner now and they seem to be very happy. She is smart, pretty, outgoing and loves to laugh. I am truly happy for both of us!

When Derek and I *finally* started dating. See what I did there? He loves it when I do that! I had already briefly met his Dad at the feed store he managed and had seen his Mom at a couple of different gigs that we both attended. I knew them to see them but was never properly introduced. Derek started to bring me around his families homestead and I got to meet the gang. The first real family gathering was at a campground near Shediac, NB. It was a place where their extended family resided during the summer months, at the time. Even though they weren't blood, they were still considered family. I suggested that we pick up Derek's brother and then stop a restaurant for a something to eat, along the way. This way I could meet and get to know him a little before we went on to the evening's events. We had a lovely meal and some great conversation and then off to the campground we went. Derek's brother and I seemed to connect which was pleasing to me. I knew he meant a lot to Derek and I wanted to make a good first impression.

Once we arrived, I got to meet some of the others, all of whom were very welcoming. This particular night, Derek's brother from another mother, as they jokingly refer to themselves, was playing a gig at the campground's rec centre. It was a great night filled with food, drink, music, and laughter. Just my kind of night! I got to know Derek's parents a little better that night and everyone made me feel very welcome. Derek's Dad even gave me a thumbs up. Which was his way of saying that he approved of me and thought I was a good match for Derek. He was a man of few words. It made me feel like a million bucks! His Dad's blessing meant a lot to both of us.

We had decided to stay over night because we had both been

drinking. I suggested that we put the seats down in my car and sleep in there. So, we put the back seats down and put our feet into the trunk area and laid our heads toward the front seat. This was a good idea just for the night, I thought. Although I wouldn't want to sleep this way for more than one drunken night at a time. Derek is over six feet tall and so he was more than a little cramped compared to me, I'm just a little over five feet in height. Well, I used to be. I could be shrinking now, I'm not sure! Nevertheless, he did not complain. Neither of us were in any condition to be driving and we both loved an adventure. This was the first of many adventures that began our life together.

The next morning as I woke, I was startled by a young boy sitting on his bike with his face pressed up to the car window staring in at us. I quietly sat up and mouthed the words "ssshhh, don't wake him up.". As soon as the young fellow saw me looking back at him, he took off on his bike like his ass was on fire. Derek and I still laugh about this today. Maybe we should have covered the windows but a person doesn't think about that when its late and dark, and they have a belly full of liquor.

The next time there was a family function, it was held at Derek's family home. There was a nice mix of family, friends and neighbours from the community. I was really surprised at just how many people that little bungalow would hold. It was in the summer time and there were people everywhere, both inside and out. They had a huge deck on the side and around the back of the house. Which was perfect for the jam sessions they always had at such gatherings. You see, Derek's Dad was a bass player, his brother is a guitar player and a lot of their friends and family were also musicians. It seemed that at least half of the people at this function played an instrument and/ or sang. They had these types gatherings all of the time and because they were in the country, they could play all night long if they wished. Which happened frequently! They lived on a ten acre piece of land and always made sure to include and invite the neighbours, who all loved it. No one ever complained, because they were all there!

I had a blast and loved every minute of it. It seemed that Derek had come from a whole different world than the one I knew. It was so fantastic! I felt like I was finally part of something real. Something real and something safe! I fell in love not only with Derek, but with the world that he came from and the people who were in it. The best part of it all was that they all welcomed me with open arms. It made me feel like I was really part of this magical new world that I had found. It was like I really belonged there! I had just met these people and it seemed like, to them, I had been there my whole life. It was very comforting for me!

After meeting Derek's parents, he had another very special couple he wanted me to meet. His Grandparents on his Dad's side had both died before I came along. He had somewhat adopted an older couple who lived down the road a little ways, as his surrogate Grandparents, during his childhood. The older gentleman had been a close friend of Derek's Grandfather and was the same individual, from which, he had purchased the property they lived on, some years before. We'll call him W.

This older couple just loved having people around, especially the younger folks from the neighbourhood. They were very well known in the community because their family had lived there for many, many years and they owned a good portion of the land in the area. In fact, they were, in some way or another, related to almost half of the people in the community. At one time, they even had an old general store on their property. These people were very kind and generous and even though they had lots of land they had very little money to spare. But, to them that didn't matter. They would gladly share whatever they had even if it meant making themselves short. This was something I had only ever seen on television or from my Grandparents and it was so very refreshing to me.

My first visit to their home with Derek, is something I will never forget. Their door was always open and visitors were always greeted and welcomed with such enthusiasm and kindness. They always offered something to eat, if you hadn't had your supper and a beverage, which was usually a beer. Sometimes it was coffee, but it was usually beer. Lol.

As we walked through the door I heard him saying "Come right in!" "Have a seat!". He was a balding man in or near his sixties, at the time, with a smile that went from ear to ear. There was however something very unique about his smile. He had only one front tooth. Just one. One very large and long tooth on the top and believe me when I say, this gave him an even softer demeanour. He loved to laugh and when he did you had a very clear view of his one tooth, which always made me smile. A few years later, he lost his tooth and simply never bothered to get any false teeth. It was amazing to me that he was able to eat such a wide variety of foods, with no teeth.

This reminds me of a story. One afternoon, Derek, his Dad, W, his son and myself decided to go on, what we used to call a "Saint Paul run". I say "one afternoon", but in reality this was a regular occurrence. The run was basically travelling all of the dirt back roads in someone's truck, to the local agency liquor store, where we could top up our beer, liquor and snack supplies for the rest of our weekend's festivities. Derek's Dad used to love to eat peanuts and we always offered to share our snacks and drinks with one another. So, Derek's Dad gets back in the truck after picking up his goodies and offers W some peanuts. W pauses for a second, then looks right at Derek's Dad and says "Well, I would love some, but, could you chew them up some for me, first?". It was a one of those precious moments! We were all half in the bag and to hear that come from a toothless man was hysterical. I thought we would all pee in our pants laughing!

I want to come back to my first visit to their home for a moment. At that time, they had a small white poodle. W absolutely loved dogs and was never without one, that I can remember. I too have been a dog and animal lover, my whole life, which was one of many things we had in common. This little dog was so very cute and friendly and we really hit it off. So much so that I needed to know what his name was and eventually asked. The response I got was, "ask him", or at least I thought that's what they said. I laughed and then after some time passed, I asked again what the little guy's name was. Once again, I got the same response. Kind of strange, I thought but okay. Then the third time I asked, they all laughed. Finally, Derek spoke up and said the dog's name is, ASKEM. Which after a few pints, sounded to me like... Ask Him! Lol. Then I couldn't help but laugh. In fact, I laughed so hard that it brought tears to my eyes. It was a nice way to break the ice! He loved to play this prank on every new person he met and got a lot of mileage out of it. They always had such a fun loving nature.

His wife was as much of a prankster as he was and she too loved to laugh and joke, with her quick and witty come backs. Which was a must if you were going to survive in that crowd. Lol. They would always drop whatever they were doing to make time for anyone who stopped by for a visit. (*Ah, life before Facebook.*)... I always felt welcome there! They reminded me a lot of my own Grandparents, on my mother's side, minus the drinking of course. They were country folks through and through. The conversation was always pleasant and comical, which was mostly because, as W used to say, "half the lies he told weren't true!". This was the first of many, many visits. Many visits that would eventually blossom into a loving friendship that lasted until the end of their days.

We spent vacations with them at their camp. It was a quaint little spot located about a mile back in the woods, behind their home. There was a shallow hand drilled well with a cistern hand pump for water, an outhouse, lots of candles and a very old radio that was wired to an old car battery. Which was always playing some classic country music. The parties and gatherings we had back there were some of my best times and are some of my fondest memories. Along with all the back road driving in four wheel drive trucks, I love that. We went on many road trips together because we would all get roaming fever at about the same time. Back then, you could do that. We always went real slow and stayed off the main roads. Mostly, we would head for the nearest dirt road or roads we could find. I think that we went so slow simply because we did not want our adventures to end. The people I met on these adventures, in the farthest parts of the woods, were some of the nicest people I have met anywhere.

There is one particular trip that W and I took together that stands out and is worth sharing here. During one of our stays with them, Derek had a gig booked in Sussex, NB for a night. We had been talking about it and W mentioned that he knew people up that way but that he hadn't been there in a very long time. By this point in W's life, he wasn't as fond of night driving as he had once been. I took this to mean that he was interested in going to see the show and maybe look up or call on a few of his old friends, along the way. So, in the spirit of a good adventure I offered to drive so that W and I could go see the show. Derek had to leave earlier in the day with the van and trailer in order to pick up his band mates and their gear so they could set up for the show that night. Then, W and I would be along later in my car, after supper. All while making a couple of stops along the way, of course.

One of W's friends lived in a small village on the way to Sussex and the other lived in the town itself. Before we left the house, he made a couple of phone calls to his friends to let them know what we were up too. The first gentleman was very excited to know that his old friend was coming for a visit but there was no answer from the second friend. There was however an answering machine, so W left a message stating when and where we were going to be in town, for Derek's show. He said that he would love to see him and buy him a beer, if he could make it.

We left shortly after supper that night and headed toward our first stop. Which was approximately halfway to Sussex. When we arrived, W's friend said that we had shown up just in time for happy hour, as he greeted us at the door. Come on in and have a seat he said, as he asked his wife to bring us a round of drinks. I told her that I was driving so water would be fine for me please. It was too far of a trip to take any chances. I might have one beer at the club, but that would be it for me. So after about two or three drinks in, W's old buddy asks me if I could do him a favour. "Of course." I said. "What can I help you with?". Then out of nowhere, he throws his prosthetic leg at me. He says "Here!", "Catch!". "That damn old thing is heavy to drag around with me and besides it chafes anyway!". I was completely shocked as I fumbled to try and catch it. I had no idea! He walked like it was real. Apparently, he had lost his leg a long time ago and it was a trick they would play on the newcomers. Those old men had a great laugh while I tried to pull my heart out of my throat. His wife said, "they think they're funny!", "But that joke is getting real old for me!". I giggled and let them have their fun. After a couple of hours, I pointed out that if we were going to make the show and meet up with W's other friend we had best be on our way. We thanked them for being so pleasant and opening their home to us and we were on the road again.

By the time we got to the club, Derek and the boys were already on stage and playing and the place was starting to fill up. Derek's band played there often and were one of the local favourites who had developed quite a following. W and I tried to find a table that was in the open so we would easily be seen, in case his friend did show up. It wasn't long after we got seated, that I noticed a lady come in who was looking around and seemed somewhat puzzled. She scanned the room and then looked in our direction. Then she walked over to the table and tapped W on the shoulder. He turned with puzzled look, as she asked if he was the man who had left a message about meeting at this club, this evening. W replied, yes of course, as he asked her to sit down. As it turned out, W's friend was her father and he had recently passed away. I could tell when she spoke the words that W's heart sunk. She explained how he passed and told W not to feel bad. It was very clear to her as well, just how upset W was in hearing this news. He wasn't very good at hiding things like that.

She tried to explain to W how deeply touched she was that he would make such an effort to connect with her father. She told us of how her father would recall and tell stories about himself and this W character and the fun they used to have. She felt bad that she was not able to find any information about this W character she had heard so much about. If only she could have found a last name, or a phone number, anything at all so that she could tell W of her father's passing. This nice lady stayed all night and talked to W. They exchanged stories of her father and threw this process I believe they were both able to heal a little and say goodbye to the man who they both cared for. W would listen with such compassion and when things got a little too serious or sad he would come back with a funny story and make her laugh. I wish there were more people out there like my dear old friend W!

It's funny how things play out sometimes? Isn't it? I could easily tell more stories of my dear old friend and fill an entire book with them alone. Maybe I will. A book on the life lessons he taught and the adventures we shared.

Derek's grandparents, on his Mom's side, were still living when

Derek and I got together. They too were very warm and welcoming people, who were very social and lead busy lives. They were always very kind to me and made me feel like one of the gang. They hosted many large family gatherings and attended some of the functions that were held at Derek's parent's home.

Derek and I were together for about six months when our first Christmas came around. I'll never forget it. He gave me the most beautiful wooden jewellery box and inside there was a gold, three diamond promise ring. I was over the moon happy with this gift and with him. You did good DW!

That particular Christmas was the first time that I met his Grandparents. They hosted a holiday gathering at their home and there were people from wall to wall. Their family consisted of twelve boys and girls, spouses and what seemed like an endless number of grandchildren. Of which, Derek is the oldest. It was almost overwhelming at first but they were all so friendly it didn't take long to settle right into the crowd. I will say that I have never seen that many people in one mini home, at the same time before in my entire life and probably never will again. I think the walls were starting to bow out at one point!

Derek's Grandfather who was also a musician, played guitar, harmonica and sang and his Grandmother had a beautiful voice. Derek gets his talent from both sides of his family. Music was a huge part of their lives too. As was their Acadian heritage. I can still remember the first time I helped them make Poutine Rapee at Christmas. It was something I had never had or experienced before and wasn't sure about it, at first. His Grandmother could sense my hesitation and subtly leaned in and said "you know dear, if you sprinkle a little sugar on them it brings out the flavour.". What a game changer! Lol. I miss them both!

## Our move to Stewiacke, NS

Neither Derek nor I had ever lived anywhere but the Moncton and surrounding area and toward the later part of 1997 and after moving out of Grampy's home, we were both starting to feel like maybe it was time for a change. We were looking at it like it would be an adventure. All of the stars had aligned just right and it seemed that it was all meant to be. We had both recently been offered jobs in the same general area and Nova Scotia seemed like a great place for a new adventure.

So, we packed up our animals, and our belongings and moved to Stewiacke. It was a very small town, just twenty minutes from Truro, where Derek's company headquarters and my new job were both located. Their Stewiacke store location that Derek was to take over and manage needed some TLC and it turned out that he was just the guy for the job. I'm sure most of you have heard about how small towns can be and how news travels quicker than people? (*Again, in the times before Facebook.*) Well, Stewiacke was one of those small rural towns. My first introduction to it was when I went to the post office to get a key for our mail box. The clerk behind the desk took one look at me and said "you must be Derek's wife Tanya?", all before I had even opened my mouth. We were the talk of the town and I stuck out like a sore thumb, as my Grandmother would say.

I was shocked and after a brief pause, I agreed. "Yes, I am Tanya". She said, "just sign here on this card and I will get you your mail box key.". Then as she handed me the key, she welcomed me to Stewiacke and I thought, wow, what a small place. It was like something right out of a movie. This was certainly going to be an adventure, all right!

We had many adventures before moving to Stewiacke. Especially when travelling on the road with all of the different bands that Derek played with. Those times were some of the best and most fun times I had as a young adult. The different people we would meet and the antics of young musicians always kept things interesting. From watching the crowd getting into a bar room brawl, to watching one of the road crew tell a story on the top of a table, in a late night dinner, at four in the morning, while having a bite to eat after a great show and a very long day. I loved, loved every minute of it!

We travelled, ate, slept and played together for many of our younger years. I wouldn't trade that time in my life for anything in this world. There are still days when I miss those times, but it is for the young at heart and body. I can remember one particular gig that had a funny outcome. Derek's theatrical telling of the story is the best! It involves a broken headlight pot on the band van and someone having a very bad interaction with a stone fireplace. Good times! All of them!! I'm sure I'm still catching up on the sleep I lost in those days. Lol.

So, as I said we packed up our stuff and moved our little family, which consisted of Derek, myself, Bear, Patches (a rescue cat from a pet store where I worked for a short time after graduating from grooming school) and Spanky our pet rabbit to small town Stewiacke. Which for us, coming from the Greater Moncton Metropolis, seemed like the slowest moving place on earth. We quickly realized that we did not want to rent the spot we had found in the town, long term. We wanted a place of our own, with some land and a place where we could stretch our legs and have some privacy. We were really happy to be there, just not right in the town. The duplex we rented was nice and so were our neighbours, but it was temporary. It was just a temporary fix, until we found some place to call our own. We were going to give it our best shot, but needed a place of our own, if we were going to thrive.

We decided to look for a house somewhere in between our two jobs so that we would each split the travelling time. Our search led us to a lovely two and a half acre piece of property with a large mini home and addition, in Shortt's Lake. It needed some work, but we could see the potential in it. This property was just a very short distance to Brookfield, which had a small grocery store, gas station, bakery, pizza joint and a butcher shop. There was a turn off to get onto the highway or you could travel the old secondary highway in either direction to both of our work places. It was perfect for what we wanted. The highway was a fast, divided highway, so my preferred route was the slower, scenic country route. However, if I was running a little late in the morning, it was convenient to just jump on the highway and make up a little time.

Our families were not used to us being away and as a result, we ended up travelling to Moncton about three weekends out of four, for sometime. This got old very quickly! As I mentioned, we had a growing family of animals. Patches was our first cat and she was a feisty young feline who had been brought back to the pet store, where I had worked, at the time. Our policy was not to take animals back once they had been placed, but then this man came in and said that if we did not take her back he was going drop her off along side of the highway. She was past the really small kitten stage and I think he just didn't want her once she started to grow.

I couldn't have lived with myself if she had been harmed in anyway. So, I said we would take her back and I would try to find her a new home. As the days past, I kept talking to Derek about her and told him how it seemed that people just wanted the tiny kittens and not a five month old. She was so loving and just wanted to be right under my feet, all of the time. I realized that my chances of placing her were next to none, considering that we had small kittens right next to her in the store. I took a chance and brought her to see Derek at his work, one day. I walked into the store with her in a kennel. He took one look at her and said well she will need some supplies so let's get her set up. That was it, she was part of the family from that point on. I started to wonder if I had made a mistake in bringing her home when she started to swing from the curtains with a devilish look on her face. In a frazzled state, I called Derek at work one day, to ask what was wrong with her. He said this is your first cat right? My answer was yes because my father hated cats, so I had no idea what I was in for. He said "well that is normal for a young calico", as he laughed. We got through it eventually and I have been hooked on cats ever since.

Once we moved to Stewiacke and I started working at the vet clinic, the next feline addition to our family was when little Babbles came along. We hadn't been in Stewiacke very long before we, well I, added another member to the family. That day, it seemed like it would be just another average day of grooming. That was until I entered the building and found a particularly heart wrenching sight. I entered through the rear entrance of the building, as it was closest to my work station and I would not disrupt the other procedures that were already in progress, in the clinic. This section had my grooming tables, a small bath tub and a number of kennels that could house animals who were waiting for surgeries or other procedures. Or, there could be animals who were in recovery and even some who were waiting for a grooming, if they had been dropped off early. On the odd occasion, we would have a lost or wounded animal and maybe a boarding client or two, as there was a need.

On this particular day, a cute little grey tabby caught my eye, as I walked in the building. I immediately wondered what her story was and my heart sank as I approached the sad looking little female. I could feel her sadness and discomfort. She looked right into my eyes and it was then that I really noticed what poor condition she was in. My eyes filled with tears. Her coat was thin and brittle and you could count every rib. I have to say that she had the saddest eyes I had ever seen on any animal. She looked so broken, not just physically but mentally as well.

Once I got myself settled for the day, I inquired about this poor little girl who had become our new tenant. I was told that she had been brought in by the clinic owner's husband, shortly after I left the day before. She was found by a babbling brook and after assessing her injuries, it was concluded that she must have been thrown from a moving vehicle and then possibly hit by another motorist. After I got a closer look at her, it looked like her back end had been crushed. I was very concerned and asked if she had a fighting chance. The vet said that she was going to do all she could for her. This little girl was in some of the worst condition I had seen, up until that point. That did not stop her from purring up a storm when I opened the cage to show her some affection, though. I would just pet her ever so gently and with whatever energy she could muster, she showed affection gratitude to anyone who showed her kindness.

The vet said she thought that she had been nursing at least one kitten and had been injured for sometime. This little tabby did all she could to keep herself and at least one kitten alive, unfortunately the kitten was not found. The search was extensive but there was no sign of her baby. They thought that maybe a wild animal may have gotten to it first. But, there was really no way of knowing what had happened to the little one. The decision was made to name her after the babbling brook she was found next to and so she was given the name Babbles. I thought it to be very suiting, considering she liked to talk. It was quite amazing to me, just how vocal she really was, all things considered. I was also amazed at how friendly she was, she didn't seem to have an aggressive bone in her body. Which was shocking to me considering the pain she must have been in and all of the procedures she had to endure in order to be mended and become well. Most cats would have been very cranky and aggressive but not little Babbles. She was full of love, kindness and gratitude.

All of that being said, I watched her get better day by day and in the process totally fell in love with her. I called Derek to tell him all about this little sweet heart and of course, he knew where the phone call was going. Babbles needed a home and Derek has as big a heart as anyone I have ever known. He knew by the way I was talking that I had gotten attached. So, he said it would be a good thing to have another cat to keep Patches, our fun loving ball of psychotic energy, company. It would be good for her to have a play mate we thought. He told me that I didn't have to sell him on the idea that I could just bring her home. I was over the moon happy on the day she was finally well enough to come home! I wasn't the only one who was happy, much to my surprise. Patches took to her right away. As soon as I opened the kennel door, Babbles ran out and down the stairs to hide underneath the bed in our spare room. We all went down to try and convince her to come out and reassure her that she was finally safe. But, it was Patches who soothed her fear and worry. Patches slowly crawled under the bed and gently touched her nose to Babbles'. Shortly after, they both came out from under the bed and almost instantly became best buds. They slept on the same chair together, they ate together and they played together. It was meant to be and was a great match for both them and us.

Derek was right about bringing Babbles home and making her part of our family. It was one of the best decisions we could have made, especially for Patches. I was so happy to have Babbles be part of the family and I believe she was equally as happy to have a loving home. A place where she didn't have to fight to survive and hunt for every bit of nourishment. Or, be abused by any more stupid humans. I totally understood that feeling.

She hadn't been home very long when she ended up with an

infection in one of her teats. In the bovine world, they call it mastitis. Poor little Babbles was not able to relieve the milk she was still producing which led to her having a nasty open sore. She was so very good about letting me treat her, though. I knew just by the look of it that it was a very painful situation. She healed well and it wasn't long afterwards that she started gaining weight. When we first got her she was a rack of bones but as she aged she gained a fair amount of girth. Maybe even a little too much! But, she was happy and lived a long healthy life.

Once we moved into our home in Shortt's Lake, our little family settled in quite nicely. The cats enjoyed having more room to run because the house had more square footage and Bear enjoyed the nice big private acreage we had. Not that she used it for anything other than napping in the shade or smelling the flowers. Irish Wolf Hounds can be such couch potatoes! Our pet rabbit, Spanky loved it too because he also had more room in the house. We would let him run around and he would go to the cat litter box to do his business. What was comical about it, was that the cats would go in after him and cover it all up. We used to take him outside and just let him run around the yard. He was a lot like a dog in the way that he would come when I called him. Eventually, we decided to make him an outdoor enclosure because he seemed so fond of being outside. This way, he had shelter and was also safe from predators. That was until he figured out how to get out of the pen. He was extremely intelligent for a rabbit. One day, I came home to see him hanging out with a wild female rabbit. I was glad he was able to live out the rest of his days with a mate.

# CHAPTER 6

*Friday, November 13, 1998*

It's probably fair to say that most of you reading this have or know someone who has a "Friday the 13th" story... and while this maybe a little unpleasant at times, this is mine.

It was kind of a strange day, right from the get-go really. The energy just felt weird all day. Both Derek and I's energy was unsettled, all day. I couldn't really put my finger on it, but something just felt off. After some discussion, we decided that we were going to go to town after supper. "Town" at that time, was Truro, which was about a twenty-five minute drive from our home. It was Friday, November 13, 1998. We thought it would be enjoyable to take some time to do some shopping. I clearly remember seeing all the newly hung holiday decorations and lights in the stores that night. I remember thinking of how excited I was getting for the holiday season that year. It was the time of year when we would start to plan what we were giving out for presents and start discussing what we would like our schedule to be for the season. There was a careful art to planning it all out, because in those days, we were concerned with trying to accommodate everyone's wants and needs in an effort to keep them all happy.   With that in mind, we were the one's travelling that year, in order to spend time with our families and loved ones. We always tried to divide our time up in a fair and equally manner.

It was a rather dark and cold night and I can recall Derek pulling onto the ramp to take the highway home that night, after we had finished our shopping. I can remember thinking to myself that I was glad we were taking the quicker route, as I was getting tired and was looking forward to crawling into our warm, comfortable bed.

As we drove onto the highway and passed the new structures that were being built, I remember thinking about how that stretch of highway would get much busier, once the new complex was finally finished. There were plans in place to have a string of new stores and restaurants and a new cinema.

Then, all of a sudden, a couple of miles down the road, without warning and out of the darkness a man appeared right in front of our vehicle. He was right there on the road right in front of us. Unfortunately, Derek had no options, there quite simply was nowhere to go. The man had been crouched down on the highway and once we got up close enough, he stood up. He committed suicide and used our vehicle and us as his means of doing so.

We were horrified, as we helplessly watched this tragic event unfold. There is no other way to explain seeing a man hit the front of your vehicle, then hitting into the windshield right in front of Derek's face and go flying straight over the top of the vehicle. The noise of his body hitting was chilling. We both screamed in horror!

Derek pulled the vehicle over, as soon as he could get it stopped and we quickly jumped out. In shock from what had just taken place, I started to run toward the lifeless body that lay on the highway. All I could think was that I needed to help this person. I recall thinking that this just didn't make any sense to me. None at all. What the hell just happened? How does something like this happen??

In a state of confusion, I started to run out onto the highway towards the individual. I didn't give a second thought to the traffic coming toward us. I don't think I even saw the oncoming vehicles. Even though they were close enough that they lit up the highway, well enough for me to see where the individual had landed. Just then, I felt a hand grab my arm with such intensity and strength that it instantly stopped me in my tracks. As I turned to see what this force was, I saw Derek's face. He was pulling me back to the edge of the road.

I screamed, "We need to help him!". We started to try to get closer to the body staying on the shoulder and then exactly what I was afraid would happen, happened. Another car hit his lifeless body and kept on going. Then, another car came up the highway and, in trying to avoid hitting the body, went into the ditch. All we could do was watch. It was like being in a real live horror film. Moments later, a woman approached to offer help and called 911.

It didn't take long before the police showed up. Apparently, ours was not the first vehicle he had tried to do this with that night. He had already jumped out in front of a couple of other vehicles, but his first two attempts had failed. With that, he decided to change his strategy and crouch down to become less visible by the head lights. Then, when we came along he stood up at the very last moment. Perhaps hoping to be unavoidable? Well, it worked. The drivers of the other vehicles had managed to avoid him and had apparently called the police to report what he was doing, so they were already on their way. Unfortunately, however, we got there first.

I could tell that the there was no hope in saving this man especially after seeing him get hit again by another motorist. There was no doubt in my mind that he was dead.

Derek and I were both in shock when the police arrived, and a very kind police officer put us in his car and put the heat on as I was shaking. It was a cold night and after seeing and experiencing what had just happened, I felt icy cold. Our vehicle was totalled, and we had to have it towed to the nearest body shop/scrap yard. Even if it hadn't been totally wrecked, I don't think that either of us would have ever driven it again.

Derek saved me twice that night. Firstly, because if he had not reacted the way he did during the accident and kept our vehicle from getting out of control, we too could have been killed. Then secondly, if he hadn't grabbed me by the arm and kept me from running out onto the highway, I too could have been hit and possibly killed. He grabbed my arm so hard, that there were bruise marks on my arm from where his fingers were. He felt bad afterwards, but I wish he hadn't. He did the right thing. I believe that his actions saved me from something even worse than the hell we had just experienced.

The police officer asked us a lot of questions and at one point I started to get a little concerned about where things was going. He must have sensed it because at that point, he started to offer the information that concerned citizens were calling in about the man who was jumping out in front of cars on the highway. I think that was his way of telling us they knew what he was trying to do. They weren't blaming Derek and there were no charges laid. I should hope not, we were deeply impacted by a man choosing to involve us in his suicide. I understand he was deeply disturbed and feel sorry for someone who feels they have no other choice. But, that said, his choice deeply affected and impacted both of our lives, for a great many years.

I will never forget watching them lay a sheet over the lifeless broken body. My heart sank into the deepest depth of my soul. I can recall thinking this can't be real. I was just hoping that I would wake from this horrible nightmare.

After the police officer finished with his questioning, he asked us who he could call for us, to come to pick us up. We looked at one another and I think in that instant, we both thought the same thing. Well, there is no one close by to call. We had just moved there from New Brunswick and our closest family was about two hours away and we really hadn't made any friends that we could make that type of call to, at that point. How very alone we both felt in that moment. We had each other and that would be enough for us. It was enough to get us through that Friday the 13<sup>th</sup> night.

So, our response to the officer was that we had just moved here for work and all our friends and family were in New Brunswick. He kindly got on the radio to report in that he was firstly, taking us to the hospital to be checked over, due to the state of shock he felt we were in. Then, he would be taking us home, when we were finished. All we had to do was call him and he would come back to the hospital and pick us up. As we drove through what seemed to be the darkest of all nights, the officer shared with us that after all the events he had experienced and lived through in his years of service, that he too had gone to counselling and felt there was no shame in it. He told us that he felt that it really helped him to deal with the imprint that some of those situations and experiences had left on him. He also told us that by going to counselling he was able to resume a happy life. He then warmly encouraged us to seek help, considering what we had experienced that evening.

Both Derek and I clung to one another. My heart was so broken for him. I could tell he was struggling, as anyone would have in that situation. He was driving and I could only imagine what was going through his mind at the time. The police officer said that if Derek hadn't reacted the way he did there would have been three deaths on that night, instead of just one. I hoped that hearing those words from the officer would make him feel a little better.

I would like to say that Derek is one of the most responsible drivers I have ever known. I have teased him about going so slow and upsetting other drivers with his attention to detail on several occasions. His response is always the same. He says that he is paying for the repairs and that reckless driving is irresponsible and expensive. Even though I hate to admit it, he is right. I certainly was thankful for his ways and driving abilities that night.

I can recall locking the doors and checking them twice when we got home. Then, I promptly closed all the curtains. I did not want to look out into the darkness, at all. I was afraid of what I might see. After all, that man had just appeared out of nowhere in the darkness. My mind was running away on me, and I did not like it.

Derek and I called our parents and told them what had happened. We decided that as soon as it was daylight, we would take our other car and drive to his parents place for the weekend. We both were very shaken and felt like we wanted to be with family, in a what we hoped would be a more comfortable setting. So, we went to bed a little later, but neither of us slept. We just laid there holding each other waiting for the sun to come up. Once daybreak hit, we loaded up our little family and headed out. I wanted Derek to get in the driver's seat after what happened. I really wanted to encourage him to get back behind the wheel driving again.

When I was younger, I had a friend who had gotten into an accident and really did not want to drive ever again, afterwards. His parents made him get behind the wheel and drive again as they didn't want his fear to take over and keep him from driving in the future. The memory of this kept rolling through my mind. My friend later told me that if his parents hadn't made him get behind the wheel and drive that he would never have driven again. Derek didn't argue at all. He got right into the driver's seat, and we set out for Moncton. You see, as a child, he had literally been bucked off a horse, many times and his dad always made him get right back in the saddle and carry on, afterwards. However, it did seem like a very long drive that day. Neither of us spoke very much. We just drove. I think we were both still in shock.

We were very happy to pull in the driveway at his parents place. Once we got settled, we told them the whole story, as we knew it. We still had some unanswered questions but as the days passed most of those answers came. Of course, Derek's family didn't know how to comfort or help us. It was a difficult situation for everyone involved. We didn't really know what we needed, what to ask for or even what to do. We just needed time and to know that they were there, if we did need something, and they were.

Shortly after we arrived, I called my mother and told her that we had made it to Derek's parents place, if she would like to come out and see me. Really, what I wanted was for her to drop whatever she was doing and come to support me. I felt like I wanted her there. I was upset and I wanted a mother figure with me. She told me that she had plans to go out with her sisters and she would try to get out to see me after she was done with her other plans. I was very upset by this. On top of everything that I had just been through my own mother choose a shopping and a lunch outing with her sisters over me. I should have known better than to look for support from her, when I needed it. I mean really. It's not like I was getting divorced and looking for someone to move back in to my house and help me through it. How serious or important could it really be? I mean it is not like someone died. Oh wait.

We decided to stay in New Brunswick a little longer than just the weekend. Derek and I struggled with our emotions from this horrible ordeal and it was all over the news. We tried to seek help in Moncton but quickly realized that we would have to go back to Nova Scotia in order to get the help we needed.

Once we got back home, I went to see our family doctor and

explained that Derek and I were having some difficulties since the accident. I explained to him that I couldn't go outside after it got dark and that I felt very anxious and scared. I just couldn't bring myself to do it. I wasn't sleeping very much and when I did I had horrible nightmares and flashbacks of the accident.

My doctor said it was anxiety and possibly panic attacks. He said we needed to go seek professional counselling and that he would refer us to someone he thought could help. I didn't want to go see someone unless Derek went with me. I was very scared and nervous. I had so much going on in my head that I felt like I was going crazy. During my visit to my family doctor, he discussed the accident with me. He told me that the gentleman did indeed commit suicide. Which is what we had thought, but it was nice to have it confirmed by someone who knew a little about the situation. The doctor also told me that the gentleman had struggled with substance abuse and mental health issues.

He told me that he been living in a halfway house and that he had told his councillor that he was going to take his own life by laying down on the railroad tracks. Even after they knew this, they let him out on a pass but he did not come back when expected. The reports from his autopsy said that there was an extreme amount of alcohol and other substances in his system. My doctor also said that they concluded that he must have changed his mind on the way in which he chose to end his suffering. I guess we were just in the wrong place at the wrong time. My doctor told me that this gentleman had struggled with mental illness his whole life. As a result, he never married or had children. His parents were the only family he had.

The last thing the doctor shared with me was that literally every bone in his body was shattered on the first impact and that he would have died instantly. He did not suffer as a result of the accident and that it was a quick death. He was definitely dead before the second car hit him and there would have been nothing I could have done, even if I could have gotten to him.

We quickly got an appointment with a psychologist for both of us to go together. I think that this was comforting not only to me, but to Derek as well. We anxiously sat together in the waiting room until a very pleasant woman, whom I recognized, invited us into her office. This was the first time that either of us had been in a situation like this. I had not placed the name but realized that I knew her when I saw her face. She was the owner of a Collie that I knew very well. I had groomed this beautiful dog on several occasions at the vet clinic, where I worked. You see, there was a particular wine vineyard that she liked to visit frequently with her lovely Collie, so they could walk among the grape vines. The problem with doing so, however, was that ticks also like to hang around wine vineyards. I spent many hours picking ticks off of her very patient companion and probably just as much time bathing and brushing her. She was a beautiful dog and just loved all of the extra attention she got as a result.

I can recall thinking to myself that if anyone can really help us, it would be a fellow animal lover like her. What were the chances we would end up being referred to someone I knew? We hadn't lived in the area very long so it was a pleasant and comforting surprise for me. We went into her office and sat down holding each other's hand. She explained that she would see both of us at the same time for now and that we would eventually work toward individual appointments, in order to get the most out of our treatment. She was thorough in explaining that we would have different issues and that, in her opinion this was the best course of action, to which we agreed. Neither of us had ever seen anyone for that type of help before and we really didn't know what to expect. We were struggling and I think we both knew that neither of us would be able to return to our original quality of life until we accepted the type of treatment she was suggesting. I was scared to go into this treatment on my own, without Derek right there with me. However, I did my best to push my fear aside and move forward with treatment anyway, and in doing so, I realized that I had faith in this pleasant animal loving doctor.

I got the feeling that she was well versed in that type of treatment, by the way she approached us. I felt she really knew how to proceed in order to get the best results for us both. Our therapy sessions continued for a very long time. My experience with this event scared me in a very profound way. At the time, I was going because of our accident so that is what I focused on. But in the process, I started to realize that I hadn't completely understood just how damaged I really was, mentally. Later on in life, I came to regret not starting to address and work through some of the other issues, from my past, at that time.

She helped me to be able to feel safe in my own home again. Eventually, after a lot of hard work, I was able to go outside after dark again. As time went on, the flashbacks and nightmares lessened and I started to feel that I was slowly returning to a somewhat normal life. Well, normal for me at least. But, it was a start even though I knew it would take more time and hard work, on my part, to really get there. She gave me the tools and showed me how to use them. I just had to open the box and put them to use. *I* had to do the work! Can any of you relate to this premise? Have you ever chose to do the work? Have you ever chose to put the time and effort in to making the changes or improvements that you want for yourself?

The fact that someone had taken their own life and involved me without my consent made me feel violated on such a personal level that it was very hard for me to overcome. I now understand how it is possible for someone or that particular individual, to feel that suicide is their only option. Or put another way, how it can look like the only way out of their pain. Maybe he wasn't thinking about, or maybe didn't care about the pain that his actions would cause others. Maybe all he could see was that he just wanted his pain to stop. Maybe the substances just didn't work anymore. I don't think anyone can really know how, or what another person is going through or how they truly feel. Most often times, those in the deepest of pain will only let you see what they feel it is safe to reveal, at the time. It's easier to bear the pain than open one's self to further judgment or condemnation. Something like "walk a mile in my shoes" comes to mind. Or, my new mantra, especially when I have to listen to someone complain about their trivial problems, "live my life for 20 minutes, then we'll talk!"

I have to believe that we, as humans, are only given as much as we can handle. I have to believe that! Without it, I don't see the point anymore!

We're not even half way through this story of mine yet. Stay with me now.

I also believe that something good will come from or as a result of a bad situation. "In every blessing there is a curse and in every curse there is a blessing". It may be difficult for us to see at the time. I certainly couldn't. But, in my experience, it will eventually come to be clear. All of my difficult times have taught me lessons and have sometimes sent me in a direction that brought me much joy and happiness.

As I continued to work through my November, which rolled into December and so on, I was searching for something positive to look forward to. I found that in my upcoming birthday celebration. It was going to be my thirtieth birthday and it was approaching quickly, as it is in March. What a birthday it would be!! I will never forget it. You see, Derek planned a birthday weekend full of surprises and surprise me he did! He told me we were going away for the weekend and that we had to go to Moncton to drop Bear off at my mother's, to have her looked after.

He had even packed my bags because he wanted for me not have the slightest clue for what he had planned. This was very exciting for me because I knew whatever he had planned it was going to be fun. He has both a romantic and an adventurous side and when the two collide it is sheer bliss for me.

As an example of just how romantic he can be, I want to share the story of a night in the first apartment we shared. I had been working a lot of late night shifts when we first moved into this tiny one bedroom apartment on the third floor of a very old building in downtown Moncton. Because of these shifts Derek and I weren't able to spend very much time together, as he was playing a lot at the time. It seemed like we were always just passing each other in the hallway.

One night as I drove up to our building, I looked up at our window from the street to see if the lights were on. If the lights were on, that usually meant that he was still up and awake and I just might get a little time with him before he crashed for the night. As I looked up, hoping to see the lights on, all I saw was darkness. I felt disappointed as I parked my car and started to make my way up the stairs. The closer I got to the third floor, however, the more I could smell something absolutely delicious throughout the hallway. As I unlocked the door to our apartment the smell of herbs and something slow roasting hit my senses and I realized that Derek had been cooking. He is an awesome chef and when he has the time, creates some true masterpiece dishes for us to enjoy.

The apartment was very dimly lit and he was sitting on the couch with wine and soft music playing. I had to look twice to make sure my eyes weren't deceiving me. Was he naked I thought? I mean hoped.... lol. He wasn't but he did have on some of his best attire and looked very handsome. He had set the table and was waiting for me to enjoy some Hors d'oeuvres and wine before dinner. He had marinated and slow cooked the most beautiful piece of lamb and had all the fixings to go along with it.

I have to say that we had the most beautiful night together. He knew I had been missing him and created a most special and memorable evening. It was a night I will always remember. I love him for many reasons but he outdid himself that night.

He does cook whenever he has the time and sometimes he will pop a bottle of champagne even if it isn't a special occasion. One night he popped the cork on a bottle of bubbly and as he did the cork flew into the wall, bounced up to hit the ceiling then changed direction again only to land directly into a bowl of seafood sauce that was sitting on the end table between us, to be served with some shrimp. Which is one of my favourite apps I might add. It was hilarious that it could change trajectory three different times and land right in the middle of the bowl of seafood sauce. The sauce was everywhere! There was even some that landed on the dog. I can recall Bear licking some off of her coat. It was another memorable night!!

Back to my thirtieth birthday getaway, after we dropped Bear off at my mother's house we got back into the car and Derek blindfolded me. We ended up at a lovely hotel in the Moncton area. The room he had arranged for our stay was beautiful! He informed me that we had dinner reservations and that there was a dress code. I looked in my bag and could not believe what I saw. That man had even packed me nylons. I couldn't believe he even thought of nylons! There was even some champagne to sip on while we were getting all dressed up. We made a very handsome couple, all decked out in our best attire, if I do say so myself! He was in a suit and me in a dress. You know it is a special occasion if I am in a dress! Derek seemed like he was a little uncomfortable. I thought maybe it could have been the suit, maybe it was too warm or not fitting quite right, so I didn't think too much about it.

A cab was called to come and take us to our destination, which was still unknown to me. I was glad for the cab because it meant that we could both enjoy our evening and not have to worry about driving. The cab showed up and it was actually a nice van that Derek's uncle drove for a living. We had a great chat on the way to the restaurant. Once we got to our destination, I realized he had taken me to one of, if not the best seafood restaurant, in town at the time. It was a very old house, on the bank of a river that, had been renovated into a restaurant. It was very inviting and romantic complete with a wine cellar where you could go and pick out your own wine, if you were so inclined. Derek wanted to pick out a bottle of wine and asked if I would care to join him. Of course I wanted to see more of this lovely old building.

He seemed to be getting more uncomfortable by the minute. At which point, I started to wonder if maybe he wasn't feeling well and was just going through with the evening because it was my birthday. He seemed as though he was adjusting his jacket as we walked down to and through the cellar so I asked if he was doing okay, to which he replied, "Of course!". Once we had picked out our wine and were seated at our table again the waiter took over and attended to our every need. Derek seemed to relax a little after a couple of sips of the delicious nectar we had chosen. We dined and sipped and talked and really enjoyed the truly wonderful atmosphere and the view. It was almost picture perfect!

Before too much longer, Derek reached into his pocket and pulled out a little box and passed it to me. As I opened it, he asked me to marry him and of course, I said yes! The most beautiful three diamond gold ring was in front of me with the man of my dreams asking me to share the rest of our days together. I was in heaven! Our evening was perfect and I guess we all know now why he was so uptight leading up to dinner.

I have to say that I was surprised that he asked me to marry him only because I had always told him that we didn't need to be married. It wouldn't change anything for me. I loved him and knew I wanted to be with him for the rest of my life. I knew I wasn't going to go anywhere unless it was with him. It was just a piece of paper in my eyes. Once he asked though, it did feel much different. A very good kind of different. He told me that after everything we had been through he realized that he wanted to marry me and make me his wife. The psychologist told us both that the accident would either pull us apart or bring us closer together. She was right because we have been happily married for twenty three years now.

So you see this is one of the blessings that came from the accident. We were married in September of the same year. Six months didn't seem like much time considering we would be married in Moncton, NB and lived in Shortt's Lake, NS. But, it just seemed to make more sense considering the bulk of the guest list resided there.

We also had another blessing that came as a result of the accident. Our dog Bear was getting very old and I was still a little nervous about living in such a secluded area after our accident. So we discussed getting another dog while Bear was still spry enough to teach the new pup her ways. Derek had always wanted a German Shepard and one of his customers had a female who would soon be having a litter of puppies. So we decided that Derek would go and pick out a pup once she had her litter. He visited the litter three times before bringing home our new little female.

I didn't want to go and visit the litter in case I influenced his decision on which one he would choose. I wanted the decision to be all his. A small part of me also thought that if I did go, we would end up bringing two puppies home, so it was best that I didn't go. We already had enough animals, all of which I had brought home. Our family was growing and I was elated. I very much wanted Derek to have a special bond with this new pup and I got my wish. I can still remember the day he brought her home and still have the picture of the two of them standing in the doorway at our home in Shortt's Lake. He was holding her with a look of pure love and joy. I also fell in love with this little cutie, which he named "Lee".

She was a very active little girl. I had forgotten what it was like to have a puppy, not to mention such an active one. She turned out to be a fantastic and loyal friend. We felt safe with her on guard, in our new home, in a new area. She was very protective and loyal, almost to a fault, you might say. We exercised her regularly in order to keep her extremely fit, as we wanted her to live a long and healthy life. We had to throw a ball for her every evening for at least an hour, in order to meet her energy burning needs. Otherwise, nobody was going to get any rest at night. She was a very fast and alert dog and was always watching and listening for anything that might be out of the ordinary. Those that she loved were held in her highest regard but there was absolutely no doubt that she was Derek's dog, through and through.

As I mentioned, she was a very active girl and it was very hard to keep her entertained. That was until I brought home a new friend for her. Someone to keep her company, as the other animals in the house were no match for her energy. Another story that starts with, one day at the vet clinic, where I worked. So this particular day, there were some farm kittens brought in to be put down. They were very sickly and the farmer didn't want to see them suffer. Those were heartbreaking days for me. This particular farmer would bring the cats from his farm in, the one's that he could catch, that is, to have them spayed or neutered. He was responsibly trying to control the population, as best he could. As most people know, cats can multiply pretty quickly, given the right circumstances. Though it was a difficult thing to do, it was better for the kittens to be put to sleep if they were suffering, or so sick that they would pass something on to the other, more healthy cats. Most of the time, this was the only option. I understood, if there was no hope for them to survive, but it was still very sad and hard to see, especially the little ones.

As I was saying, I came into work one day and there were some kittens sitting in a kennel. They were very sick, scared and unsure of their fate. Most of them were so sickly that they almost seemed like they had given up all will to live. One by one, the vet on duty, who was also the owner of the clinic, came in to get them and do what she thought was best by putting them out of their misery. She was a kind soul and I could see that she truly hated that part of her job. When she got to the last kitten, she scooped him up in her arms to take him to another section in the clinic. As she laid him on the table, he looked up at her with his big sad kitten eyes and reached up with one paw and touched her face ever so softly. It was at that moment, when she was just about to administer an injection that would surely end his life, she decided to stop. This cute little orange tabby male stole her heart. I think he was trying to ask her to give him a chance. She stopped and put the needle down. She then asked one of the vet techs to start giving him a couple of different medications. She decided to give him the chance he had asked for. Her heart melted and when she told me the story, so did mine.

Every day I would go in and see him slowly gaining strength, as he continued to fight for his life. He was a true little warrior. Such a sad looking little thing. I couldn't help but love him for his determination. He was like no other. I would play with him on my breaks and every time I walked by his kennel he would reach out to touch me. The weekend was fast approaching and

I knew that there would not be anyone around to give him his medication. He had come so far and I was concerned that his progress would stall if he didn't get his meds at the proper times. Once again, I called Derek to tell him of this poor little sickly creature. I laid it on thick and asked if he would mind if I brought him home for the weekend. It was just so that I could make sure he got his medication and stayed on track. We both knew that if this little guy came home with me, he was staying and once again, Derek said yes sure you can bring him home.

We figured he was only about four weeks old by the size of him and the information the farmer had given us. I could not believe the energy he had. He was everywhere, all at the same time. He ran circles around the other animals, all except Lee of course. She could keep up to him. They played together, slept together and ate together. They were always together. They instantly became best buds and we quickly got attached to him. We called him Fast Freddy. It seemed suiting considering his level of energy and of course, once we named him, he was staying. The female cats we had at the time, weren't quite sure what to make of him at first. In fact, I caught them trying to hunt him one day. So, to be safe, he slept in between us at night, until I felt that the girls could be trusted not to eat him.

One night I woke up scared that I had suffocated him in my sleep. When I woke, I realized that I had been laying on him. I was mortified. I thought for sure he was dead. In my panicked state, I woke Derek and as I started to shake Freddy, all of a sudden he opened his eyes, looked up at me and yawned as he stretched. It was as if I was disturbing his slumber. Almost like he was saying, "What?? I was sleeping!!".

From that point on, we absolutely had to keep Freddy. Fast Freddy! He was the only one who could keep up with Lee's energy. She was the only dog I knew that had her own cat. Everyone we knew thought it was all very comical. As it turned out, he was just the right fit to our little family.

Years later, after we moved back to New Brunswick and out of nowhere, Fast Freddy became sick. He started dragging his back leg behind him, which was very swollen. Right away, I took him to our vet and after some testing, she told me that he had a fast acting cancer and it had basically eaten all of the bone and tissue in his leg. She said that all that was left was a tumour and skin. Our options were to remove the leg as far up as she could and hope that she got all the cancer, or put him down. She also said that even if she did operate, the cancer would probably come back and attack a major organ within six months.

I would not hear tell of putting him down so she amputated his leg. When I first saw him after the surgery, I wondered if I had made the right decision. He was so sad and pitiful looking, it broke my heart.

Freddy lived six more healthy years, until his last three days. It wasn't the cancer that eventually took him though, it was his heart. He ended up with heart failure and we had to put him to sleep. It was one of the saddest days of my life. I guess in the long run, however, I made the right decision in amputating his leg. He had a very happy long life and the funny thing was that he still ran circles around the other animals, even with only three legs. He recovered and recouped extremely quickly. I believe it was because animals, unlike humans, don't feel sorry for themselves. They just live in the moment and get on with things. They adapt and adjust and keep moving. We humans could learn a thing or two from these wonderful and intelligent creatures. Fast Freddy definitely used all nine of his lives.

# CHAPTER 7

## *Planning our Wedding*

Remember earlier on when I was telling you about the wonderful birthday evening dinner we spent at the lovely, character filled, old house on the river bank when DW proposed to me? Well, I can still recall how excited I was, when I decided to call my father to tell him that I was engaged to be married. As I was trying to tell him what we were thinking of for our wedding, his first response was that he didn't think that the date would really work for him. He then asked me if we could provide him with an alternate date. For which he made a suggestion, of course. The second thing he said was, "I suppose you want some help paying for this wedding?". I was not surprised, but I will say that it hurt a little. We were talking about my wedding here. You know what the worst part was though? It was that, in the end, we went with the date that he had suggested and we did it because that is what I was trained to do. I was trying to please him, at the expense of my own wants and needs and now, it was at the expense of Derek's too. Where do you suppose I learned this behaviour?

I'm not sure why it is always expected that the bride be "given away", or be walked down the aisle by her father? It seems that more and more people are getting away from those traditions and looking back I wish I had too. I wish I had started my married life by sticking to all of my original plans and just focused on what made me and us happy. It was wrong of me to change anything I, or we, wanted to suit my parents. It was simply a continuation of their manipulation and me bending to their wants and needs. I would have been happier with having a goat walk me down the aisle and standing up on my own!

When Derek and I first talked about getting married and how we wanted to proceed I suggested it might be easier to just go away get married and then come back and have a big party. His response was that neither he, nor I would want all those people to be disappointed. I laughed and realized that he wanted the big wedding and I would do anything for him. He later said that my original suggestion is the way we should have gone. He said that he really did not understand what was going to take place, like I did. He said that if he had, we would have gone to the Caribbean, gotten married, had a huge party on the beach and not told a single one of them!

Once we finally set the date, you remember the date that was most convenient for my Father and his... well, never mind. Once we set the date, I found that my excitement started to build and from that point on, it seemed like I made at least one, sometimes two, trips to Moncton per week. Just because of all the planning that was required and of course, I did it all while I was trying to work.

At that time, I thought, well, maybe I came to believe, that mother was one of my closest girlfriends. So in a moment of weakness, I asked her to stand up with me. You see, she complained non-stop that my father and his wife were going to be there and how uncomfortable she felt around them. All of this incessant bitching of hers, eventually got to me and then I started to get worked up about it too. I guess maybe I thought that if I asked her to stand up with me it would make her feel even more special because then not only was she the mother of the bride but she would also be the matron of honour. So here I was going out of my way to try to keep her happy too, on our special day. Again!

Derek and I discussed what we thought we would like our colours to be and came to a great decision, I thought. It was something that we both really liked. We were stuck on either navy or burgundy, which was a good choice for us. When I told my mother about our choices, her response was that the colour would be whichever colour she could find a dress in. She had absolutely no consideration for the fact that I might want to pick the colours. Once again, I mean still, it was all about her. Maybe I should have had a goat stand up with me too.

She very quickly tried to make our wedding an event that she alone was planning. Not an event that Derek and I were planning. Every single time I told her what I wanted to do, she had an opposing comment, idea or suggestion. She was so concerned with her own appearance and all that it entailed, that I don't even think she thought about the fact that it was *my* wedding.

My mother used to sew a lot when I was younger and made feeble attempts at making some of my clothes. All so there would be money to outfit my brother in his latest new hockey gear or custom built, child sized golf clubs, I suppose. I can recall having to wear a dress she made that I hated. I was in my early years of school and really didn't need any help in drawing anymore unwanted attention to myself. I pleaded with her, "Please don't make me wear this!", "Oh, come on it's cute!", she said. So, off I go to school in this stupid looking dress with my stupid looking, boy style hair cut and all so she could tell people what *she* did and how wonderful she was. It was a very bad day! Can you just imagine what school playground bullying was like in those days of the mid 70's? Dressed like that? I'm mean really!

I told her that I wanted a very plain and simple dress for my wedding and I thought that maybe we could make it together. She used to sew and I've always been good at that sort of thing. Maybe it would be fun, I thought? "Absolutely not!", she said. She would not hear tell of any such thing. I was getting worn down having to fight with her on every one of my choices, so I caved. I decided to ask Derek's aunt to make a dress for me. I designed it and she came pretty close to what I wanted. I was a very big girl then and I thought it would be hard to find what I wanted, so it seemed that maybe that was my best option. I'll have it made, then maybe I can get close to what I want. To this day, my mother insists on keeping my dress. Even though I have asked for it multiple times. I guess maybe she thinks it's her property since she chipped in a little to help pay for it.

Big weddings can be very stressful to plan, as anyone who has ever planned one knows. My mother was quickly making it about her and what she wanted and not considering us at all. I know that she helped to pay for some of it, but she wasn't the only one who chipped in and that did not give her the right to take over the whole decision making process. Contrary to her thoughts at the time, of course.

I had a meltdown one night when talking to Derek about it and, of course, he did what he always does and tried to save the day. He told me that he was now going to get more involved with what was left to plan and my mother wouldn't dare fight him on any decisions we both made. It was nice, since he is the one who wanted the big wedding in the first place. Which was quickly turning into a colossal shit storm. My hope was that she would back off once he got more involved.

Derek and I decided to go pick out our flowers together. Mother, of course, wanted to be part of that process too and was very unhappy when we informed her that we would not be needing her help, nor was she welcome to join us. I guess maybe that's why I had to arrange my own stag party. I always thought that it was sort of the responsibility of the matron of honour to plan the party. She response, "Well I had a shower for you, wasn't that enough?". That didn't stop her from attending my party though. She wouldn't want to miss out on anything. I even bought most of my own drinks during the night. I really should have asked a goat!

I let her get away with this behaviour and always have. She played the victim because my father and his younger model would be there, and as a result, I felt that she needed be treated special and put ahead of my needs. It was the worst thing I could have done. She just needed to face her own demons like everyone else, but I couldn't see that at the time. Maybe I was still feeling guilty for "being the one who caused their divorce".

I felt bad for her boyfriend at the time. Many times I wondered if she showed this jealous side to him, on matters concerning my father. If she truly loved this new man in her life, it should not have mattered what, or who, my father was doing. She said that she always felt that she was too weak to fight during their divorce or that her lawyer was no good or countless other excuses. But really, it all boiled down to her feeling like she had gotten cheated and that my father had gotten everything. Maybe he did, I don't know. The one thing I do know is that it was unfair to try and make others feel responsible for her life choices and decisions. I know she has, and maybe even continues to blame me for their divorce. After all, I was the truth teller. I even wrote her a letter about it one time, many years ago. In the letter I stated that I always felt that she blamed me for their divorce and how her actions and never ending list of "comments" made me feel. This was after one of our many, many disagreements. This particular time we were on the phone, she was going on and on about the same old "do you know what your father did?" bullshit and I told her that I just didn't want to talk about it anymore. I did not care what or who he was doing and that she should just get over it and let it go already! She was so mad that she hung up and never called me again.

Months went by and I didn't call her either. Almost a year had gone by and her birthday was fast approaching. It was a milestone for her and our fight had been eating at me. I had never gone that long without talking to her before. I knew she would never forgive me if I didn't do something for her milestone. Not that it would matter, however, nothing I ever did or tried to do was ever good enough anyway. So, feeling sorry for her, I tried to arrange a party in her honour and the only people who would attend for one reason or another was one of her sisters, my brother and his family. I thought that knowing that no one would attend her party would hurt her, so I cancelled it. Instead, I reached out to my brother and asked him if we could just have a small private party at his home for the immediate family. I offered to do the bulk of the work, which of course he thought was a great idea! That way, he didn't have to go anywhere or do anything, as usual. Perfect for him! For me, I wanted to see her for the first time on neutral ground, in case it went badly.

We had the get together and she was very cold toward me. There are days now when I really wish I had just stayed away. I say this because I know that if I hadn't been the first to reach out, she never would have. It would have been easier, in some respects, to just live without her in my life. But, my upbringing was such that I thought Grammy would have been disappointed in me if I didn't tried to mend fences, as it were. I wonder now, if Grammy is watching, if maybe she would have offered some different words of wisdom? A different lesson maybe? I wonder if she would have a different perspective on it all, now? After feeling and seeing the impact that it all had on my young life.

On the day of our wedding, I spent more time getting my

mother ready and doing her hair than I spent on myself. In fact, it made us late because of it. On *my* wedding day!

I want to say that even though there were a lot of hurdles to overcome and a whole lot of unnecessary, frustrating bullshit in planning our day, I would do it all over again, in a heartbeat. When I looked up and saw Derek standing at the front of the church, I felt pure love and sheer joy at the fact that I would be his wife, friend and lover for the rest of our lives. I'm truly blessed! It was a beautiful celebration of love and togetherness!

Not everything about our wedding was negative, although the way I just explained some of it, it might seem so. We had two showers that our parents held for us which were a lot of fun. All of my favourite people in the world were there celebrating with us, and Derek's aunt held a lingerie shower for me where I received all kinds of sexy, lacy things to wear on our honeymoon. It too, was a lot of fun! I had never attended a party like that before.

All of the events and gatherings leading up to our wedding, as well as, the rehearsal party were a blast. The day itself, however, was a blur. It was like I blinked and the day and evening were over. I wished I could have pressed a rewind button so I could go through it again and slow it down. It was a fairy tail wedding and wouldn't have changed it for anything. I was glad Derek convinced me to have a big wedding I think I would have regretted not doing so, in the end.

We got married in a little country church that is just down the road from where Derek grew up. In fact, he attended Sunday school and youth group there, as a child. He also attended this church with his grandmother when she lived with them, when he was very young. It was a quaint country setting. We had our pictures taken in front of the big pine tree in Derek's parent's front yard with all our friends and family around.

The reception followed at the local community centre down

the road. Derek and his many musician friends played all our favourites for the first part of the night and for the rest of the night we had recorded music. I had asked my brother to make some mixed tapes for us, as I have always loved his taste in music. It was nice because it gave us a chance to spend part of the evening together as a newly weds and socialize with our guests. I still have the mixed tapes (we used cassettes in those days) that my brother made and I still listen to them from time to time. They bring back some good memories.

We enjoyed a private night at a hotel in the city after our reception. It was a beautiful room with all the bells and whistles you could imagine for our first night together as husband and wife. I don't think we slept at all that night. The adrenaline from the whole experience and the day just kept us on cloud nine.

My mother insisted on us going to her house the next day to open our wedding gifts. She wanted a big show and invited some people over. Really, I think she just had to know what we received and who gave us what. I think she even took notes. Honestly, we just wanted to go on our honeymoon. It wasn't that we were ungrateful, it was just that we needed some time for ourselves. Time away from all of the hype and arguing.

Once the gifts were opened, we got on the road and headed toward home. We needed to drop some things off, make sure that our animals were well cared for and pack some more luggage to get ready to head out the next morning. We were heading to Prince Edward Island for a few days to be alone, first. From there, decided to visit the South Shore of Nova Scotia. It was there that we found the best night's sleep, on the most comfortable bed I have ever slept in. It was a bed and breakfast right across the road from a beach in St. Margaret's Bay. It was a beautiful old home with a wonderful honeymoon suite and the sound of the waves crashing on the beach just a few metres away made for a wonderful night. It made a perfect getaway for us. We have both always loved the island and any part of Nova Scotia.

Now we both joke and say if we had known what having a big wedding was really going to entail, we would have eloped to a hot beach on a remote island somewhere. I believe that we both may have had some regrets with that decision though. Especially after having had the most beautiful wedding I could have ever imagined. Or would we?

## Returning to life in Nova Scotia

After our little break, we returned to Shortt's Lake and our life there as best we could. It wasn't long, however, before the stress of working at the vet clinic started to really take its toll on me and especially on my mental health. I couldn't seem to separate myself from what I saw and was in the presence of, on a daily basis. The cruelty that some humans posses and the things they are capable of doing to innocent animals is simply beyond me. Sometimes, more often than not really, I would leave work in tears after witnessing animals suffering at the hands of stupid and cruel humans. I worked in the back section of the clinic, where all of the animals were housed and it seemed that, after our accident, I was even more sensitive to seeing such sad or horrific sights.

I now know that I am an animal empath and that I can and was feeling everything that the animals were going through and it was horrible. Although I learned a great deal more about animals, from a medical perspective, in working there. I found that constantly being exposed to and in the presence of the pain and suffering of the animals wore on me and to the point that I had to make a change. I had to leave my job behind and try to move forward in building my own grooming business. Maybe out of my home, I thought? I didn't want to stop grooming, I just wanted all of the anxious and sad feelings I was getting from being in that environment to stop.

For a while I made it work. I developed a small clientele, which was amazing, because where we lived was not a heavily populated area. But, word travels fast in a small town, remember? I offered some pick up and delivery service and some people would come and watch while I groomed their dogs.

As time went on, we decided that we had enjoyed our time in Nova Scotia, but it was time to move back home. Sometimes I think that I just wanted to run away from there. I think I wanted to run away from that place and all of the memories of the terrible things that happened during our time there. Don't get me wrong, I also remember a lot of the good times we had. I remember the neighbours we had and the friends we made. I remember the community events we attended and the fun times we had. I loved the life we had built there, in some respects. But, at the same time, it seemed to me that maybe it had just been a chapter in our lives and maybe that chapter was done. Maybe it was time to move on to our next chapter. Have any of you ever felt that way?

Not only had we had our horrible accident during our time there, but we had also lost Bear and Spanky and a couple of family members back in New Brunswick had passed away suddenly, during our time there. I felt like we were missing out on spending time with our loved ones and friends back home and that I wanted to be closer.

We decided to build a small dwelling on a piece of property that Derek's Dad passed on to him. It is the same property where Derek's very first childhood home was located. In fact, there are still some small remnants of it in our front yard. They have mostly been covered over by heavy brush and some small trees that have grown up, now.

I had suggested we just build a camp like structure and live in it for a couple of years, then if we liked it we could build something a bit more permanent. The road out home can be hard to navigate in the winter and I wasn't sure whether I would be comfortable with the long drive to my new grooming job in the city.

A part of me didn't want to sell our place in Nova Scotia because we had worked so hard at cultivating it to our liking, but, even after all of that, it still didn't feel like home. Not compared to being here in New Brunswick.

We knew it would be a lot of work to clear the grown up piece of property in New Brunswick but neither of us were scared of hard work and we didn't want to clear anymore land or take down anymore trees than was absolutely necessary. If we had hired someone else to do this work, we thought that they might not treat the property in the same way that we would. Being good stewards of the land is something that is very important to us both. We wanted to build in such a way that there would be a very long driveway. In this way, we would be further away from the road noise and have lots of privacy. Our long and curved driveway leads to a little clearing surrounded by trees. Which is where we built our camp. Well it turned into a tiny home on a concrete slab. At a mere six hundred and twenty-four square feet, it is a small dwelling, but it is all we have ever really needed.

Our home has an open concept. The living room and kitchen are all in one big open room, which has a wood stove in the centre. The bathroom has a corner shower, toilet, vessel sink and a floor to ceiling cabinet in one corner and a wall cabinet, that we built for linens. We built most everything in our home really. Another plus with the layout we came up with, is that we were able to have our washer and dryer right in the bathroom, which is nice. Most things are cleaned and stored within close proximity to one another. The bedroom is large enough to have two small dressers, a good sized closet and a queen size bed with drawers built underneath. We also have a small storage room with a couple of freezers, a hot water tank, water pump and pantry shelves.

Our house is all on one level and was built on a concrete slab because neither of us wanted a basement. Having everything all on one level just made sense to us. I think a big part of it was because, in her later years, we had to lift Bear up and down the stairs at our home in Nova Scotia. She was a big dog and it took a lot of effort. Being such a large dog, her hips were weak and we didn't want her to strain will trying to navigate the stairs. We remembered this when we decided to build something of our own. Having everything on one level would be easier in case we found ourselves in a similar situation again. Besides we had lots of land and we could always add on later, if we chose.

Derek's idea was that we would build a house later and then turn this structure into a garage, if it made sense, down the road, and so building on a slab gave us more options. After we had finished cutting and clearing as much as we could by hand and with the chain saws, it was time for the dirt work to be done. We were so proud of our accomplishments and were very excited for the next phase. Then all of sudden and out of nowhere, our progress came to a screeching halt.

By this time, my brother was in the process of taking over my father's construction business. Father made it very clear that he wanted to help in getting the dirt work done for us and because my brother still owed him some money, he would use the dirt work as a way for my brother to pay some of it back. He also said that, where he had done so much for my brother, he wanted to do this for us. If we were measuring however, which we were not, it would not even have come close to all that he had done for my brother. But, maybe it would ease his conscience a little. It's hard to say really. I think that a big part of it was also pride. He wouldn't want us to hire another company to do our dirt work, what would people say?

I agreed, but wasn't thrilled about the idea. I had made arrangements with my brother for a start date for our dirt work and based on that Derek and I booked time off from our new jobs so that we could start building. Then, after we had all of our arrangements made, and at the last minute, my brother cancelled and postponed. He said that he was busy and there were other jobs that had to take priority over our project. It was not the first time he had put us off, but it would be the last. I lost it! I told him he was fired and not to step foot on our property again. A couple of hours later, my father called and told me that I need to be reasonable. He was trying to defend my brother but very quickly realized he wasn't going to get anywhere with me, with that approach. He spent a great deal of time on the phone with me trying to convince me that it would look bad for me to hire someone else. I told him I did not care and that I had been living in New Brunswick far too long without a home of my own and I simply wasn't waiting any longer. Finally, he said that he would do the work personally and that my brother would have nothing to do with it, except that he would be using his equipment.

This may seem harsh, but I have been put off and discounted by my whole family, my whole life. It wasn't like I was asking them to do the work. It was them who insisted on doing it! I just wanted it done and would have gladly paid someone else to do it so I wouldn't have to deal with my family and their bullshit. It was all about appearances and hiding how they have really treated me all along. My father did do most of the dirt work himself but he needed a couple of truck drivers to haul the grubbing waste away and to bring in fill. We had told him what we wanted for the lay out but he convinced us to go another route, I think it was because it was easier for him. I wasn't impressed but at least we were making some progress. So once my father was done with his part, he told his foreman to leave this big gaping hole in our yard to the side of where our building was going to go. The foreman took it upon himself to fill it in. He told us afterwards that he couldn't, in good conscience, leave us with a mess like that, as it would have been very difficult to deal with, after the fact. I was very grateful for his kindness and that he put his own neck on the line so that we wouldn't be left in a huge mess. I will never forget his kindness. Or my father's short cuts!

So finally and just as soon as the concrete slab was poured and dried enough, we could start building. I think it was mostly dry, at least. I couldn't wait to get things going. We had a tonne of help from Derek's family and my mother's boyfriend, at the time. One of my Uncles, on my mother's side, even came to help for a day. They have my sincere thanks and gratitude for all that they did to lend a hand.

Derek and I worked very hard all summer trying to get it weather tight so that we could be in it before the snow fell. Even if the inside wasn't finished, that didn't matter to me, just as long as we were warm enough, that's all I was concerned about. Besides, we weren't completely sure on how we were going to finish it anyway. We decided it would be better to just finish it as we went along. As it has turned out, our plans have changed several times but always for the better it seems. We are living and learning as we go. I love our home and I am very glad we decided to build and stay here. Building one home is enough though, especially when you are constantly adding and changing to best suit your needs.

## My career as a groomer in Moncton

Before we left Nova Scotia, I started looking for a grooming job in the Moncton area. I had seen an ad for a grooming position and decided to go visit the shop to see if it was the kind of place where I would like to work, before even applying. I had my resume in hand, in case I got a good feeling about the place. The young lady who owned the shop and was a groomer herself, was looking for some experienced help, as she also had a teaching facility attached to her shop. She met me at the door, as I entered her establishment and greeted me in a very pleasant manner. As I looked around, I noticed that the place was clean and the dogs seemed to be calm, which was a good sign to me. She and I had a nice long talk and got along nicely. We seemed to have a fair amount in common, with our thoughts on grooming and animals and both decided to give each other a shot at working together. The grooming shop was fairly busy, but the amount of students she had at any given time, had a direct effect the amount of work she had for me. I knew I could help her build her business even larger, if I gave it a little time and effort. At that time in my career, I was still young, fast, and very efficient at finishing, especially when it came to scissoring. I could do as many dogs as she could give me, the business was growing and things were going well.

Along with the growth of the grooming business, however, the school started to grow as well. She started to get more students which meant less work for me because the students needed dogs to learn and practice on. Eventually, this led to lack of work for me and so I started looking for a place to rent, so that I would have my own shop with my own clients and would no longer have to rely on someone else. I wanted a place that was in town but not a long distance to travel everyday. I also thought it would be good to be in a high traffic area with not a lot of competition in the vicinity. I approached a young couple who had rented a spot that used to be a community general store. They were renovating it and had a small corner that they were interested in sub-letting to me, to help pay their bills. It was exactly what I was looking for, there were many homes close by and it was in a high traffic area. It was only a fifteen minute drive from home and the rent was reasonable. I could do this!

It wasn't long before I had set up shop and was grooming. In fact, as soon as I put the sign up I was getting calls. I hadn't even opened the doors yet and people were already inquiring. I was over the moon happy. Finally, I could build on my own clientele and do it my way. I would not have been able to do this without all of Derek's help and moral support, however.

It didn't take long before I needed to hire some help because I was just that busy. It was very difficult to find the right people to help me though, as I had to completely train everyone that I had come to work with me. My clients expected my quality of work and that is what they were going to receive. The shop was very small, but I made it work. My client list just kept growing larger by the day. I realized that if I was so inclined I could expand and have a store as well. I saw an opportunity to sell to pet products and supplies and maybe even have a couple of lines of top quality dog food, too.

Derek had been in this business for many years and I thought if I could get his help, we could expand the business and run it together. So, that's just what we did. Derek was amazing and we soon outgrew the original spot. Before long, we moved to another, much larger location. Before I knew it, I had over six hundred grooming clients, the store was selling all kinds of pet related products and we had thousands of dollars worth of inventory. We had a staff and all kinds of new opportunities and responsibilities. It was all very exciting for us, at the time. I was running on excitement and pure adrenaline for the first couple of years. But then, all of a sudden, I started to feel ill and extremely tired. All the hard work was starting to take its toll on me. We did well for almost 5 years and then things started to affect both Derek and I, in a negative way. It was getting more and more difficult to find qualified, reliable staff and I was running out of steam. I knew I wouldn't be able to keep up that pace and maintain our quality standards, on my own much longer. Shortly after that, during a visit to my doctor, she told me that the stress of my work was starting to affect my health. I knew that I needed to make a change and so we sold all of our products and found someone to take over our lease. I have learned over the years, that if you don't have your health you don't have anything.

Typically, dog groomers will stay in the trade for an average of about six years, or so. This is because it is very taxing work, on both the body and the mind. I knew that I needed a break but I wasn't really sure, at that point, if I wanted to give it up completely. I had passed the six year mark, long ago and so, it was time for a break, at least.

We closed the store, cleaned it up and gave the frontage to some folks who could make good use of the space in expanding their business. The day we were moving out and cleaning up our space, my mother, in one of her many asinine states, jumped out of or into a moving vehicle, I can't remember which. At any rate, she had fallen and needed to go to the hospital. Of course, *she* needed attention on this a very important and difficult day for me. My brother knew about her situation and did nothing to help, as usual. So, I went with her. Thank you to Derek's Mom who helped us with cleaning and then went to sit with my mother at the hospital, while I tied up some loose ends with Derek. We got through it but, as always my brother looked out for himself. He knew I would be the one to look after our mother, again.

Derek decided to go into carpentry and renovation work and started his own business, after we closed the shop and did very well. He had lots of work and plenty of satisfied customers. I took three months off to rest and figure out what my next move would be. Where do I go from here, I wondered?

Eventually, I did decide to go back to grooming but on a smaller scale, this time. I had customers calling me at home checking to see if there was any way I could groom their dog, either at their house or my own. My next thought was that I could renovate one of our outbuildings and just take back enough clients to keep myself going, at a comfortable pace. I decided that I would groom from home and offer a pick up and delivery service. This way, I could schedule and control the flow of my work a little better. I could make a decent living and not wear myself out. I could get back to enjoying my work and the time I spent with the animals.

I talked to Derek and he agreed to help get me up and running. It wasn't long before I had over two hundred clients again and my phone was still ringing. I didn't advertise and was located in the middle of the woods. Some people came all the way from Nova Scotia to have their dog groomed, which was amazing to me. I tried my best to provide top quality care and service to as many dogs as possible. My plan was to only work part time, so that I could then work on my other passion, which was my art. Painting and sketching have always been things that I absolutely love to do. It's an outlet that centres and relaxes me.

Before I knew it, I was juggling both because I wanted to sell my work as an artist. I got a table at one of the local farmers markets in town and was working that into my week as well. I didn't really realize just how tired I had started to become, again. I knew and could feel that I wasn't in tip top shape, so I decided to go see my doctor. I told her that I had been feeling really tired and that I had mostly chalked it up to my age and what I thought were some early menopause symptoms. She suggested that we do some blood work and have a closer look at what was going on. She ordered a full work up and my numbers were fantastic, she said. Nothing to worry about, go and live your life. My idea was to start to retire from grooming and focus on my art work. That way, I could fill my days creating and selling my pieces and prints at the market and/or online.

Suddenly, I found myself trying to meet the demands of my grooming clients and trying to schedule time to work on my art and commissioned pieces that clients had ordered. Anyone who is an artist knows that you create when the inspiration or mood strikes you and that trying to schedule time to be creative typically does not work very well. It can actually be more stressful than therapeutic and relaxing.

It wasn't long before I was getting really tired and was not feeling like myself, at all. Looking back, I realize that the extra strain added by trying to force myself to be creative and work on deadlines, made it feel more like a job than something that I just loved to do. In the midst of all of that, and in addition to what I was trying to do for me, it seemed like I was also being pulled by our families. I tried to spend ample time with everyone and be efficient at everything, I was involved in. But, it just kept getting more and more difficult, as the months passed. It came to a point where I wasn't even making time for my friends. I wasn't sleeping well. I had zero balance in my life and started to take my frustrations out on Derek. It felt like he or we were spending more time helping others than we were spending quality time together, trying to make our own dreams become reality. I used to get so irritated, saying that we hadn't even finished our own tiny home yet. It was not like me to act in this manner. It wasn't just helping one person or another out, that was frustrating me. It was the fact that I couldn't say no. I was at the height of the "over-achieving people pleaser" phase of my life and my health was paying the price, again! My life was out of balance and the inertia of it was running me, I wasn't running it. Have any of you ever experienced that? Can you relate?

If we were doing something for one person, all of sudden someone else would see it and the they too would ask. We decided to buy an old travel trailer to fix it up and take it to my father's cottage on the Lake. He had offered us a spot where we could park it on the beach. It was a beautiful spot to relax near the water. Except that there was always something to do around there too. My father always had a project on the go or needed something to be fixed and of course there was always yard work to do. Not to mention all of the endless meals we prepared and provided. I figured it was the least we could do to share in this lovely oasis. It was nice of him to invite us but it came with, what felt like, a high price. We worked almost all weekend and then would go out on the boat for a couple of hours and return home more tired than when we had left. We had just moved the same behaviour to a different location. I thought maybe that spending some time at the cottage and working around with my father, might bring us closer together. The boat rides felt like we were getting quality time and I enjoyed them thoroughly. I thought he did too. Well, that's what I thought.

It was a long weekend and my father wanted to go out on the boat to meet up with some friends of his, on a neighbouring lake. So, the four of us packed up our coolers and got ready to go. My father, his wife, Derek and I. We loaded into the boat and headed out for a lovely cruise. When we met up with his friends, I happened to know him but I never met his wife until that day. In fact, I used to groom their dog at one time. The weather was perfect that day and I was really enjoying myself. We had tied the boats together so we could cross over from one boat to the other and were all talking and having a few drinks, except for my father. He was trying to stay away from alcohol at the time because of some of the medications he was on, which seemed to be making him irritated. This coupled with the fact that I was drinking and when I have a couple I get a little louder, just like the rest of my family. Where do you think I got it from? Derek said I wasn't over the top and trust me, he would know. I could kind of feel some tension in the air coming from my father but I just chalked it up to him not drinking. At one point, he and his friend jumped over to his boat and went to the bow of the boat, to have a pee. He didn't like to use his bathroom that was on board because then he would have to clean it. He then says to his friend, "now you see why I divorced my first wife, to have raised the likes of that!!". He was referring to me, of course. As he was saying the words, he didn't realize that Derek had stepped onto the boat to grab a drink and overheard his comment.

Derek came back onto the other boat and sat right beside me and put his arm around me. He remained very quiet for the rest of the day and didn't speak unless spoken to. I thought maybe he wasn't feeling well, so I didn't question him. Sometimes he is quiet, that can just be his way. Besides, I talk enough for the both of us anyway, at times. So after our little boat party, we left the others and made our way back to the cottage. Derek continued to be quiet on our return trip and we spent the night in our own trailer. The next day Derek insisted that we take our trailer home and that would be the end of our season. There were only one maybe two good weekends left to the season anyway and so I agreed. I wasn't sure exactly why he wanted to leave early, but it was tiring for him to be there, working all the time. I thought maybe he had just had enough for that season. So we packed up, thanked my father and his wife for their hospitality and headed for home.

Three months went by and every time I would say something about my father or the cottage Derek would get quiet. I could feel that something wasn't right. Finally, I asked him if something had happened at the cottage between him and my father. "Did he do something?", I asked. Derek and I never lie to one another, it's just always been that way. His reply was that he didn't think I really wanted to know and that he really didn't want to tell me. He said that it would hurt me and he didn't want to do that. Of course, I said that if something had happened that I needed to know. So, he told me what my father said on the boat that day. I have to tell you, that it's far from the worst thing he ever said about me or my mother so I wasn't shocked. Now, the remaining members of my family, when the heard what had been said, felt that it was just an "off-handed comment" and was nothing to be upset about. However, Derek being the man of principle that he is and knowing that my father was sober at the time, felt much differently about it.

The thing that bothered me the most was that Derek heard him say it and I think maybe it hurt him a little too. I think he thought that we meant more to my father by that point in our lives and I think he felt somewhat used. But, the biggest part about it was that Derek didn't want to hurt me. During our time at the cottage, we had gotten close with our nephews, my brothers two boys. They seemed to be around a lot during the last three seasons we were there, which was really the only time we saw them. My father and his wife would bring them up and keep them when my brother and his wife had functions to attend. The boys spent a lot of time with us and we watched them very close especially around the water. My father and his wife could have been more attentive, but Derek and I enjoyed watching them, so it all kind of worked out. I will always have fond memories of the time we spent together.

Now, I felt that Derek too had been affected by my father's antics and I couldn't ignore this behaviour. My heart broke a little more after hearing Derek tell me what he heard on the boat that day. The look on his face, as he told me, was sheer sadness. I believe my father lashed out that day because he wasn't the centre of attention. He always needed that. He hurt my mother, me and now Derek with his comments and I just couldn't ignore it or let it go. I made a choice that day to go no contact with my father. A couple of weeks went by, and even though he would call, I totally ghosted him. It was at least a month after him trying to call and me ignoring him before he decided to drive out to our house. Thankfully I wasn't home. He even went next door to Derek's parents place to ask them if we were okay, as we hadn't been returning his calls. That night Derek's mother told me about our visitor. I hadn't told anyone what he said at that point.

So, in order to stop any further aggravation I answered his next call. I told him that I knew what he had said and done on the boat that day and of course, he played stupid, as he always did when he was caught doing something. I told him that I was really hurt and so he asked me tell him what he had said. My reply was, "Really, you have to ask me?". He wanted me to repeat it to him. I guess it must have been hard to keep track of all the hurtful things someone like him would say. I told him I needed time and to just leave me alone. He did say he was sorry and didn't really mean it the way it sounded. But, he was not joking. Derek made that very clear in telling me and he does not lie.

My father kept calling and calling. Eventually he would say, in his messages, that he couldn't even remember why I wasn't speaking to him. Or, what he did wrong. This was a man that remembered everything. He said in a couple of his messages that he hoped that some day I would find it in my heart to forgive him. I actually forgave him long ago but that didn't mean that I would continue to let him talk down to and disrespect me. Any contact with him always ended in some form of disrespect or abuse for me. He continued to call for a couple of years and then the calls just stopped. I would get the odd call, or snarky little text message from his wife, every so often, pleading with or trying to bully me into forgiving him. I didn't answer those calls or texts either. In fact, I chose not to speak to him or acknowledge her for five years.

# CHAPTER 8

*For the love of Dogs*

So, I was grooming again, from home, which was good. It was better than the pressure I felt at the store. But then, at some point, things started to change. It seemed that all of a sudden, I was constantly getting calls from new clients again. Maybe at first, it seemed like a feather in my cap, but then with me not being able to say no, it wasn't long before things started to spiral and I was getting more and more tired by the day. I'm not even sure how I managed to get out of bed some days. It seemed that people had forgotten why we had to close the store in the first place. Once again, it felt like it was my fault for not being able to saying no. Being a people pleaser is exhausting! I wonder where I learned this behaviour? Oh yes, now I remember.

I even started trying to accommodate people during what was supposed to be my off time or closed hours. It was all spinning up just the way it had been before. It was running me, not me running it. Then, shortly after, I started trying to do all of this, another horrible thing happened. We lost our last cat Babbles, due to old age. Suddenly, after about fifteen years or so, we found ourselves without a cat, which was very strange. I found myself missing having cats around and so we decided to get a couple of kittens from one of the local farms. They had found themselves with a couple of litters needing some forever homes. Between the time we lost Babbles, and the time that we got the kittens, the only animal we had left was a sweet little old mix breed dog named Jessie. He looked like a miniature golden retriever and was a great little dog, full of life and love. He was about eight years old when we adopted him. The lady who had him before us was a retired lady who liked to travel and her daughter had dumped him on her doorstep before moving away. She really didn't want to be "saddled" with a dog at that stage in her life. She just wanted to have the freedom to come and go as she pleased and did not want to worry about something else to look after.

One of my grooming clients, who happened to be a friend of this lady, told her of me and my services and recommended that she give me a call. So after talking on the phone, she decided to bring Jessie in for a grooming to get him looking and smelling nice. She thought it might be easier to find him a new home if he was a little more presentable. This all took place when I was still in my very first rented grooming shop space. When she arrived with Jessie she told me why she had come to me and why she wanted to find Jessie a new home. I thought I might be able to help as I had developed a fairly long list of dog loving clients, some of whom may be interested in him or could help us find him a home. He was small, friendly, fun loving, non-aggressive and cute as hell. I told her I would do my best to try and find him a loving home. She had told me she wanted to go away for a weekend and did not have anyone to look after him. I told her I would check with my husband and see if he would be okay with us taking Jessie for the weekend. This way I could see if he was good with cats, which would make it easier to place him in a good home.

So I groomed the little guy, who was a perfect gentleman and really enjoyed the time that we spent together. When she picked him up she seemed to be pleased with my service and the job that had been done, she paid her bill and they were on their way. A week or so later, I got a call from her asking me if she should drop Jessie off to me, or would I be picking him up, as she was leaving in the morning for her weekend getaway. I had totally forgotten about making this offer and I hadn't talked to Derek about the situation. I asked her if I could call her back in a few minutes. So, I thought for a moment or two about how I could spin it and then I called Derek to explain the situation. He laughingly agreed, as he always does, to letting me bring Jessie home for the weekend. I guess he just can't resist my charm!

I went to pick Jessie up that same day, after work. It was a nice home but Jessie was only allowed in either the kitchen when it was cold, or in the garage when it was not and the garage is where he spent most of his time, she explained. He seemed lonely until I picked him up and put him in the truck to come home with me. He was a dog that would just stand in the middle of the lawn with his nose held high smelling the fresh air and wagging his tail in sheer bliss. He got along really well with all of our cats and our German Shepard, Lee. Derek and I fell in love with the little guy and decided to keep him. He seemed to appreciate his new home and fit right in with our routines. It was just like he had always been here.

So, with only having little old Jessie left in the house and him being sixteen years old, we really didn't know how much longer he would have a good quality of life. We needed some more cats! We had never been without animals in the house and I really did not want to be. So, up to the farm we go! Going to get me some kittens!

After having a look at the litters and observing their behaviour and play for awhile, Derek picked out a very lively and spirited black and white male kitten. In the early days of bringing them (him) home, I thought he was possessed by Beelzebub himself. I of course, picked out a quiet little grey and white female tabby with extra toes on all of her feet. She was sitting all by herself on top of a barrel looking out through the window in the barn. After some thought, and debate, we decided to name them Jim and Jam.

It wasn't long after we got the kittens that Jessie's health took a turn. I could sense that it was coming and sadly, it was time to say goodbye to our sweet little friend. As hard as it was, it was the right thing to do. He was pretty well blind and deaf and his back end had started to weaken drastically, which is no quality of life for anyone. Especially a friend like him. We had to say goodbye to Lee, our German Shepard, about a year before that. Sadly, we had lost a member of our family every year for a few consecutive years. Initially, we had acquired them all within a year or two of one another and so this pattern can exist, in the circle of life, sometimes. They had all grown and aged together which meant that we would mostly likely lose them all, at around the same time. Which we did.

Suddenly, it was just Derek and I with these two little kittens who were only four or five weeks old. The farmer said that they had been drinking and eating on there own, so they should be fine to go to their new home. So I, I mean we, gladly took them home. I suppose there are times when a farm of that size can be a dangerous place for tiny kittens. I really thought it best that I, oh sorry, I mean we, bring them home as soon as possible. At that time, we always had people around our place. We had family and friends who liked to visit, almost every weekend that summer, as we had decided to put in an above ground pool. This meant that the kittens got lots of handling and attention, which was great socialization for them.

They were now my whole world! All of our other animal family members had passed on and they were getting all of our, I mean my, attention. I spoiled them and gave them everything they needed and then some. Bet you didn't see that coming?

Up until that point, we had always had indoor cats and as I said earlier, we live in a tiny home. These kittens were full of energy and very active. They were used to having lots of room to run and play in the barn. I thought maybe they were missing having all that room to run and play. I started to wonder if it would be better to let them outside. Maybe just while I supervised them, I thought? So, I decided to try it and they absolutely loved it! We have a long driveway and if they started to go down the driveway, toward the road, I would herd them back up to the house. I thought long and hard about this decision and talked to a lot of people, with varying points of view, before I decided to try it at about ten months of age. I did my best to show them that there was danger toward the road and that we had lots of space to run and play up close to the house. Eventually, I felt comfortable enough to let them out unsupervised. They were attached to us and mostly stayed right with us, or quite close by, when we were outside. They seemed to follow our lead. If we were outside, they were outside. If we went inside, for lunch, they did too.

Jam liked to disappear in the woods, on occasion, but for the most part she would come back if she was called. Jim loved attention, so he would always come when he was called. He would meet and greet me as I got out of the car, saying what sounded like "mama" to me. It doesn't matter to me if the sound he made actually meant that or not, that's what I heard and I loved it! He wanted to be picked up and he would wrap his little front legs around my next and nuzzle his face into my neck as he would say it. It made my heart melt, every time. I would never go to bed until they were in the house for the night, though. Then one afternoon, November 16, 2016 to be exact, when I was normally finished work for the day, I decided to take a client after lunch. We had all come inside for lunch and then when my client arrived, we all went back outside. I went to the grooming shop, Derek went to his workshop to work on a carpentry project and the cats went out to play.

When my grooming client showed up she told me that she had decided to wait outside until the grooming was done, as it would save her some extra driving. After the grooming was finished, we were outside talking when I noticed that Jam was hanging around close to the house, but Jimmy was no where to be seen. Which was very unusual for him. It was typically the other way around and I thought it to be quite strange. I called for Jimmy, as I frequently did, and usually he would come right to me. Jam, on the other hand, was sticking close and coming to me. Looking back now I realize that she was trying to tell me that something was wrong. At the time, I thought maybe she was just looking for some attention. I was very tired that day and didn't pick up on the messages she was trying to send me.

I went to Derek's shop and asked if he had seen Jim, but he hadn't seen him since lunch time. I decided to sit and talked with him for a bit, while he was working. At the time, I was thinking that Jim would show up any minute with a little present for me, which he was famous for. My thought was that he was hot on a trail of a rodent and wasn't giving up the hunt until he succeeded. After a couple of hours went by, I started to walk around the yard looking for him. I checked with some neighbours and went to all his usual hang outs, but there was no sign of him. By this time, I was getting very worried, as he never missed supper and it was that time of day.

I made another run around the back yard calling his name, in an almost panicked state. I don't know what made me think to go over to the pool, which we had recently drained down about half way in preparation for winter, but I did. What I found was absolutely horrifying to me!

There was poor little Jimmy floating lifelessly in the stupid pool. I screamed at the top of my lungs as I tried to get to him and pull him out. We had put the ladder away for the season and I was straining to reach him and at the same time screaming for Derek. It was an easy fill pool and I was determined to break it all to pieces, if I had to, in order to get my little boy out. Finally, I was able to reach his cold lifeless body and I knew he was gone. I screamed as the tears poured down my face while I walked toward Derek's shop with his body. Derek came out and saw me holding him crying and he knew what had happened. I don't remember what he had in his hands as he ran out of his shop that day, I just recall him throwing something in complete despair, at the sight of poor little Jimmy.

I tried to revive him, even though I knew he was gone. I didn't want to accept it. My guilt for wanting and having a pool that took my little boy's life was almost more than I could bear. I couldn't look at it anymore.

As I cleaned up little Jimmy's body I noticed some blood on the towel I had wrapped him in. All of a sudden it made sense. He must have been picked up by a bird of prey. We had spotted a very large bald eagle hanging around and several large hawks. We also had osprey that were constantly circling the farm yard. I did not realize until after Jim's death and doing some research, that those birds of prey can easily take a cat. Jim must have been too heavy for the bird to maintain the hold it had on him. He was a big boy. I think the bird must have then dropped him in the pool and Jim had no way of getting out. He was always doing his best to protect Jam from harm and it is even possible that maybe he was trying to protect her from the nasty predator. I guess we will never know for certain. I do know however that he might have survived if the pool hadn't been there and I now had to live with this gut wrenching guilt. I also had to live with the guilt of deciding to let them go outside. I really thought they would be okay and they would be healthier having the wide open space, fresh air and lots of room to run and exercise.

Once Derek and I cleaned him up, had his funeral and buried his little body, we decided that the pool had to go. We tore it down with great anger and sadness. As we threw it away at the dump, I said good riddance. I can't even imagine how I would have felt if it had been a child that had fallen in. I don't even want to think about how horrible that could have been. I had done nothing but clean that damn thing, entertain and feed people, to the point of exhaustion, since we got it anyway. Now after all of that, this is what I have to show for it? My little boy was gone forever! My heart ached then and still does now. I miss him and his antics every day. He left a mark on my soul. He loved very deeply. I could tell by his actions toward his sister Jam. He was always looking out for her and protecting her from harm. I could also tell by the way he offered his loving snuggles to anyone that he deemed worthy. He was very selective when it came to this though.

He was a comical little guy and was always doing something that made us laugh. For instance, sticking his head out through the tiny little access hole that we had cut in the porch wall for the garden hose. Or climbing the rafters in the porch and hanging off them like a monkey. When he first came to live with us he was obsessed with sticking his head in the fridge to the point where we had to put a large sign on the fridge for guests to remind them to watch out for him. We did this so that he wouldn't get his head caught in the closing door, again.

One day after returning from an ATV trip, Derek was a little, let's call it distracted and closed the door on little Jimmy's head. We were horrified. Jimmy scrambled and flopped away like he was having a seizure or was about to die, or maybe had something neurological happening. We really weren't sure what was happening. I jumped up and scooped him into my arms to evaluate the situation. I think he just was hurting and had the wind knocked out of him. Poor Derek was beside himself. The look on his face was nothing I can describe. He loved that little guy and would never dream of hurting him. I could tell that he felt horrible. I told him that I thought Jim would be just fine, if I just held him around my neck for a little while. After about an hour or so, Jam decided it was time to play and as she touched her nose to his, he looked up at me and they were off running. It was like she healed him in that one touch. That was the next line to come out of my mouth at the time, which inspired a song from DW. Maybe we'll feature it on my Youtube channel someday. We used to tease when Jim would do something awkward or silly, that it must have been because of his head getting slammed in the fridge door and laugh.

He was famous for running through doors without any consideration for the person operating it. In fact, after the fridge incident, I slammed him in the entrance door, twice. It never seemed to hurt him however, he would just give a little shake and keep on trucking. He was a tough little guy but, I guess the bird of prey and the water were his last two lives. He had a short life but he received more than 10 lifetimes of love from us.

Little Jam took his death hard. They were very close and I could tell that she was missing him. I used to take her for a walk in the woods behind our home everyday after that, as she didn't seem to like being out in the open for quite a while after that. Neither did I, for that matter. All I had to say was, "do you want to go for a walk Jam?", and she was right beside me waiting for me to open the door and lead the way. I never put a collar or leash on her. She would just walk along beside me. We were like two best friends just enjoying our freedom and nature, she just chose to stay with me. We would walk the many trails that Derek and I have created on our ten acre piece of land. This daily ritual was good for both us. It was a way for us to help one another grieve and heal a little, I think. We would have lovely little conversations on our walks and sometimes she wanted to be picked up and held. Sometimes we would visit Jim's grave and she would go over and sniff the stone I painted to mark the spot. She watched us bury him, so I think she knew. I believe that she saw everything and knows more about what happened than we do.

At first Jam wouldn't go outside without me, which I was fine with. Taking her for walks everyday got her out regularly and she stayed inside with us the rest of the time. During this time, our bond became much stronger, though I didn't think it was possible, as we were pretty tight from the beginning. I guess we both realized it was just the three of us now and so we needed to look out for one another. Jam still sleeps right in between Derek and I almost every night, even now.

It wasn't a full year after Jimmy passed that one of my clients, who has a farm near our community, asked me to go and pick up their dogs for a grooming one day. They told me that when I dropped the dogs off, after the appointment, that I should make their place my last stop, as they had something they wanted to show me. I agreed and was excited to see what they wanted to share with me. I think I might have even rushed through my appointments a little that day, in anticipation.

Derek was working from home that day and I asked him if he would like to join me for the drop off drive, to see what our neighbours were so excited to show me. He seemed interested as well and agreed to come along. Once we unloaded the dogs from the van they proceeded to take us to one of their many barns. As we entered the barn, we saw that there was a miniature horse who had given birth to a foal, just the night before. It was a beautiful sight, seeing this tiny new foal nursing and trying to stand on her new and very awkward long legs. As Derek and the farmer talked horses, his wife said I have something else to show you in the other barn and asked me to follow her. I anxiously followed along, of course, to see what else there was to see. She took me to a dark section of the beef barn and as she knelt down, she picked up a tiny little black creature, from a small cavity in the wall. As she stepped into the light and moved a little closer to me, she passed it to me to hold. I could not believe my eyes, it was a tiny black kitten with the exact same markings as the ones Jimmy had. Jimmy had a very clear and sharply marked white moustache while the rest of his face was black. It was almost, too perfect. He also had a white patch on his chest and all four of his feet were white. This little bundle of joy, that I was holding couldn't have been more than a week old and he looked just like my Jimmy. I took it to be a sign that this little guy would eventually be coming home, to live with us.

There were four kittens in the litter who were all equally as adorable. One of the females had already been spoken for and I could see why too, she was a beautiful little long haired female. A little girl from their neighbourhood had picked her out just a day or so before. The other three were short haired, which I prefer. A long haired cat requires a little more care and grooming and I already had enough in the way of grooming responsibilities, with my job. As she passed me this little Jimmy look alike, I started to tear up. Then, as I looked a little closer at him, I started to sob. The poor lady didn't realize why I was crying and quickly asked if she should go get Derek. All I could do was nod my head yes, as I cradle my new friend in my hands. Derek came into the barn to see me holding a kitten. As I turned him around so Derek could get a better look him, he responded in saying, "Well look at that now.". I smiled and quickly asked them both if I could eventually take him home when he was ready to go. I believed that these events playing out the way that they did, was a sign. It was a sign that he was to become part of our family. He may even be Jimmy reincarnated, I didn't know at that point. All I knew at the time, was that I felt better when I was holding and loving him.

As the weeks went on, I could not stop thinking and talking

about this new little addition. Derek had mentioned that maybe it would be good to get one of his siblings, as well. We weren't sure how Jam would react to the little guy and the thought was that if he had another playmate his own age, it might ease the transition. I had been giving her lots of extra special attention lately and the upcoming change in time and attention allocations, along with the age difference between them might take a little getting used, to for her. I agreed that two is better than one especially were kittens were concerned, so we decided that Derek would pick out the other kitten. He picked a little short haired female who also had some white markings. Her back feet are both white and she has a little patch of white fur on her chest, the rest of her is completely black. Well, all except for her whiskers, one side of her face has black whiskers and the other side has white, which I found to be most unusual. I had never seen that particular combination before and so with that, I figured she would fit in just fine with our little group of misfits. We decided to name them Jelly and Berry. That way we would have Berry, Jelly and Jam! I love their names and they make nice additions to our little family unit.

I want to take a few more sentences to talk about how special Jim was. As I said before, Derek had picked him out of a group of several kittens at the farm, as there were many to choose from that year. Derek picked him because he was fearless. I did not know this until we had already brought them home, but what had attracted Derek to little Jim was the fact that he had been playing with the other kittens in a very unusual way. He would climb up to the highest point of the water tank that he could get to and then jump head first into the large group of kittens below. I can just imagine that he was probably yelling "cowabunga" in kitten talk, as he leaped head first into the crowd. Derek has always liked animals with spunk and Jim had spunk, ten fold. If I had known what he saw I might not have agreed to bring him home. Well, on second thought, I probably would have. Once I saw him with his little "Sylvester the Cat" markings, it was all over. I guess that Derek knew not to tell me until I was already attached, which did not take long.

I had picked Jam because she was quiet and sitting all by herself. I have always picked the underdog so to speak, for the most part. I guess I know now why Jim was always getting into the weirdest situations. He would crawl into Derek's sweater with only his head peeking out from the sleeve hole. He would climb up on the roof of our barn. He got his head slammed in the fridge door. It just seemed like every day he was doing something else that would totally take me by surprise. I wanted to say us by surprise, but I guess Derek already knew what to expect. We loved him for it though! I really wish that he hadn't had his nine lives all used up at such a young age, however. But, with an active personality like that I guess I shouldn't have been surprised. He did everything full throttle. It was all or nothing from the very beginning.

I can still see him laying on my desk in the grooming shop watching me groom or saying hello to some of the friendly dogs in the shop. There were times when he would even jump right up on the table with them. I'm not sure if he was trying to say hello or maybe trying to comfort them in some way. He had his own way of doing things. I enjoyed having him there and I believe he enjoyed being in the middle of all the chaos and commotion. Just like when he was a kitten, he was right in the middle of it all!

I miss him and I believe he sends me messages from time to time. It has been six years and up until just recently, I blamed myself for his death. That was until just a little while ago, I was gazing up into the sky, as I often do, and in the clouds I saw a very familiar sight. What I saw shocked me speechless and those who know me know that it takes a lot to make *me* speechless. I love to talk!

I saw the formation of Jim's head and face appear, as clear as it could be. It was like looking at him in real life. It was an exact picture of him. It was like he was sitting right in front of me. I started to tear up and then next formation I saw was a very large heart shape. It was like it had to be that large so I was sure of what I was seeing. The next formation that I see brought tears to my eyes. Maybe you can guess what it was. Yes, it was the formation and shape of an eagle.

I have to be honest, at first I really thought I was seeing things. Then I realized he was trying to tell me that it wasn't my fault. I think he was trying to tell me that it really was an eagle and that he loved me and was watching me and waiting for the day when we can be together again.

After seeing that my heart healed a little bit and now I get a little peace of mind in thinking that at least I was able to share in his life. Even if it was only for a short while. Rest in peace Jimmy, my sweet little boy.

Derek and I brought our newest kittens home when they were five weeks old because we got a call from the farmer telling us that the kittens on his farm were disappearing from the barn. He thought that perhaps coyotes were somehow getting into the barn, catching them and taking them to the woods to feed their young. There was no way to know for sure if this was the case, but I wasn't about to loose another animal to a predator. So, we went to pick them up and bring them home shortly after we got the call. They stood a better chance in coming to live with us at only five weeks of age than to stay at the farm and possibly get eaten by a coyote.

I was glad we brought two kittens home but, as I suspected Jam was not impressed. It took her a little while to warm up to the idea of sharing her people and space with these new bundles of energy. So it was good that they had each other to play and sleep with, especially where they were so young.

Jelly might have looked just like Jim at first, but as he got older his markings started to change slightly. As far as his personality goes, Jelly is, well, unique to say the least. Derek and I tease sometimes and say that Jelly is in fact Jim reincarnated because I have accidentally slammed Jelly's head in the entrance door, just like Jim. He loves to follow me, in my blind spots and with my walking challenges now, I don't always see him, until it is too late. He always just shakes his head and keeps on going, just like Jim used to do. I don't close the door with as much force as I once did, however. I'm not sure how many more knocks to the head the little guy can stand. He and Jim do have some similarities, but they are also very different.

He is very entertaining, when he performs his regular clumsy and goofy antics, which he does quite often. We always comment that it must be all of the knocks to the head from a previous life and laugh. He has a huge heart and was just born to play. Though he does not have the same level of intelligence that Jim had, he does however have his unquestionable loyalty, protection instincts and huge heart.

Because Jelly is, for the most part, an indoor cat his street smarts and hunting skills are not quite as refined as Jim's were. That said, we decided to build a very long outdoor cat run with a large pen at the end of it, near the tree line in our backyard. It is open to them for their entertainment and exercise, twenty hours a day, three hundred and sixty five days a year. They are still able to hunt if something wanders into the enclosure and on the odd occasion they bring us a little gift. Plus in the colder months, they are also able to access our wood shed which they absolutely love. The wood shed is attached to the side of our tiny home and has translucent sides and roofing. When the sun is beaming in, it makes for a nice, warm spot for those winter afternoon cat naps, meanwhile they can still see what is going on outside. The cats love to go out and watch the wild life and it gives me piece of mind knowing they are as safe, healthy and happy as possible.

Because Derek and I never had human children, our pets are our family. They mean the world to us!

# CHAPTER 9

## *My Event*

It was November 28, 2017, and it was a bright and sunny morning. I got out of bed early to start my day, as I usually did. But, little did I know, that within the next few hours, my life would be changed forever. As I mentioned a little earlier, the momentum of my grooming business had been growing steadily and I was starting to feel the effects of that again. On this particular morning however, I felt more tired than usual and not quite myself. I had somewhat of an uneasy feeling, but chalked it up to the stress of the Christmas rush and everything that goes along with it and the holidays.

You see, my grooming business always started to get very hectic at that time of year. Typically during the month of November, things were a little more quiet than during the average month. It was like the calm before the December storm of Christmas madness. Most of my clients liked to hold off until as close to the holidays as possible before having their dogs groomed. This way the dogs were looking and smelling their absolute best for Santa and their holiday guests. December, for me, used to be completely booked up by the first of October. Some clients even booked their appointments a year in advance, just to make sure that they had a spot as close to the big day as possible. It was serious stuff!

While my clients were getting all of their holiday preparations completed and looking forward to another happy holiday season, I was starting to get into my usual holiday state of being. I think it is best described as a mixture of very mildly controlled anxiety and chaotic bewilderment. I hadn't done any Christmas shopping yet. I hadn't put up any decorations or done any baking. All of the things that seemed to be subtly prodded to the top of my list of holiday priorities, by expecting family members. Oh yes, not to forget I was running my own business, by myself. This was the third time that I had built my clientele to this level. All on my own.

All of these things played over and over in my mind and in my ear. It was a constant reel of suggestions and demands for what they, and by they I mean, my immediate family of course, wanted to make their holiday just perfect. I mean they even blessed me with the pleasure of doing most of the work, even when I was invited to their homes for a holiday dinner or gathering. Knowing that I would always offer to help, they always had a list of things for me, both in prep and clean up. So thoughtful! So, with these imposed expectations, I did my best to manage it all and to be somewhat prepared ahead of time. Because, after the Christmas grooming rush, I was spent! I put everything I had, and then some, into trying to make Christmas just perfect for everyone! Well except for me, that is. I would always say, this year I've got it. I've got everything just so and I have picked out the perfect gifts. It is going to be a great holiday! Everyone will be so happy! I can't wait! Yet with all of that, they still managed to find something that wasn't to their liking and I would come away from the day feeling like I had not done enough. Again, and again. I was really starting to hate the holidays and really just thought I would rather spend them alone. At least then, maybe *I* would be happy!

I just want to say that November seems to be a bad luck month for me. Even today I seem to almost hold my breath until the month is over, every year. I pray that nothing else bad will happen in November.

On this particular day, I got up, did my chores and went through my regular routine to get myself ready for the day. Just as I did every other day. I left the house at around seven o'clock, so that I could pick up the dogs I had booked for that day's grooming appointments. Part of my services at that time, included a pick up and delivery service. This service was convenient for a lot of my clients considering that I ran my grooming shop from my country home.

I only had four dogs booked that day, which I was thankful for considering how I felt that morning. My plan was to groom those four dogs and take them back home by lunch time, so that I could do some shopping in the afternoon. I always had the best of intentions to be ready for the holidays before the rush, but it never seemed to work out that way. Every year, Christmas would come and go and I was left feeling like I could have done it better. I stressed about it constantly and my mental state was such that I always felt like I should have done more. I wonder what that came from?

By the time December rolled around, I had very little energy for waiting in long line ups or standing to do baking after a long day of grooming. Sometimes, I would book eight or nine dogs per day, so that I could get all my regular clients in before the holidays. I put a lot of pressure on myself to try to make the holidays perfect, especially for my mother. She always had such high expectations for that day. She would always say, every year, all that work for a few hours and then it is over. Every year I thought that maybe this year I could make her happy and every year, she always seemed to be disappointed. Every year I thought, this year, I have finally out done myself and she will tell me that this year was the best Christmas ever and that she appreciated my efforts. Nope! Never happened! She blew a truck sized hole in every single one of them!

I went to the first home to pick up my client's two dogs and they were ready and waiting. I loaded them into the van and was off to the second home, for their two dogs. It was great, only two stops and four dogs, so far the morning was going smoothly. I told both households that I would be returning around lunch time or shortly after. After loading the last two dogs, I started to feel worse than I was when I left home. I can recall thinking to myself that it would pass. It was probably just indigestion or something like it, I thought. It had to be because this my last light day. After this day, I was totally booked right through until Christmas. There wasn't one spot left available. So, I was going to have to push through this too, whatever it was. That was simply all there was to it.

As I started my drive home, I started to feel worse and worse. My chest was very uncomfortable. It sort of felt like I had some severe heartburn. I was only a couple of miles from home when I thought to myself that maybe I should pull over. Then I thought, well maybe I'll just roll the window down and get some fresh air. That seemed to make me feel a little better, so I continued on. I was almost there after all.

I was thankful when I pulled into the driveway and saw Derek was still home. He was just loading his truck for the day's work he had ahead of him. As I parked my van he came over and looked at me in a puzzled manner. He said that I didn't look very well and I told him that I didn't feel very well. We had bought take-out lasagne the night before and I told him I thought maybe it was making me ill. He suggested that maybe the dogs would be fine in the van for a few minutes, so I could get some fresh air. He thought that maybe if I got out and walked around the yard a little it, maybe it would help whatever was happening to pass, thinking that maybe it was indigestion or gas perhaps.

We started to walk together and after a couple of minutes I

told him that I needed to go to the washroom, as I thought I was going to be sick to my stomach. I got into the house and headed straight for the washroom and sure enough, I was sick to my stomach. While this was happening, I broke out into a full sweat. At the time, I was thinking that maybe I had food poisoning. As I came out of the washroom, I started to feel faint and as I walked through the kitchen, I fell on the couch when I got to the living room. It was like my legs just gave out from underneath me. I looked up at Derek and told him that my arm felt funny. He quickly asked which arm. I replied that it was my left arm. At which point, I was starting to get the feeling that whatever it was couldn't be blamed on some bad take-out.

I had absolutely no strength. Derek picked me up and practically carried my weak body to the van and put me in it. He jumped in the driver's seat and we were off to the hospital, dogs and all. There was no time to waste. The drive to the hospital would normally have taken at about twenty five minutes. It only took us twelve to thirteen minutes. At one point during the drive, I told him to slow down a little because the discomfort didn't seem to be as bad, but that didn't last. As we arrived at the hospital emergency parking lot, the discomfort was really increasing again. I swear by the way Derek drove in, it felt like we were taking the corner on two wheels. I was really starting to get concerned at this point. After all, Derek does not drive fast!

Derek ran in to get a wheelchair and ask the security guard for some help. All I can remember is being put in the wheelchair and Derek rushing me in. I was not breathing very well and grasping my chest in agony. The triage nurse was evaluating an older man when we rushed through the emergency doors. She took one look at Derek and I and, after a little coaxing, asked the older gentleman to go wait in the seating area. I believe he was a little upset at the fact that he was getting pushed aside because I don't think I have ever seen anyone move so slow. Even Derek made the comment, "Please hurry sir, she is all I have in this world". My eyes started to well up hearing those words coming out of his mouth. I knew then that he was sure of what was happening to me. Just as I am writing this, the tears are flowing. The thought of us being separated from one another in this world was absolutely crushing then, and still is today.

The nurse took my blood pressure and asked a couple of questions and then quickly took us back to the emergency room. There, I was met by an intern and the ER doctor on duty. They began connecting me to several machines and gave me a shot of Nitro under my tongue. They did all of this while continuing to ask all kinds of questions to both Derek and I. As time went on, I quickly started to feel worse. I was thinking that maybe it was just anxiety. One of the last things I said actually was, "I'm going to be really embarrassed if this is just gas or indigestion.". The thing is that the doctors and nurses were not treating it like anxiety. They were treating it like something much worse. As the pain worsened again, the intern gave me another shot of Nitro. Within minutes, the ER doctor came to me and told me that he did think that I was having a heart attack and that they were going to prep me for transport to Saint John Regional Hospital, by ambulance, immediately. Saint John Regional is, without a doubt, the best hospital in our province for cardiac care. At that point, I looked up at Derek and told him that maybe he should call my mother. Just then, the intern came over and gave me another shot of Nitro. That was the last thing I remember until I was woken up about two weeks later. As Derek walked away to go call my mother, I went into full cardiac arrest and the intern started chest compressions.

Derek called my mother and his own family members thinking that maybe they could help us in returning the dogs to their homes, as they were still in the van. In addition, he thought that maybe someone would take our vehicle somewhere to be parked as he was going to accompany me to Saint John Regional. It took two phone calls before my mother arrived. Derek was very clear about what had taken place and told her that she may not get a chance to say goodbye before I died, if she did not get there soon.

At the time, she was working for my brother at his gravel pit. She worked at the weighing station and apparently had to wait for someone to come and relieve her of her duties.

She was the last to show up at the hospital and when she did finally get there, she pushed her way through people to get to me and from what I was told, was very rude. Then, as she approached me, she said to me that I needed to get through this because there were people who were depending on me. The next thing out her mouth was asking my husband, who had just been kneeling on the floor beside my lifeless body, trying to find the words to say good bye and let me go, if he was trying to rub the skin off my forehead. She had absolutely no consideration or concern for the details of what had just happened or how those things might be affecting others, just how it was affecting her, as usual! My father was out of the country with his family. His much younger new bride and her, (their) daughter. The daughter he always wanted but never had in me. I guess maybe I just didn't portray the right image or keep up the appearance they needed. I wouldn't keep up the facade. I wouldn't hide all of the dirty little secrets and lies. He never did come back. We had been somewhat estranged, because of something that he did and said. So, his comment was that he didn't want to waste money on a plane ticket, where we hadn't been talking and he wasn't sure if I would see him.

Before my mother showed up, the medical team had been trying to revive me for over 35 minutes. I was clinically dead after suffering what I am told was a widow maker. For those of you who aren't familiar with the term, a widow maker is a massive heart attack, from which very few people survive.

They believe that a small piece of plaque broke off from one of the main arteries going to my heart. When a person cuts themselves the body tries to clot the blood and  stop the bleeding, in order to heal the wounded area. My artery did just that, it clotted and completely blocked the flow of blood in that artery. They believe the artery was 100 percent blocked and the only thing that saved me was that the medical team gave me a clot buster cocktail and they continued to do CPR. They believe that this approach along with continually shocking my heart trying to get it to start beating again, is what saved my life. All the while, Derek would not leave the area. They tried asking him, coaxing him, then even tried to make him leave. But my husband is 6' 2" and weighs two hundred and forty pounds. If he does not want to go somewhere or do something there is really no way of making him, without a fight.

Mostly they were trying to do this for his own well being, as most folks do not deal well with seeing and experiencing this type of trauma. However, I could sense his presence and I am glad that he did not leave the room. Derek and I have a very special bond and love for one another. He was sending me messages to come back and I did not want to leave him. Although, where I went was a hard place to leave. There was no pain. I had a feeling of complete peace and contentment. One of which I had never experienced in my waking life.

It was so very dark in this place and yet it had a glow about it. It's like when you look up at the sun and it sort of blinds you. Then you close your eyes and what you see is an overwhelming brightness that seems so bright it actually starts to turn into other colours, as you try to focus. I think I was in some sort of limbo area. Not here, but not there either. It was beautiful and I am no longer scared to die. But, I am scared to be without my soul mate, even if it is for a short while. Time seems to pass much differently when you are not in the realm of consciousness.

Ever since I was a very young child, I had these episodes. Well, that is how I referred to them. It was a situation where I would faint and lose consciousness. My mother used to say that they seemed like seizures but the doctors who ran the tests when I was a child never found any evidence to suggest that they were epileptic in nature. I believe it was stress that brought them on. During these fainting spells my eyes would roll back into my head and I would completely black out. Sometimes, my bowels and bladder would release while I was out, which was very unpleasant when I woke. I was usually only out for a matter of a few minutes, under five most times.

During this time, it felt like I was dreaming, but then in the commotion of waking up, I would usually forget most of what I had experienced in that state. I now believe that I wasn't dreaming at all. I believe I am a traveller. I am a traveller, who travels between realms. I believe that we all have a soul and it is born into a vessel. When your vessel is no longer able to carry on due to physical ailments or other conditions, your body or vessel dies but the soul lives on. Our soul then goes to a different realm and is matched with another vessel and the cycle continues. I believe I have lived many lives and continue to come back to this realm. I believe that this cycle has been continuing so that I can continue to learn. I can continue to learn and to teach. I think, or maybe hope would be a better word, that I have completed the learning portion of my journey, this time around. I base these statements on my experiences, opinions and the recollections I have of my experiences I have lived through. I believe these things to be true, for me.

So, while I was flat lining, I could feel a pull back to Derek. I heard him say, "come back to me". He says he didn't physically say it but I could feel his energy calling to me from beyond this realm. I could not deny my soul mate or our connection. I knew I would have to go back, even though I did not want to leave this new place. It was a peaceful place, somewhere I had never been before. It was an experience like nothing I had ever felt. I felt no pain or discomfort. I did not feel bad about myself for not living up to another individual's expectations of me. I did not feel bad about what I should or should not be or do. I did not feel bad about how I should talk or act, or any other critical crap that I had heard my whole life. So, as hard as it was to leave this new peaceful and freeing place I was in, my time in this vessel was not over just yet. Somehow I think I knew that it would be a long hard road but I had to go back and if I'm being honest, I never really have done *anything* the easy way. With that said however, I did not really have a true understanding of just how long or how hard this road of mine was going to be. If I had, I would have stayed.

So at this point, I have been out for a little over thirty five minutes. There has been a team of three performing CPR on me for the duration and they have continued to shock me repeatedly, all the while. It seemed that nothing was working or going to work. It was at that point, that the charge nurse conferred with the ER doctor who was calling the procedures and suggested that they try doubling the defibrillator pads in one last attempt to re-start my heart. After a minute or so of discussion, they prepared and applied the pads for one last attempt. This was not a common practice and was only considered or attempted in extreme cases. Derek later told me that it was like nothing he had ever seen before. My body sat straight up, limbs fully extended and eyes wide open, it was a chilling site to say the least. Once my body returned to the gurney below, my CPR team resumed their efforts. It was at that point that Derek told the Managing Director of the ER, who had been with him for about the last fifteen minutes of this ordeal, trying to focus his attention and energy, that he wanted to go over to my bed side. He had been standing just outside the team of medical professionals, giving them space to work and watching them the entire time. She replied that he could do so, all the while trying to prepare him for what she thought was to come.

They walked over together and then she let him go. He knelt down and sat on the floor beside my lifeless body, holding my hand and trying to some how comfort me while trying to find the words to say good bye. When all of a sudden he heard a voice behind him say "Just call it already!". As he look up, in complete disbelief, he saw that the respiratory technician standing to his right, who made the comment, did not realize that he was there and quickly removed himself from the group. As I'm sure you can imagine, this was anything but comforting. So, as Derek held my head and hand, kissed me on the forehead and whispered in my ear, the doctor called for one last check for a pulse. With complete surprise and astonishment, the charge nurse replied that she had a pulse! It was very weak and very faint, but there was a pulse. Derek quickly stepped back while the team took the next steps to prepare me for transport to Saint John Regional.

The clot buster cocktail of medications they had given me had helped to open up my artery about five to ten percent, they figured. I was in extremely critical condition, but I had a chance. The doctor came to Derek and told him that if he had anything to say to me, that he should do so now as there was a real good chance that he may not see me, alive, again. He said if she has a fighting chance, we need to get her to Saint John Regional, right away. He also told him that they didn't know, or even think that I would survive the ambulance ride, but they were going to try. He then said that if I did survive the trip, the specialists, equipment and knowledge of the Saint John Regional team and facility were my absolute best chance at survival.

As Derek started to climb in to the ambulance with me, the nurse grabbed and held his hand. She told him that there just wasn't enough room for him to go with us, as they needed the space to do their work. Especially, if I crashed on the way. She too, urged him to say anything that he may have wanted, or needed to say right then, as it may very well be his last chance. She told him that she did not normally make these types of trips, but given the circumstances, she was going to accompany me and do her very best to help me get there, alive. She told him that he could, safely, follow along behind them but that if he happened to find them stopped along side of the highway, not to approach the ambulance. Just pull up behind them and wait. She said that they would be working on me and that she would come to him once they had either me stabilized, or it was over. So, he said his good byes and they loaded me into the ambulance.

Saint John Regional Hospital is a little over an hour away from the Moncton Hospital, where we were leaving from. After we left, Derek then had to make arrangements to get the dogs, who were still in the van, back to their homes. He asked his brother if perhaps he would be willing to call my clients and make the necessary arrangements and deliveries. He agreed and a plan was made, for which I am forever grateful! I know that they were well looked after and returned safely, even though they did not have a grooming that day. I always kept my appointment book and client contact information with me, which made the process much easier.

Once Derek made the arrangements and passed on the information, he grabbed my mother's car keys and got into her car along with her and his own mother and took off, trying to catch up to the ambulance that I had left in just moments before. They were unable to catch up to us. I figure that we were probably going as fast as regulations would allow for that sort of thing. Derek told me that the car was completely silent during the ride to Saint John Regional. He crested every single hill with almost paralyzing anxiety of what he might see or find waiting for him. Luckily however, the ambulance was nowhere to be seen. Once they arrived, he jumped from the vehicle right in the middle of the parking lot traffic and rushed into the hospital. He then proceeded to ask for directions to the Cardiac ICU, only to find that the medical team had already taken me into the Cath lab. In talking to the first nurse he could find, he was told that I was in surgery and that he could wait in the small family room just down the hall. The pleasant nurse told him that the porters and nurses would be wheeling me right by the door of the room he was in, when I was brought up to my room. She then said that when or if they had any more information, they would come to the room and bring him up to speed. As he got to the family room he had been assigned to, he heard the words "code blue, Cath lab" over the intercom speakers. He immediately rushed back to the nurses station where he was met by a very calm and soft spoken nurse who assured him that there were three different ORs in the Cath lab and that this code did not necessarily apply to me. She then calmly told him that as soon as she had any information, she would go see him immediately.

Throughout this whole journey, Derek has been my hero, soul mate, and is the absolute best man I know. He has given and sent me more love and strength than I could only have imagined was possible. Even when it had a depleting effect on himself. He has and continues to give me his all. I have been truly blessed to have found him. He is my best friend and our relationship has been like a fairy tale. It is like something that I believed only existed in books, although he has made it very real for me.

I am completely convinced that if Derek had left the room while they were working on me, I would not have come back from the darkness that was quickly consuming me. It was a state of peace and calm that I had never felt before. It was the most comfortable I had ever been. I had no fear and was welcoming everything that I could sense. I was moving toward and welcoming what I thought was coming next. Derek pulled me back and for that, I will be forever grateful. He sent me messages, love and most of all the strength that I needed to fight. There was a big part of me that didn't want to fight anymore. I was so tired and had been fighting, for what seemed like absolutely everything, for so long that this feeling of peace and contentment was appealing. It was very appealing and relieving, but yet I did not want to know an existence without him. I'm not sorry I came back. Although it has been tough, there have been many good things and experiences that have come, as a result. It was all worth it, to have even just one more day with my love. I am happy to say that as of these writings, I have been blessed to have had many. When my time does come to pass over, however, I will not be afraid.

So, he waited and waited and waited. I can only imagine what he must have been thinking and the range of emotions he was feeling. I hope that he will share what went through his head in those moments and what happened when he saw me being wheeled by, at some point.

As I mentioned, my heart attack was a widow maker. This is a hundred percent blockage of the left anterior descending artery (LAD). The LAD artery carries fresh blood into the heart so that the heart is supplied with the oxygen it needs in order to pump properly. This type of heart attack is most often fatal.

I was fortunate to have been transported to the Saint John Regional hospital very quickly and that the doctors were able to do surgery and placed two stents in the artery to open it back up again. As a result of my widow maker however, there was a portion of my heart that was not able to receive enough blood, before the stents were put in, which caused what the doctors refer to as scarring. Basically, it means that part of my heart is dead and no longer works. At this point in time, however, my cardiologist says that the rest of my heart is working well and seems to be strong. I now have an irregular heart beat, which most definitely gets worse if I get stressed or worked up about something. It can get much worse depending on the cause of my stress and discomfort. The damage and scarring that my heart endured during my event is permanent and irreparable.

The doctors in the Cath lab at Saint John Regional decided it would be best to go in through my right arm to put the stents in, which meant that they would not have to open me up. They did not think that I would have survived it if they had and neither do I.

Once they were finished with me in the Cath lab, I was taken up to the Cardiac ICU where I was placed in a private room with a nurse present in my room, twenty-four hours a day. Once there, I was placed in what's known as *Therapeutic Hypothermia*. This is a process wherein, healthcare providers use cooling devices to lower your body temperature for a short time. Hopkinsmedicine.org describes it as the following. I have no affiliation with hopkinsmedicine.org, I just liked the summation for this purpose.

*"Therapeutic Hypothermia is a type of treatment. It's sometimes used for people who have a cardiac arrest. Cardiac arrest happens when the heart suddenly stops beating. Once the heart starts beating again, healthcare providers use cooling devices to lower your body temperature for a short time. It's lowered to around 32 C to 34 C (89 F to 93 F). The treatment usually lasts about 24 hours."*

It was decided that my Therapeutic Hypothermia would go on to last a minimum of 36 hours, due to the severity of my case and situation. They go on to say the following.

*"The heart has an electrical signal that helps coordinate the heartbeat. If this signal is disrupted or abnormal, the heart may not be able to pump the right way. That can result in cardiac arrest. During cardiac*

*arrest, blood doesn't flow to the organs of the body. The brain may also not get enough blood. That's why many people don't recover after cardiac arrest. The lack of blood flow can cause lasting damage to the brain. The person may be unable to regain consciousness. Lowering the body temperature right away after cardiac arrest can reduce damage to the brain. That raises the chances that the person will recover."*

As I stated at earlier, I was in full cardiac arrest for about thirty-five minutes. So, for the next thirty-six hours, I would have a nurse present in my room every moment of the day as my therapeutic hypothermia progressed. During this time, Derek lived in the family room just down the hall from my room, where he was joined by both my mother and his own. They too, stayed in the family room. Derek's mother did her best to offer support and encouragement and also remind Derek that he would eventually need to eat and maybe sleep. At about the mid point of my therapeutic hypothermia, he had slept maybe two hours of the last thirty-six to forty.

At around three o'clock or so in the afternoon on the last day of my treatment, as they were getting ready to start the process of warming me up very, very slowly, I started to wake up. The nurse who was with me at the time was very puzzled by this. She said to Derek and his brother, who was present at the time, that there is absolutely no way that I should be waking up, at this point or in this state. They both looked at each other and said well, you don't know Tanya. Which they followed up with, and if you let her wake up now, being this cold, she is going to be very angry!

That was the last day of my Therapeutic Hypothermia and it was now time to start warming me up and with any luck waking me up. As the day progressed, however, and my body temperature started to slowly come back to a normal range, the true nature and seriousness of my condition would become very apparent and very real, very quickly.

You see, my husband is an empath and a strong one at that.

His perceptive abilities are very strong and he rarely misses even the most subtle changes in energy or mood, in any room. So you can only imagine how heightened his abilities were at that point, after forty some hours of running on maximum adrenaline and in a constant state of sensory overload. What some refer to as the "fight or flight" state. Let's just say that all of his senses and perceptive abilities were extremely sharp and very keen.

As evening progressed and I continued to warm up, my blood pressure continued to drop and would not seem to level out. In addition, my kidney function was worsening and at one point, had completely stopped. The nurse on duty, along with the charge nurse, were very concerned with these factors and frequently consulted with the intern doctor on duty that night. After some discussion between them and a couple of phone calls placed by the intern, presumably to a consulting cardiologist. There was some tension between them and a clear difference of opinion, well it was clear to my husband, on the best course of action to be taken with me. As the hours passed and things continued to get worse, both with me and between the staff members, which was increasingly concerning and unsettling, well for Derek at least. It didn't seem that any of the others who were present had a true or realistic grasp of what was really happening.

He listened carefully to what was being said, and of course what was not being said, by both the nurse and intern. He found that the logic of the nurse's desired course of action seemed to be the most in line with what he felt was the right thing to do and so he made efforts to keep a very open dialogue with her about what was happening and what could or should be done. This helped to develop a level of trust and open communication, or so he felt.

Basically, as my body temperature continued to rise and I got warmer, I started to bleed out, internally. During the thirty-five minutes or so, that the team of three was performing CPR on me, trying to keep blood flowing to my brain, I ended up with some fractured ribs. This led to three lacerations in my liver. So, as I warmed up and my blood flow increased, I was bleeding, which is why my blood pressure was so dangerously low. With this, the nurse felt it best, well essential really, to continue to give me blood. Each time she did, my blood pressure would stabilize for a little while. As this continued, my kidneys simply stopped working all together, which led to an extreme build up of fluid in my body. As the time passed, into the early hours of the morning and the fluid pressure continued to build, the nurse insisted that I must go for an emergency CT scan, immediately. She was met with much resistance from other staff members who either did not see things in the same way, or were already stretched to their limit. She persisted however, and had me taken, or should I say, took me for the scan. The results confirmed what she had suspected all along. I was bleeding internally and corrective action had to be taken right away.

The decision was made that a "pic line IV" had to be put in ASAP. However with all of the internal fluid pressure, seeing, let alone, finding and hitting a blood vessel was nearly impossible. They called several individuals in to try, but none of them could get what they needed. Eventually, they called or found someone who was considered to be the absolute best individual on the premises to do type of thing. Even though they struggled for some time, they eventually got what they needed so that dialysis and other treatments could begin.

During the later parts of the above process Derek stayed very close to the nurse. As close as she would allow, in fact. There were times when she asked him to step out to make her and their job easier but he was told to stay close and she would come and get him, as soon as she could. Because they had all basically been living in the small family room, not far from my room, Derek and the mothers were somewhat spelling each other and taking small opportunities to get an hour or two of sleep here and there. After I had gone for my emergency scan, my mother decided that she would try to get a couple of hours sleep.

During the worst parts of the above process, when things were quite serious and it was looking like they may lose me. Derek asked the nurse if they were at the point where he should wake my mother. She replied not yet and suggested that he give her a little more time. Then all of a sudden, my mother woke on her own and came out into the hall to see all of the medical staff in my room trying to help me. She went off and was going on and on about how I was her daughter and she should have been woken up and she should have been informed and on, and on, she went. She was told of what had happened and the steps that had been taken, but it didn't matter. She just kept going, in that hateful, vindictive and aggressive way that she does. She truly had no real understanding of what was happening or the severity of my condition, but, it wasn't about her and how she thought things should be, so on she went, with those sinister eyes and constant digs and pokes. Like Derek didn't already have enough to be concerned about and have enough things to watch and observe. Now he had to put up with my mother throwing one of her famous temper tantrums. Great! Eventually, he had to manipulate the situation and say just a couple of the things that he knew she wanted to hear, just to get her to stop.

Just close your eyes and imagine it for a minute. You have been living in a tiny hospital family room for days. You have only eaten and slept just enough to keep your body functioning. You have been "showering" or washing up in the tiny hospital bathroom down the hall. You have been told twice, so far, that your spouse, your partner in life, the person you love more than anything, may not make it. You can sense the disagreement and the difference of opinion between the very people trying to save her life and now, you have to deal with this too. Even though, a very rational explanation of the events leading up to that moment in time, was given. Still, she persisted.

Eventually, he just had to find a way to make her stop.

# CHAPTER 10

### *The next 48 hours*

As morning, or more specifically, daylight arrived, things started to change very quickly. All of a sudden there were new staff members arriving and appearing. They all seemed to be taking a far more regimented and serious approach to my care. As they started to accumulate in my room to assess, question and evaluate my situation, with Derek present, he got the sense that they would be more comfortable doing their work if he was to excuse himself from the room. So, he moved to the hallway to wait and observe. As more specialists were called in to assess and evaluate my situation, the charge nurse came over, put her hand on his shoulder and told him not to worry. She said that all of the best minds in the building were in my room and that they would figure it out. Immediately after which, the head of the entire facility came to Derek to explain what was happening and which course of action they thought would be best to move forward with. Though he was the only one to understand and grasp what the Director had just told him, he found it somewhat comforting to know that the Surgical Intensive Care Unit (SICU) team were taking over my case.

As Derek and our mothers waited for me to be assessed and prepped to move, the doctor in charge of the SICU came by to introduce himself. He offered his assessment of my situation and explained his immediate plan of action, saying that *if* I made it and we got through the next 24 hours, this was his plan. "She is very, very sick!", he told them. They determined that as I was bleeding out and my body was filing with fluid. As a result, the sac around my liver had developed both interior and exterior pressure sufficient to temporarily stop the bleeding from the lacerations in my liver. So, the nurse doing what she did, in continuing to give me blood and thereby building fluid pressure inside my body, saved my life.

One of the immediate side effects of this was the development of compartmental syndrome in my right arm. WebMD describes compartmental syndrome as the following: (Again, I have no affiliation with WebMD, I just liked the way they describe it in this application.)

*"Compartmental syndrome occurs when excessive pressure builds up inside an enclosed muscle space in the body. Compartment syndrome usually results from bleeding or swelling after an injury. The dangerously high pressure in compartment syndrome impedes the flow of blood to and from the affected tissues. It can be an emergency, requiring surgery to prevent permanent injury."*

Just as soon as Derek arrived downstairs, following me to the SICU and was shown to the room they could wait or reside in, the head of plastic surgery entered the room, and asked for Derek and the room. As the others gathered their belongings and left the room, he closed the door and sat down. He explained to Derek that as a result of the build up of fluid pressure in my body, I had developed compartmental syndrome in my right arm. The same right arm that had been used to put two stents in my artery, just days before. The same right arm that I use to paint and draw. The same right arm that I use for, well, almost everything. He told him that compartmental syndrome had developed over night and that we where now in another emergency situation. He told him that there were two options. Either he do surgery and cut me open to relieve the pressure immediately. Or, he do nothing and I would lose all function and use of my right arm and hand. It would still be there, but it would just be a crumpled up stump, that I would not be able to do anything with. He told him that he needed a decision and authorization to move forward, immediately. There was no time to waist! Derek had to make a decision right then. His main concern with surgery was the risk of infection, of course. But on the other hand, if I did survive and there was a chance they could save my right arm, then they should take that chance. The decision was made, the paperwork was signed and the surgeon left, ready to move forward. It all happened in under five minutes.

Immediately after that, the doctor in charge of the SICU came into the room and again closed the door to talk to Derek. He explained a bit more about their immediate approach, especially over the next twenty-four to forty-eight hours. He explained that there would be a nurse present in my room twenty-four hours a day to constantly monitor me and the eight to ten life sustaining machines that were connected to me. He explained that he would be able to come in and visit for just a few minutes every couple of hours. He then looked Derek straight in the eye and told him that he needed to look after himself better, if he was going to be of any good to support me. He told him that needed to sleep, eat and shower because, if I did make it, they were looking at weeks and most likely months of recovery and rehabilitation. He then told him that at the end of the day, he was to go to a hotel, have a meal, take a shower and sleep in a bed. Or, he feared that he would have Derek as a patient also.

Derek took the doctor's suggestions and complied. He went to a hotel and did all of the things he was urged to do and the long process of watching, listening and waiting began. It was at that point that he decided to start writing everything related to my case and situation down. He kept a journal book where he recorded every conversation he had with every member of my large team of medical professionals. It was the only way to keep it all straight while assessing and evaluating what was happening. It allowed time to ponder, reflect, research and question. It provided a basis for a strategy in knowing which questions to ask next, when an opportunity for a conversation with a member of my team presented itself.

The plastic surgeon made an incision from my wrist to my elbow, in a snake pattern, on the inside of my right arm. The incision was to the bone and was left completely open to drain, for a period of five weeks. I had a detailed and up close view of the inside of my arm when they were changing my dressing, while I was in this state. It looked like something out of a horror film to me, when I did finally see it. Of course, I was in a coma initially, while all of this was going on and I remained in that state for about two weeks or so, after my heart attack.

With the massive build up of fluid pressure internally, I just kept getting larger and larger. My right arm took the worst of it, as I described earlier. After I woke up and some time had passed, Derek told me that he had never seen a human arm that big before. Having said that, I have learned first hand just how far human skin will stretch and, just how little it will retract! My whole body now has extra hanging skin. Some of it is in places I never thought possible!

I am somewhat grateful that I was in a coma for the first two weeks because I think that the discomfort would have been more than I could have tolerated. Or, so I thought at the time. As it was, once I was out of the coma, I was extremely uncomfortable and I am putting it mildly. What I really mean is, I was in excruciating pain!

As the days progressed, it didn't seem that I wasn't getting any worse. Though it may not seem like it, that was something! There were several times when everyone wondered if I would even make through the night, or the next couple of hours, for that matter. All of the life support and dialysis measures continued for the next two weeks, or so. Eventually, I started to stabilize, and so it was time to try waking me up. It was time to see if I would wake up, and if so, what type of cognitive function would I have. Would I have any function at all? There were a lot of unknowns and a lot of uncertainty.

When the doctors finally decided to bring me out of my coma, Derek had requested that he be there. Of course the medical staff knew just how traumatic this type of thing can be and proceeded without him being present. My thought is that they were concerned that I may not react well to be woken in such a manner. In addition, they did not know if or what type of brain function I would have and were trying to shield him from further upset and trauma.

The first time they tried to wake me, it did not go well at all, from what he was told. This was not surprising to anyone but it was a place to start. I certainly did not react well to all the tubes sticking out of every natural orifice in my body. Not to mention the ones connected or attached to the new holes that had been made! The second time was the same. I do not remember it but I was told that I was biting at the intubation tubes and was not happy, at all. I had been intubated in the ER in Moncton and stayed that way for as long as possible in the SICU in Saint John. That was until the time came when the surgeon removed the tubes and put in a trachea tube (trach), so that they could continue to artificially support my breathing. My lungs were not strong enough for me to breath on my own, so I still needed some help.

The third time, the third time, I remember waking up. Third time is a charm, they say!

As I slowly opened my eyes struggling to get a clear view of my surroundings, I could feel this excruciating pain everywhere in my body. It felt like I had been crushed in a press, like a piece of scrap metal being made ready for recycling or something. I could barely focus my eyes on the things around me. As the blurriness started to clear, I scanned the room trying to figure out just where the hell I was and what the hell had happened to me. "Is this a bad dream or is this real?", I questioned. At first, I couldn't tell. I soon realized that it was very real and I was laying in a hospital bed. I was unable to move my arms or my legs. The only thing I seemed to have any control over was just a tiny bit of movement in my neck.

There were tubes coming out of every natural orifice in my body and there were a few new holes that had been made for additional tubes and needles. I was intubated and had tubes in my mouth and down my throat. I was hooked up to a machine that was breathing for me and I was connected to eight different other machines, all injecting life sustaining medications. I was very frightened and all I could think of was my husband. Where is he? Is he okay? My eyes scanned the room for him and then finally after what seemed like several minutes, I saw him. He was right there, by my side. Then, I immediately thought to myself, well if I had been in some kind of accident either he wasn't involved or if he was he wasn't hurt. Either way, whatever is going on with me he is here and watching over me so I will be okay. Then, I closed my eyes and everything went black again.

The next time I woke up, the extreme pain was still present and, in fact, it seemed to be worse though I didn't think it was possible. My right hand and arm were bandaged to the elbow and had some kind of brace on it to keep it from moving. It felt like there was something seriously wrong with it. I was so confused! What was all of this? What was happening? But once again, I saw my love right there beside me and then after a moment or two I could hear my mother's voice in the background.

As I tried to focus, I thought to myself maybe I was in some kind of car accident and had been thrown from the vehicle. Or, maybe I had pulled someone through a car window trying to save them. Maybe that would explain what happened to my arm? My right arm. The hand and arm I use to sketch and paint and create. What is wrong with my right arm? Why can't I use it? Why wouldn't it move? Maybe it got slashed open by the glass from a broken window? That must be it, right?

It seemed like a lot of time passed, though it really wasn't very long at all, and then Derek told me that I was there because I had a massive heart attack. This was confusing because I still could not understand why my hand and arm were wrapped up and why I was unable to move either of them. Then I tried moving other parts of my body again, nothing would budge. I tried to speak. Nothing! I thought to myself what the hell is happening?? Then I remembered that there were tubes down my throat preventing me from speaking or making any sound at all.

Anyone who knows me would definitely say that not being able to speak must have been one of the hardest things for me. Why you ask? Because I love, love, love to talk and sing and truly just make noise all of the time! When I wake in the morning I start talking to whom ever is present. It doesn't matter who it is, I talk! It could be my husband or one of our three house cats, the dog, it doesn't matter. It is usually Jam, our oldest indoor cat, she is typically lying right beside me on the bed. I start talking and singing in the morning and I do not stop until I go to bed. Unless I am creating or I get into a good television show. Then I'm quiet, for a little while, maybe. Sometimes I even talk in my sleep, just ask DW! Lol.

I thought to myself, this is going to be quite a challenge for me, not talking. I certainly hope it isn't going to be too long before I am able to speak again! The next thought I had was, that it all must be very serious, and why can't I move? Damn it! Derek could tell I was confused. But then after a few moments, I started to remember going to the Moncton Hospital with chest pain in a fast moving van and some pieces started to come back to me. Slowly, I started to remember the things leading up to the moment when everything went black in Moncton.

He told me that I was in Saint John and I knew what that meant. It had to mean that I was transported there for urgent care and probably by ambulance. I knew it must be serious, but I still wasn't clear on what had happened. It was however, enough information that I could at least process the severity and realize that I was not out of the woods yet.

Derek looked so tired, but relieved to see my eyes open again. He told me afterwards that he didn't want to try and explain everything to me all at once as it might have been too much, too soon for my mind to process and I agree. It would have been very overwhelming to have been told every detail of what had happened to me in those initial moments after waking up. In fact, at that point I had no idea that I had been in a coma for two weeks. I think that knowledge alone would have been very upsetting, in my fragile state.

He could tell that even though I could not speak, I was able to understand what he was telling me in that moment. This was a huge relief because none of the doctors were really sure what level of brain function I would have when I woke up, considering how long I was in full cardiac arrest. Not to mention all of the other complications that followed during the time I was asleep and there were a lot of them. By this point, Derek had been told on three different occasions that he should prepare as this could be it, I could be gone.

As the hours passed that day, I started to understand a little more of what was happening, he started to talk to me about things we had done and experienced together. He started with things from way back, when we first met, and slowly and subtly, throughout the day, worked his way to the present moment. I did not realize it at the time, but he was trying to get a feel for my cognitive function and memory retention. As the day progressed, it was a huge relief for him and a win for the doctors. My mind was showing good signs of a full recovery. As time passed and I worked through my lengthy rehabilitation process, my doctors and other medical professionals had me perform many tests in order to find out exactly how much brain function I had managed to retain. I have lost some of my abilities and my capacity for memory retention, but all things considered, I am very happy with progress I have made.

As my recovery continued, I had to have dialysis almost every day for about 5 weeks. While my team continued their efforts to get my kidneys functional again. I have to say that going through dialysis, in the condition I was in, was awful. I was very weak and my lungs were not working well at all, even with the ventilator support. Anyone who has experienced dialysis knows that slow relaxed breathing is best for the process, but I was struggling just to breath at all and at every moment. Then, you add the process of dialysis to that and it made it much, much worse for me. As a result, I would get very worked up and anxious when dialysis time rolled around again. I would tell Derek that I just wanted to go home. Why wouldn't he just take me home? Please? Just take me home?

He explained to me that I was still very sick and that he could not look after me properly at home, just yet. He told me that I had to hang in there and try to focus on getting better. He said that he wasn't going to leave me and that when I was well enough and it was time, we would leave and both go home together. I had to trust him. He had never lied to me, let alone anyone else, why would he start now.

I recall one day of dialysis that was unusually hard for me. I believe I had been going on very little sleep and they were trying to wean me off some of the pain meds because I was having such horrible hallucinations. Derek hadn't arrived at the hospital yet that morning and they had started the procedure anyway. I was very worked up and started to have a lot of difficulty breathing. I was trying to get them to stop. I literally thought I was going to die. It was to the point, during dialysis, where it felt like every breath I took could be my last. I honestly thought dialysis was going to kill me, right then and there. It was so exhausting. I had to fight with absolutely everything I had left, for every breath I took.

When Derek arrived, I was in a frenzy. I was shaking and crying. He rushed right over to me as soon as he saw the state I was in and grabbed my hand. As I clung to him with all my might, I mouthed to him that I didn't want to die and that I couldn't do it anymore. At one point, I looked up at Derek with an intense look of consuming fear in my eyes, (a look that he tells me he has only ever seen in one other individual, one time in his life) and begged him, "Please don't let me die!".

Every day, since I woken up, had been a struggle and on this day, I realized just exactly how sick I really was. Derek made them stop the dialysis and made them put the blood back into my body. The doctor tried to convince him otherwise, but Derek plainly stated that I needed a break from it and that was going to have to be it for that day. Derek was angry but then, later that day, the doctor took him aside, put his arm on his shoulder and thanked him. He thanked him for reminding him that sometimes they need to look at more than just the numbers on the screen. He said that he reminded him that there is a person connected to those machines and screens and that sometimes they need to take a step back and consider what is happening right in front of them. He said that he was trying to see how far he could push me in order to stimulate my recovery progress. He said that they were trying to get me strong enough so that I could be transported back to the Moncton Hospital.

In the end, everyone decided that it was best to try again the next day. I could and would push through it now, as long as

Derek was by my side, and now, I was focused on getting back to Moncton. At least I would be in my hometown and Derek could sleep at home, with the cats, while I worked on getting better. I also thought that just maybe my mother would go home and with any luck give us a break from her craziness. I wasn't sure how much longer we could take her presence, in every moment of this experience. I suppose it could have been okay, if she would have just shut up and stop picking at every little thing, trying to make it about her.

The best days were the ones when they would give me pain meds just before dialysis. This would relax me and if I was lucky I would fall asleep while they were hooking me up to the machine. It was shear hell otherwise. My mother was always there telling me to breath slowly. If I could have reached up and slapped her I would have. I already knew that! Her telling me didn't help, it just frustrated me even more. All I could think at the time was, "Oh shut up, you idiot!", I know what I'm supposed to be doing. I'm scared and I'm fighting for my life here! Just shut up!

It got to the point that one day, I mouthed to Derek not to bring her back. She just made things worse for me. She just kept repeating herself over and over again. It was torture! She was constantly picking at me and yet when I needed her to do something helpful, she would not. I wanted her to leave and not come back. During my time in a coma, my mother would talk about me and my condition to anyone who would listen. Though she really had no grasp or real understanding for what was truly happening. As soon as a doctor or nurse would start to talk and try to explain something, she would start talking over them. Trying to string a few words that she could remember into some sort of verbal thought. She didn't then, nor has she ever, really listened when someone else is speaking. It made it very difficult not only for me but for Derek, as well. In fact, it was harder on him because I could at least sleep through some of it. He had to try and really listen to what my medical team was telling him. He had to really try to absorb and remember it all so he could write it down for future reference. All the while, she was going on as she does.

I believe that she only stayed because Derek stayed. It was like a competition to her. A battle of wills, perhaps. I truly believe that she was happy I was sick. Not to mention the amount of attention and number of free lunches she was now getting because of it. This was also pleasing to her because for the first time in a long time she wasn't alone. As you might be starting to gather, she can be unpleasant to be around.

Shortly after I woke up, my team decided that it was time to remove my intubation tubes and replace them with a trachea tube. The concern was that if they didn't take them out then, I would have permanent damage to my vocal cords. I was told that having someone intubated for that length of time is very unusual, but do to my circumstances, they felt it was necessary.

So authorization was given and the surgery was scheduled, which I was thankful for. At least I had a little more movement and the opportunity to try to mouth some words. Derek quickly became very good at reading my lips. My mother, on the other hand, had no clue. Even the nurses started to catch on some, which made it easier for me, especially at night. It was still very frustrating for me, however, when I couldn't get the message across that I was trying to relay. Derek tried to help by buying me a white board and marker so that I could write down what I was trying to say. It was a good idea and a nice thought but my right hand was totally immobilized and my left hand was so weak and awkward that I could not use it effectively. As a result, the marks I made were illegible, which only frustrated me more. Maybe we should have tried an alphabet board? If any of you ever find yourselves trying to help someone in a similar position, try an alphabet board.

The third time they tried to wake me, I can recall looking at my right arm, before I passed out again, and thinking that I must have been a car accident. My hand and arm were completely bandaged, wrapped up and braced. At which point, I was sure that I must have been a car accident. Why else would I be in this kind of shape? In my mind, I thought that I had pulled someone through, or crawled through a broken car window. Or, maybe I had gone through some broken glass of some kind. Why else would my arm be cut open like it was? I had this picture in my mind of a car upside down and a woman inside crying for help. I think the reason why I thought this was because my mother had been talking to a lady in the waiting room who's daughter had just been in a very bad car accident and she talked about it constantly in my room, while I was in a coma. She just kept going on and on about the poor little girl who had been in the bad car accident.

If anyone says you can't hear anything while you are in a coma state, they would be wrong. She would sit at my bedside and repeat the story to Derek or anyone who would listen, over and over again. I must have thought she was referring to me. Maybe this would explain why my arm had been cut open from my wrist to my elbow on the inside and why my hand had been laid open in three other spots on the top, I thought.

Let this be a lesson to all, coma victims can feel and hear and they know you are there. Even the doctors would be very careful what they said in my presence. My advice to anyone who may find themselves with a loved one in an unconscious state fighting for their life, is to talk to them. Say positive things, tell them you love them and give them encouragement. They can hear you! It might be a matter of life or death for them. Help them know that they have something or someone to fight for and come back to. I believe it made a huge impact in my recovery. Derek would talk to me and touch me lovingly. I felt it and I fought to come back to him.

Once the trachea tube (trach) was put in, I did feel some relief. That is except for my overwhelming thirst. Drinking water with a trach in, was totally out of the question, of course. But, that didn't stop me from wanting it, or trying to get it for that matter. Even though it was completely unacceptable for me to have anything by mouth. I was being tube fed and all of my fluids were being put directly into my system through a small tube that went up my nose and down the back of my throat, into my stomach. Technically I didn't need anything I suppose, but that didn't matter, I wanted it! I had no appetite but my thirst almost drove me mad!

I did not have my teeth brushed until many weeks later. I guess it was the least of my concerns, at the time. They were just trying to keep me alive. I would not have been able to brush my teeth anyway. Someone would have had to do it for me. That said however, I was not permitted to have any amount of water in my mouth. I used to dream of drinking a large glass of water constantly and thought to myself when Derek finally springs me from this place of torture, I'm going to get him to stop at the first store we see that has a slushy machine. Slush was also something I craved. My dream of having something cool and refreshing just kept repeating over and over again! Maybe it was a combination of the drugs and the dry hospital air, I am not sure. What I am sure of, however, is that I desperately wanted something cool to drink.

I would beg for a drink of water to anyone who came close to me. One night, a nice young nurse, in training, came into my room to check on me. I begged him in the most pitiful way I could muster to give me a drink of water. He did not realize what my situation was or he would not have brought it to me, I'm sure. I must have looked just that pitiful and sad, because he rushed over and got me a glass of water with a bendable straw. Deep down maybe he did realize that I probably shouldn't have it because I recall him telling me to take just the smallest of sips.

When I think back about it, I was overjoyed to feel the water in my mouth but, when I tried to swallow, I did not get the satisfaction I was hoping for. I just wanted to chug it down but I was not able to. I was however, satisfied to, at the very least, have had some moisture in my mouth. He tried to take it away and I motioned for him to leave it, thinking that I would be able to wet my mouth again in a few minutes. He left it close to the edge of my table, so I could get my mouth close to it and then he was off to tend to another patient. I am forever grateful that he granted my wish. Thank you unknown and kind young nurse!

As I was about to try to wet my mouth again a few minutes later, another nurse came in to check on me. I was never alone for very long. She saw the water and said that I should not have that and quickly disposed of it. This all happened in the late hours of the evening or early hours of the morning, as I never slept after Derek left for the day.

So now, my goal was to try and figure out how I was going to get myself another drink of water. As the nights went on, I would watch the clock and started timing the nurses. They did their rounds at pretty much the same time every night and as I said, they never left me alone for very long. So I would have to be quick, I thought. Remember now, I was on a lot of meds at the time and not all of them helped me to think straight. My plan was to wiggle my way to the floor and crawl to the bathroom. If I can just get to the bathroom, I thought, I will be able to quench my thirst.

It was a terrible plan of course! I hadn't walked or even moved my legs in weeks. I couldn't even sit up on my own. My legs did not work but yet I was trying to rock myself out of the bed! I wasn't very successful though. All I ever managed to do was get myself positioned on an angle in bed, with my foot hanging over the edge, by the time the nurse would visit me again. Upon entering my room, they would always say that they couldn't understand how I would end up in that position. Then they would put the sides of my bed up and that would put an end to my efforts for getting to some water. Well for that night at least! This went on almost every night for weeks, because I never slept at night. I hated the night time.

During the day, Derek was by my side as much as they would allow him to be. When I received my meds, it would take but 20 minutes and then I would have a hot flash. These were not regular hot flashes either. They were torturous disgusting hot flashes. The medications I was on intensified my regular hot flashes. So, in an effort to help me through this, Derek would get a bowl of ice water and a couple of face clothes to put on my face, head and neck trying to provide me with some relief. He could tell how uncomfortable they made me and did everything in his power to cool me down. For which I was extremely GRATEFUL!

All of a sudden, one day, I got an idea after seeing the bowl of ice water and the cool water soaked face clothes. I thought that maybe if I bit the cloth I could suck some of the cool water from it. This would be better than nothing, I thought. So as Derek tried to sooth me, I bit down on the cloth. Shock came over his face and he quickly realized what I was trying to do. He pulled on the cloth and as he did, I clamped down even harder. Of course, I was no match for his strength and he won the battle, in the end.

He smiled nervously because he was a little concerned. But at the same time I think he found it funny. He did not realize to what extent I would fight for what I wanted. He knew I shouldn't have anything by mouth so he was very careful not to get the cloth too close to my mouth again. Unfortunate for me! Looking back, I probably would have laughed hard if the tables had been turned.

# CHAPTER 11

## *Night time*

As I lay in my bed at night, it seemed there was very little that I could do to keep myself from going out of my mind. I felt like I was going mad. I slept a lot during the day, as I knew Derek was there watching out for me. However, it was a much different story for me at night. Fear kept me awake most nights. I would not let the nurses turn the television off in my room even though a good majority of the shows that came on were pure torture. They either had scenes containing food and drink in them, or the commercials that came on during the program itself did. Either way, I didn't like that part very much. It angered me! But, at least the noise of it distracted me part of the time depending on which show would come on. I was unable to change the channel so I would watch whatever came on, if it interested me. Most often though, it was just background noise. The majority of the shows that came on simply were not my cup of tea but having them on did seem to help me feel a little less lonely.

The feeling of being helpless is mostly what kept me awake. Thoughts of something happening inside the hospital scared me. Something like a fire breaking out and being left to burn alive because I was unable to get out on my own, absolutely haunted me. I know that even entertaining the notion is ridiculous, but I couldn't seem to shake the uneasy feelings that came from the mere thoughts of it. Even though I had a nurse with me 24/7, they still had to take a bathroom break at least a couple of times, I was sure of it. "What would happen then?", my drug induced mind would taunt. "There's less staff at night to look after the same number of patients as during the day.", it would say. "Your nurse has to look after more than just your needs at night, remember?", it did this and tortured me every single night! Looking back now, I am sure that would never have happened. But, I never thought I would one day wake up and find myself in the position I was in either, and at forty-eight years of age no less!

Every night there was a man dressed in a white doctor's coat who would come into my room. He resembled Kurt Russell, to me. He would enter my room but would not say a word to me. This man could clearly see that I was awake and yet he never spoke, which made me very uneasy! It made me uneasy because he would press buttons on the machines that were keeping me alive. He could have said something, anything at all and I would not had been so frightened but there was never a single word uttered from his lips. Until this day, I have a hard time to watch anything that has Kurt Russell in it. It was very creepy to me. Creepy and horrifying! Wait, who are you? What are you doing? Why are you touching those machines? Those machines are the only things keeping my alive right now. What are you doing over there? All thoughts that raced through my mind. Every single night!

I told one of my nurse friends about this and she said he was probably a respiratory technician and was probably just checking my breathing and oxygen levels. Which did make sense to me after the fact. But, I really was puzzled and frightened by him acting in such a manner, at the time. My fear was so overwhelming at times that there was no way that I would choose to sleep. However, if by some chance exhaustion did take over and I did fall asleep, I would have horrible nightmares. I think that this was mostly because of the drugs I was on at the time. Although, as you may recall, I have been plaqued with this affliction my whole life. So, with all of those factors in play every single night, I did my absolute best to stay awake until Derek got back. Which was usually around 6:30 am.

I had dreams of crows and ravens dive bombing me while I lay helpless in my bed. I had dreams of little elves on the ceiling baking cookies and chopping one another up and adding the bits of their victims to their baked goods. I had a dream that Derek's mom was sitting with me while Derek had to run an errand. In my dream, she was allowing kids to come into my room while they were trick or treating, except that they were looking for treats in all the wrong places. They were under my bed, looking under my covers and going though my drawers. It was very disturbing to me because she was letting them push buttons on my life support systems and found it hilarious. Then, after they all left, all she did was stare at me with a mean glare. They were all very frightening dreams and all seemed very real to me, at the time. But, I couldn't communicate to tell anyone what was happening in my head. I had to suffer in silence.

I had another dream that the hospital wanted to discharge me in the middle of the worst snow storm that New Brunswick had ever seen, because they needed the bed for someone else. I was glad to be leaving but was very unsure of how we would get home in such terrible weather. The hospital staff had arranged for Derek and I to be flown, by helicopter, to a field in our community. Once there, we would have to jump out into a snow drift at which point Derek's dad would be waiting for us in the tractor to take us the rest of the way home. For some strange reason, as if this dream wasn't strange enough, my brother's two sons were in the helicopter with us and had two Labrador retrievers who apparently belonged to them. I was uneasy about jumping but then the dogs jumped, the boys jumped and so Derek and I jumped. I remember the sweet satisfaction of climbing up into the cab of the tractor with Derek's dad. Finally, I was going home! I was so very disappointed when I woke up, only to find that it was just a dream. I know how all of this sounds, but in my drug induced and very confused state, it all seemed to be very real to me. So very real and so very terrifying!

There was a very kind gentleman who used to come in to my room every night to do some light cleaning. He always spoke to me as he could see that I was awake. I looked forward to his nightly visits and his kind small talk. I felt comforted as he would talk about anything and everything. He spoke of his son so much that I felt like I knew him. I believe he could sense my fear and wanted to be kind and maybe some how comfort me in my weak and frightened state. I was very thankful and grateful for his kindness!

The nurse on duty would tell me every night after she hung up the phone, that she had just finished talking to that wonderful husband of mine. She would say that she didn't think he ever slept and that he wanted to check to see how I was. He would call every night, or should I say morning. I so wanted him to take me home and I am sure he wanted that, too. One of the times that I woke from my coma, I cannot be sure of the timeline, but Derek told me that he was there and that he was not going anywhere. He was not going anywhere until he could bring me with him and we could go home together. He kept that promise.

I had one dream that was mostly horrifying and partly true. My dream started out with me feeling very drugged up and in the company of two "ladies of the evening". They were helping me into what seemed like an apartment, in an area that was unfamiliar to me. As we enter the apartment, I see a large mattress on the floor and the two ladies lay me down on it. I recall not being able to move except for my head. I can hear the women talking to a man. He is telling them that they should hurry up that I am expected to work that night. The man who, you guessed it, looks like Kurt Russell instructs them to finish drugging me. The two women come over to the mattress and keep telling me to be calm, that I will feel better soon. I can remember having trouble breathing in the dream. Just like in real life.

One of the ladies starts to inject something into my clavicle area and as she does, I feel relief and then she says to me, "Don't you feel better now?". So then, I was totally helpless. I felt totally trapped and it reminded me of when I was a child. When my parents used to lock me in my room. They always told me it was because I used to sleep walk, but even after I got older, the lock remained and my brother used to lock me in. He thought it was a big joke. Eventually, I had enough of that treatment and removed the lock myself. My mother was shocked that I was "smart enough" and capable of removing it on my own. She asked for the lock, but I told her that it broke when I removed it. It didn't, but I wasn't giving it back to her.

Getting back to my dream, then the two women started to implant something in me. It was something that would make it much easier for me to breath, they said. The next thing that happens is that Derek comes busting through the door. He laid his head down on the pillow next to mine and faced me. I told him that I wanted to go home now. His response was that I would be okay now and that he wasn't going anywhere until I could go home with him. The two women were now dressed as nurses and Kurt was dressed as a doctor. They were all talking to Derek and saying that I was in bad shape and they were doing everything they could for me. Derek got up from the mattress and went into the next room to talk to the so called doctor. The next thing I see is the door busting open with police officers rushing into the apartment and putting cuffs on the two women. Meanwhile, the doctor was trying to talk his way out of the situation. The police said he was a real doctor but that he had pimping out patients. Apparently, he had been under investigation for some time and finally, thanks to Derek and I, they were able to gather sufficient evidence to put him away for a very long time.

Can you see how things were getting so mixed up for me? Do you see how I was trying to process my reality in my drug induced state?

In the next dream that I can recall, I am walking outside of the hospital and a van pulls up. The driver asks me if I could get in the van and help him out with his dog. So naturally, I agree! If there is a dog in trouble and I can help, I will every time. As I climb into the van, the next thing I know I am being tied up and gagged, as they lay me down in the back of the van. The van pulls into the parking garage, where the ambulances enter to drop off and pick up patients. All of a sudden, the Kurt Russell doctor appears and starts barking out orders to another doctor, who's face I could not see because he was wearing a mask. I then feel a sharp pain in my clavicle area, and realize that he is cutting into my skin and trying to insert something. He instructs me to stay still but I'm fighting with all my might. He tells me it will hurt less if I stay still and I am literally freaking out because I can not understand why this is happening to me. After several attempts on the right side, he gives up and moves to the left. I keep fighting by moving whatever body part I can. I can tell he is getting upset and he decides to take a break to talk to the Kurt doctor. Kurt insists he keep trying so he comes back for another try. The next thing I know he says, "there I got it", and he leaves me laying there totally confused and hurting.

Later, after being told about some of the real life procedures that were performed in trying to save my life, I believe that I was, once again, confusing dreams and reality. Somewhere in my brain I knew or at least could feel what was happening to me but could not make sense of it all.

I needed to have a pic line put in before I could have dialysis and I do remember a nice lady talking to me as she inserted the line on my left side. She asked me if she was hurting me, at the time and also if the stitching was too tight, as this was the first she had ever done this procedure.

In addition, I think that I remember the ambulance ride to the Saint John Hospital being very quick and bumpy. From what Derek told me, they had me strapped down to the stretcher in order to transport me safely. They did not want me to fall off of the stretcher and onto the floor during the trip. Some part of me recalls bits and pieces of these events. Even though I was heavily medicated and in a coma, I was fighting for my life and even in that state of complete confusion, I knew not to give up.

So, even though I had been having dialysis, about every second day, the reduction of fluid and inflammation in my body seemed to be very slow. Every morning around four thirty some one would bring a portable x-ray machine into my room and then sit me up in the bed for pictures. I hated it because when they would put the head of my bed upright, I was unable to breath. Now, I think it was all of the extra fluid pressing on my organs, that made it feel like I was being folded in half. I had no idea at the time that it was fluid causing the discomfort and of course I couldn't tell anyone. So, I suffered in silence.

That is until the doctors figured out that I had fluid built up in my stomach. Upon discovering this, they performed a procedure wherein they drained eight litres of fluid, mixed with blood, from my stomach. Though it was very painful at the time, it seemed to be easier to breath afterwards. Soon after that however, because the fluid pressure within my body had been slowly, but consistently reducing with dialysis, I started bleeding internally. You see the fluid pressure that had been stopping, or maybe it would be more accurate to say slowing, the internal bleeding from my lacerated liver, was no longer applying pressure. The SICU charge nurse was expecting and watching for this, or any possible signs of it, immediately after the draining procedure had been completed. Then all of a sudden, my blood pressure dropped. It dropped to a dangerously low level and then seemed to stabilize. She ordered the nurse looking after me that day to check my blood pressure every ten minutes and to keep a very close eye on me. Though it came up and seemed to stabilize briefly, it remained low. She then told everyone in my room that if she saw one more drastic drop, they were to prep me to be moved immediately. She then escorted Derek and my mother to a private family room and asked them to remain there until she returned. Saying as she ran out the door, that she wouldn't be very long, but that she urgently needed to get me looked after.

After a few moments, she returned and asked both Derek and my mother to follow her. She was very serious and had a real sense of urgency in her words and tone. As they all sped down the hall toward the surgery wing, she told my mother to wait in the waiting room that she pointed to on her right and instructed Derek to follow her right away as they had no time to waist. As they entered a small room just outside of the operating room, Derek was met by a surgeon who was in a very serious state. He very quickly explained to Derek that I was, at that very moment, bleeding out and would be gone very soon, if he did not act immediately. He told him that I was bleeding from my liver and that he thought that there was a small chance that he could cauterize the areas that were bleeding, if they were veins. If however, the bleeders were arteries, he would then have to open me up to try and repair the damage, but did not feel that I would survive the surgery. He explained the situation and his planned approach very quickly and then in a very matter of fact manner, told Derek that he needed his approval and signature *immediately*.

Derek listened very closely. Did his best to absorb and process this information and signed without hesitation, as it was the only chance I had at survival. As soon as he signed, the charge nurse ushered him and my mother back to the small family room, where they had previously been waiting. As they returned, she told them that she would be back as soon as she knew more about my condition and asked if they would like her to call a Priest, Pastor, or maybe a counsellor to come and be with them. It was that close! This was the fourth time that they had come to Derek and told him that I may not survive, but it was the first time that they had ever asked if he wanted to see a Pastor. This could be it! This could really be the time. It really could be the time when he had to say good bye.

I was already pretty heavily drugged up before this procedure but then they had to add more medications before starting, of course. Even with all of that, though, I was still in and out of consciousness during the surgery. I can remember the doctor and nurses talking to me. They kept telling me that I was doing great and that I was going to feel so much better once this procedure was completed.

Meanwhile back in the family waiting room, where Derek and my mother were waiting to hear news of my status, Derek told the charge nurse that neither he nor I would like to have a Pastor present. My mother disagreed, of course, and said that she thought that it was something that I would want. The Pastor was not called. Then just as the severity of the situation was really setting in, well for Derek anyway, I don't think that my mother really understood what was happening. Just as the reality of it all starting to set in, again, my brother arrived and was shown to the family room where they were.

It was then that he began to tell them all about how he was finally going to be rewarded for all of his years of hard work and suffering in taking over my father's business. He was so very happy and so relieved that he was in the process of making a deal with a big corporation to buy the bulk of his business and set him and his family up, financially, for life. Isn't that great for him? He so deserves his perfect life, with his perfect family and his perfect pile of money. Good for him!

So, it's the next day and with eight litres of fluid now drained from my stomach and three veins in my liver cauterized to stop the internal bleeding, my blood pressure has stabilized and it looks like I'm going to make it, again. With all of that, I didn't seem to feel as much pressure in the early part of the day. But, when the nurses came in to wash me and clean me up, they turned me on my side and the pain I felt brought instant tears. I kept trying to tap the nurses to get them to put me on my back again but they had to get me cleaned up. I'm sure they worked as fast as they could but the pain was so very awful. Not to mention the fact that I couldn't breath when they would roll me on my side. It was so very frightening! I was already having my challenges with breathing and when they put me on my side it seemed to cut off all air flow. I would start to pass out every single time the nurses rolled me onto my side.

I had what is known as a fecal management system put into my rectum and as far as I am concerned, this apparatus is not far removed from some sort of mid-evil torture device. That said, this is a device in which all of the waste is supposed to go from the patient, into a tube that is inserted into the rectum and into a waste bag at the end of the tube. There is a tube inserted into the rectum, which has a balloon like end on it. Then, the balloon is inflated which, in theory, is supposed to keep it sealed inside the rectum. In my case, it stayed in place all right, but it leaked. It leaked all the time and as a result, I was laying in the liquid waste, which, for those of you who don't know, has a very damaging effect when constantly exposed to bare skin. The prolonged exposure seriously burned my back side and the inside of my legs. I had been tube fed for weeks, so you can just imagine what was coming out the other end.

Because this system leaked continually, the nurses had to wash me up every day and sometimes more than once a day. There was one incident, however, where the leaking stopped. Well for about twenty-four hours or so. One evening, toward the end of the day shift, my nurse that day was cleaning me up from the day's mess and it was extremely unpleasant, for both of us I might add. I would like to say, before I go any further, that with the exception of this particular incident, I received the very best of medical care and attention at the Saint John Regional Hospital. This particular evening things were very messy and I was in a lot of pain. This nurse did not like this portion of caring for me and seemed to put it off until the last of her shift. Eventually I guess, she worked herself up to it and we began. It wasn't going well and was taking longer than she had hoped. She was short on time as she had a party to attend that evening, which she talked about frequently throughout the day. Her efforts to re-insert the balloon end and seal up the discharge were simply not working. As her frustration continued to build and her time was running out, her solution, so she could get to her party, was to ball up a piece of toilet tissue and shove it up into my rectum to block the flow of waste. This would then give the appearance that everything had been sealed up and I would not be in a mess. "There you go, all done.". Now I can go to my party! Yay, me!

The next morning when Derek arrived, he questioned why there was nothing in the discharge bag, several times. As he asked this question, every time in fact, I would squirm and try to wiggle myself at the waist, trying to bring his attention to what I was so desperately trying to tell him. Eventually, when the next nurse was cleaning me up, she found the ball of toilet paper that "Miss Party Nurse" had shoved up there the night before. Though she said it quietly, I heard her say "Well now what is that doing up there?" when she found it. She finished cleaning me up, re-inserted the device, disposed of the evidence and the regular flow of matter resumed. Nothing more was ever said about it. What does that say to you? What type of person does that to someone? Let alone someone who was clinging to life as I was at that time? Think about it... just for a moment.

So for me, the fecal management system experience was a very, very painful ordeal. In fact, it was so painful I told Derek that if I am ever in a situation where they say they have to put a fecal management system in again, I want you to tell them to pull the plug. I am not going through that hell, ever again. It took months for me to heal and the scars that I now have in that area are a constant reminder.

The five and a half weeks that I spent in Saint John were the longest five and a half weeks of my life, without a doubt. Even though Derek and my mother were there every day, I still felt so very lonely. I longed to be home cuddled up with my fur babies. At the time of my heart attack, my grey tabby Jam, was almost four years old and was still getting used to the fact that we had adopted two kittens, who were now six month old. Initially, she was not happy with their presence at all and she did absolutely everything she could to avoid them. I worried about them and how they were all getting along with one another, constantly. Although, looking back, I think it was a good thing that we adopted Berry and Jelly when we did. Otherwise, Jam would have been all alone and I think that would have been worse for her. For the most part, I think the whole experience of being on their own is what helped them to bond.

A close girl friend of mine and Derek's parents checked in on them daily to give them fresh food and water and to make sure they were doing okay. I appreciate that they were all willing to give up their own time to help us out and check in on our little bundles of joy. Though I believe they looked forward to their daily human visits, it was no substitute for their human form "mom" being around on a daily basis. The cats must have been wondering what happened to me. Well, to both of us really. We just left and didn't come back. Jam did see Derek taking me to the van however and I'm sure she felt my energy. Her and I are very close. In fact, since I came home from the hospital if I'm not feeling well or not having a good day she does not leave my side. When all of this took place, I had been working from home for some time and they were used to seeing me frequently throughout the day and of course I was always home in the evening. I missed them so much I could barely stand it!!

Some time had passed since we arrived in Saint John and it seemed that things were starting to settle down, just a little. It seemed that I was starting to make a little progress in my recovery and I was starting to put my focus on getting back to Moncton. I had started to realize, not accept, but realize that it may be some time before I actually got to go home. Back to our home, where my kitties were waiting for me. Back where I belonged. Back to the only place that has ever really felt like home, for me. We had been in Saint John together, for quite awhile at this time. In fact, Derek never left the hospital, unless it was to go to the hotel, a few blocks away, for a shower and a couple of hours sleep. He didn't even leave to go and get some of his overnight things from our home. His family was kind enough to bring him what he needed and I am very grateful for their help!

As time went on, and it got closer and closer to Christmas, all I could think about was the fact that I wasn't ready. It had been a fear of mine my whole life, that Christmas would come and I would forget a gift for someone or what I gave was not right or not enough. I used to have bad dreams about it and would wake up in a sweat because of it. I think that it may possibly have been because of the examples I saw from my mother. She always seemed to put so much emphasis on making Christmas just right. Maybe growing up in that reality led me to believe that I had to do the same, or be the same way. Isn't it interesting how we can shape the future of a young mind, just by the examples we set and display? What examples are the young people in your home seeing and recording?

I was getting worked up about not having done any shopping, or baking. I hadn't even put up a tree yet. What kind of Christmas would it be? I was so caught up in my habitual behaviour that I couldn't see that being alive was the best gift of all! Still, after all that I had just and was continuing to go through, I did not realize the magnitude of what had really happened to me.

Derek only told me what he thought I needed to know as the days passed. He was concerned that telling me too much all at once would possibly have a negative affect on my mental state and hinder my recovery process and progress. I think he made the right decision. I think I would have been much more afraid, and maybe felt more defeated, if I had known the full extent of the damage that had been done as a result of my event, all at once. My mother, on the other hand, disagreed completely! She said, *repeatedly*, that she would not have done things that way and that Derek should have done everything differently. Of course, she said all of this with no more real understanding of the full extent of the damage that had been done, than I had. But, she had her opinions and felt that she should voice them.

As the big day got closer, even though I remained hopeful, eventually I was told that I would not be going home for Christmas. I was told that I would be spending it in Saint John, in the same room and in the same bed that I had been in for the past few weeks. I was also told that the balance of my recovery, once I was discharged from Saint John Regional, would be spent in the Moncton Hospital. What are you talking about? I don't need all of that! I just want to go home and get ready for Christmas. Don't you realize how disappointed my mother will be? I could not understand what was happening. Are you telling me that not only am I staying in Saint John for Christmas but then once I leave here, I am going to be in the Moncton Hospital? For who knows how long? I'm fine! Get me up and let me go to the bathroom! I'll show you!

I started to get very depressed. I felt depressed and trapped. I couldn't move. I couldn't do anything. I was completely reliant on someone else for every basic life sustaining task and function. The nurses could tell that I was so very sad. They would come in and tell me jokes and stories as often as they could trying to lift my spirits. They were absolute angels! They even got together and decorated my room for Christmas. In Saint John, the staff were not allowed to bring in decorations from outside of the hospital. Perhaps it was a sanitary issue. But that didn't stop some of the nurses from sneaking a few items in. Sshhhh, don't tell anyone! They put lights around my television and hung some cute ornaments from the ceiling. My favourite was a giant snowflake that one of the nurses cut out from some paper they had in the nurses station. She would make these lovely pieces of art when she took her breaks and then hung them from the ceiling in my room. They were all complete Angels to me and I will remain forever grateful! All of a sudden it started to feel a little like Christmas!

Derek has never been big into Christmas. He has always said that he could care less about gifts and presents. They simply were not important to him. He just liked getting together and having a nice meal and a bottle of wine. He said that Christmas had just become another commercialized holiday and he did not really wish to participate in that aspect of it. Truly, I think he just went along with whatever I wanted to make me happy.

For years, we decided to buy something for the house instead of buying individual gifts for one another. On the odd year, we might do a few stocking stuffers but it was more to appease my mother because we always spent it with her, as she was alone. So, on Christmas morning Derek showed up with my mother ,of course, and he was carrying an unusual number of bags. The tears are flowing just thinking about it, as I write these words. The man had gone out and bought some presents for both me and my mother. He even bought wrapping paper and wrapped them to make things just a little more festive. He thought that it would brighten our spirits and maybe distract me from my reality, even if for just a moment or two.

It wasn't the presents that filled my heart with utter joy, love and appreciation. It was the thought and effort that he put forth. I was in aww at the fact that he thought of doing this considering everything that had been going on. I love that man!

I felt so awful that I wasn't able to get him anything before all this happened. He said that the only gift he needed was for me to be here with him. He said that I was his Christmas miracle. I did truly feel that way. All of a sudden, it felt like Christmas! It was snowing outside and we were together and that was all that mattered!

The doctors and nursing staff also said that I was a miracle. I was told that less than 5% of the people who experience what I had gone through survive. I was young and had a really good reason to live. I will continue to fight for my life and for really living, with every step of my journey. I am used to it because I have had to fight, dig and scratch just to survive my whole life. It is all that I have ever known, since the time I was born. For me, being rejected, shamed, devalued and never heard, from the beginning, taught me a very valuable lesson, at a very young age. It taught me that in order to survive one must fight and fight hard for what they want and what they need, to make it in this world. My life with Derek seemed to come easy. His love and support taught me that not all people are mean or evil.

Christmas day was a good day! There was no dialysis that day. The hospital operated on a skeleton crew. More people could be called in, but if it was necessary. I kept thinking about how we were all so far removed from our usual Christmas experiences. Derek wouldn't even get a traditional Christmas meal. The thoughts of this made me sad. I was being tube fed and couldn't talk or even get out of bed but, I was alive! As the day passed by and was coming to an end, I didn't want to say goodbye. I wanted so badly for Derek to stay. I missed sleeping beside him and rolling over in the middle of the night to find him there. I realized just how comforting it was after being alone for so many lonely nights in the hospital.

Just the same, Derek looked exhausted and I knew he needed to get some rest and something to eat. I guess he had picked up some cooked chicken and salad at one of the local grocery stores and left it in the fridge in their hotel room for supper that night. As everything would be closed that day and evening. I was glad they were prepared but I could tell that Derek was more tired than hungry. I don't think he had much of an appetite the whole time we were in Saint John. He just ate what he needed to in order to survive. The stress of it all likely killed his appetite and any desire for substance, I think.

After Christmas, the nurses told me that they wanted to get me up and sitting in a special chair that they could strap me into. Their hope was that the doctors would see me building strength and it would get me one step closer to being transferred to the Moncton hospital. They said that they had to see me looking more lively and alert. I still wasn't what they considered stable, but if I was strong enough to sit up for a bit then maybe I could make the ambulance ride back to Moncton. Where the local medical team could take over my case and my care.

During my stay in Saint John the nurses had to help me breath by using a suction device to remove the fluid that would build up in the tubes of my trach and in my airway. This build up of fluid made it hard for me to breath and when the tubes would start to fill up, there was a gurgling noise that told us it was time. I fought for every breath and so breathing got even more difficult if this wasn't done several times a day. One day a young trainee came in to do my suction. She had been told before hand not to go down too far with the tube, because doing so could affect my heart rate and possibly even stop my heart. Well the first time, she went too far and my heart rate dropped dangerously low. Then, the second time, you guessed it, she went too far and my heart stopped. Derek was outside, in the falling snow, installing a new battery in our van so he could get back and forth to the hotel and my mother was in the room when this took place. The nurses escorted her out of the room very quickly and then called Derek.

I just remember going to that lovely limbo place again... Then all of sudden, the next thing I remember is waking with a nurse straddling me on the bed performing CPR with all her might. I recall looking at her as she was pressing down very hard while counting. I noted that her eyes were closed and all I could do was try to tap her by moving my left hand. I was trying to get her attention and tell her that I was okay and that I really needed her to stop because it was hurting me. Finally, she opened her eyes and quickly removed herself. She was very worked up and I'm sure that her adrenaline was pumping. Speaking of which as she was climbing down off me, Derek come running into the room with look of rage on his face. He was clearly upset and was pacing like a caged cat. Needless to say that trainee did not do my suction ever again. He was not angry at her specifically, but after all that we had been through up until this point, his reaction was definitely escalated.

I was all for trying to get into this chair that nurses had

suggested. It looked like a large pink recliner on wheels with straps, to hold a person in. I remember them bringing it into my room and as they started the process of transferring me into it, I quickly realized just exactly how weak I really was. As I recall, it took three people to get me into it. It was a real chore and I was completely exhausted just trying to help the process along, never mind sitting up in it for an hour. But, if it got me closer to going home, I was going to do everything I could to stay in it as long as possible, so the doctor could see me.

The nurses got me into the pink recliner twice. I had asked if I could try sitting in a regular chair but they didn't think that I would have the strength to hold myself in it. I did try to get into one with some help, but it was clear that is was going to required far more strength that I had, at that point. The pink recliner was much safer and the idea worked, the doctor saw me in it twice and figured I would be strong enough to survive the transfer and ambulance ride back to Moncton.

I was sent to the Medical and Surgical Intensive Care Unit (MSICU) at the Moncton Hospital on the 28th of December. Which was also the anniversary of my dear beloved Bear's death, so many years before. It made me think that she was with me. Finally, I would get to go back to my home town after almost six weeks in Saint John. I felt like nothing was going to stop me now.

This news made us both very happy. Derek would finally be able to sleep in our bed again and the cats would be glad to have him back home. I rested a little easier knowing he was going home. This also meant that I may have less dialysis, if any at all, once I was transferred. I was hoping for none and I got my wish. I was elated! That news absolutely made my day. I started to feel like I could see a tiny little light at the end of a very dark corridor.

In the early hours of the morning, on the day I was transferred back to Moncton, I mistakenly pulled my feeding tube out. My left arm had become a little more mobile and from what I remember I had an itch. Somehow I got the tube wrapped up with my hand and it got yanked out. Honestly, I was glad. I will never forget the after taste of that liquid as it ran down into my belly. I was mostly laying down and it tasted like it was running backward up into my throat. It was a very unpleasant taste and I was always very nauseous because of it and the cocktail of drugs I was on. That constant feeling, mixed with this food in a bag that, to me, looked like creamed vomit was disgusting. It was disgusting and I hated it. But, it kept me alive and for that I am thankful.

The next tube that I wanted gone was the fecal management system. I was not going to Moncton with that still in. In fact, I was not going anywhere with that still in. I would use every ounce of energy that I could muster laying on a bed pan, just so that I could get rid of that painful mid evil torture device. I wanted it gone!! My bottom was so sore and raw that I could barely stand it. In fact, my frequent tears were mostly from the pain that the use of that device had inflicted on me. So, before going to Moncton, the fecal management system was removed. Oh, what a happy day it was! I had to keep the catheter in but that was tolerable and besides I was sure it was just a matter of time before that would be taken out as well.

The respiratory therapist had been working with me during the day and was getting me to take a couple of different puffers trying to increase my lung capacity and function. I still had the trach but they wanted to disconnect it from the machines so I would be breathing on my own. I would keep it in but it would not be hooked up to the ventilator. This way, if something did go wrong on the trip back to Moncton, the paramedics could help me to breathe until I reached the hospital. In addition, the doctors in Saint John figured they would let the Moncton hospital staff decide what the next step should be, concerning the trach. It really didn't bother me that much, except for the fact that I couldn't communicate very well. In preparation for my ride, they did not want me to be reliant on any machines. So I took my puffers as often as they wanted me to and did whatever I could, to gain strength for my trip.

The next issue that had to be addressed before me being transferred, was my right hand and arm. As you might remember, my right hand was cut open in three spots and my arm was cut open from my wrist to elbow on the inside, so that it could drain the fluid that had been built up. I couldn't leave the Saint John hospital with that wide open, as the chances of infection were far too great!

The plastic surgeon came in with his interns to take a look at how things were progressing. He introduced me to one of his interns and informed me that they would be leaving the two cuts on the top of my hand open to heal on their own but the incision on the inside of my hand and thumb would be stitched along with cut to my arm. The young intern was very pleasant while stitching me up. He was joking and telling me that he was going to make it beautiful by adding some "twigs and berries" along the stitches, to be decorative. He made me laugh! I think he knew that I was fully aware of the scar that I would be left with and he was trying to make light of the situation. Honestly, I thought to myself this is just going to be another scar to add to my collection and it was the least of my worries. As long as I was able to use my hand and arm again, I would be happy. All of which was still completely unknown, at that time.

I watched some, as he worked at putting the stitches in but it was pretty gruesome to watch because, I could see right to the bone. He just kept talking and telling me stories as he put over 35 stitches in my arm. Those were just the ones that I could see. I know there were more under the skin to hold the many layers together. Also, he put at least six stitches on the inside of my hand and in my thumb muscle. It made me a little queasy at times to watch what he was doing. So when I felt a little nauseous, I would just look away. I did not need for anything to slow the progress of my transfer and getting sick to my stomach might have done just that. So I decided to play it safe. I had not had anything in my stomach for some time because I pulled the feeding tube out and they did not put another one back in. Which I was just fine with. But, I could have done some damage to the trach or aspirated on the bile if I had become sick to my stomach. In the end, I was very pleased that these incisions, which had been open for so long, were finally closed up.

The paramedics came up to my room with the gurney to get me and I could feel butterflies in my stomach. Derek was smiling from ear to ear. If at all possible, I think Derek was more excited than I was. He was so excited he almost forgot his guitar in my room. He used to play softly for me in the evening. It helped me from going insane, not to mention it was soothing for both of us. Some days when I think back to what the whole experience put him through, the guilt and shame almost consumes me. I know I didn't have a widow maker heart attack on purpose and the doctors say it was a freak thing that could have happened to anyone. But it didn't happen to anyone. It happened to me and Derek paid the price right along with me.

I lived my life making a lot of bad choices and if I could go back and change those unhealthy choices I would. The sad reality is that I can't and now I must live with the fact that I have heart failure and will not live as long as most people would. I won't grow as old with Derek as I once thought I would. Looking back on my past, I could have changed so much. Ignorance is no excuse and now the piper has to be paid.

The paramedics who came to take me back to Moncton were based out of Moncton. In fact, we knew one of them personally. He had been married to a very close friend of ours. We were all shocked to see one another. What are the chances? I started to feel a little more comfortable knowing who was taking me home. Our friend drove and teased me, as he always did, while the other nice young man kept an eye on me during the trip. Derek and my mother followed along behind in their own vehicles.

The ride back to Moncton was exhausting for me, not to mention uncomfortable. Those little beds they strap you to are hard and I had lost 80 pounds while I was in Saint John. Some was fat and some of it was muscle tissue. My weak muscles and frail bones felt every bump. The nice young man who sat in the back with me kept saying he was so sorry for the uncomfortable accommodations. I didn't care how uncomfortable it was. I was just happy to be going home!

I now try to live every day making choices that will help and improve my health. I now try to do this, rather than continue to give of myself where I can no longer afford to give. Or, extending myself beyond my limitations, which is and always was, to my own detriment. I still want to help others. But now, I have learned that there has to be balance in everything. There has to be a measure on it. I can no longer just pour until there is nothing left in the bottle. Some people will never understand this and some will never even try. I still have some people who expect me to do what *they* think I should, so that it makes things easier for them. Things that will make *their* life better. Things that make their life better, without a consideration for me. I have decided not to give anymore to these people or these situations. I have learned that there is no end to it. They will take as much as I am willing to give and that's okay. I can accept that they are who they are, and, they in turn, must now accept that I am who I am.

I need to live my own life without expectations from others. Don't get me wrong, if I commit to something, I will follow through. But, those old patterns of doing things and giving just to please others because they expect it, are now done. They are a thing of the past. You must earn my love, time and respect. If you don't, I do not have the time of day for you. Those who have taken advantage of my kindness in the past. Those who have mistaken my kindness for weakness, will now have to find another to be at their beck and call. It is self-preservation time for this girl. I am now looking after me!

I enjoy doing little things to make people smile and I will never stop trying to do just that. Especially when a friend is in need. It fills me up and completes me to help in this way. My hope is that in writing this book, it can help people who are struggling with similar things, to make better choices for themselves. In reading my story and coming to understand what stress can do to a person both physically and mentally, maybe it can help them to live a happier more balanced life. Let my story be a lesson for others so that they may never know the heart ache and pain that I have endured.

I was never so glad to see the inside of the MSICU at the Moncton hospital. It seemed that I knew about half of the nurses who worked there. Some of them were friends and some of them were or had been grooming clients, at one time or another. It seems that being a client's groomer can put you in a position of feeling close, to not only the dog, but to the family also. Most people who have pets feel that they are part of the family and they need to know that they can trust you to take care of them just as they would. Trust is an important part of grooming for both the dogs and the owners. I had always made a point to get to know both of them, as well as I could. I still miss some of the connections and relationships that I used to have with my clients and their families. In fact, I am still in touch with some of them.

As they wheeled me into the MSICU, Derek came right in behind us. Eventually, they got me into my room and onto a more comfortable bed. There were other nurses coming and going and introducing themselves as well as the doctor who was on duty that day. Everyone was doing their best to get up to speed on my complicated case. Some of them seemed a little nervous that I was there. I think that maybe they were concerned that I was not as stable as maybe they had hoped I would be, considering what I had already gone through. A little later on in the day, the doctor on duty came in to my room and told me that he had just finished reading through my entire chart and getting up to speed on my case and situation. At which point, I knew I was going to be okay. I knew I was going make it. The extent of my recovery was still uncertain. But, I was determined that I would be going home as soon as I could! So let's get on with the healing!

I was very tired from the trip so, in between the medical staff coming and going, I tried to nap a little. I was still unable to communicate very well, so I was happy that Derek was there to answer any and all questions they had. I just laid there and listened mostly. They had a plan and I was willing to go along with it. After all the medical system had saved me and got me back here. I was going to give it my absolute best!!

# CHAPTER 12

## *The RT*

So we've gone through some initial introductions in the MSICU and we've discussed a bit of a plan, but I'm still not completely settled yet. I've been there for a little over an hour and still my trach is wide open to the air, I'm getting tired and it's starting to get harder to breath. We were told that the respiratory therapist (RT) is on her way, about an hour earlier. Derek can see that I am getting tired and struggling to breath more and more, as the time passes. So, Derek being Derek, he starts stirring things up and before you know it, there is the respiratory therapist present and I am all hooked up and ready to settle in for the night and get some rest.

She apologized for the delay and explained that she was very busy today and was trying to get everyone looked after before her shift ended and the night shift RT arrived, to take over. As she is talking and saying the night shift RT, Derek's energy changed immediately. Having one of those feelings of his, he decided to say good night to me so I can get some much needed rest and leave for home. Or, so I thought.

As it turned out, he was unable to shake this feeling of his and decided to wait in the hall for the arrival of the night shift RT. Which took some time, about an hour and a half or so, as I understand it. All of a sudden, when the RT did arrive,

Derek's feeling was explained. It was the very same RT who uttered the words, "just call it already", when Derek was on the floor kneeling beside my lifeless body in the ER, on the day of my heart attack. This very same one who is now going to be looking after my well being, on my first night back in Moncton. It was quite unsettling for Derek. He was about to leave me in the care of a bunch of new people, after having been so close to our medical team in Saint John, and this RT was now in charge of the most important aspect of my survival right now.

As he walked toward Derek, down the long hall way toward to the MSICU, there was very little time to make a decision on how best to approach this situation. In the end, as he got within speaking distance, Derek decided on his approach. He firmly reminded this individual of who he was and who I was and that he remembered, explicitly, what had been said in the ER. Then Derek offered to shake his hand, which he accepted. As they locked hands, he looked him straight in the eye, squeezed his hand until he winced and then thanked him for providing me with the absolute best of his care during the night hours to come.

The next day, after having some rest, the plan was to remove my trach and evaluate what and how I was able to swallow. Which at the same time, would give us the opportunity to evaluate my speech. Could I talk? What sounds could I make? Could I be heard, or understood?

I thought it would hurt when the trach was removed, but I was pleasantly surprised. The relief I felt from it no longer being there was an incredible feeling. They just pulled it out, cleaned around the area and put a bandage over it. That was it! I thought maybe the hole in my neck would have to be stitched up? But nope, they just put a bandage over it, which was a welcomed surprise. They changed it frequently, cleaning it ever so gently so that I did not get an infection in that area. It always felt good when they cleaned and swabbed that area of my neck. I was very surprised at just how quickly the hole healed over.

My speech pathologist was a kind young woman with a great sense of humour. She told me not to expect to hear my normal voice when I tried to speak. She explained that because the tubes had been in for such a long time, that it would be a long road to regain the original tone of my voice or have any amount of volume. She said that she was unsure if I would ever be able to sing again and thought that only time would tell. She was, however, sure that I would be able to speak. She said that it would just be a matter of time and patience, along with some vocal exercises, on my part. The first time I tried to speak the noise I made was more of a raspy whisper. The sound was so quiet that I could barely hear it myself, but at least I made a noise. It was a start and I considered it a big win!

I think that at this point, it would be good for me to remind you all that, as I mentioned earlier, I have ALWAYS been a big talker and usually a fairly loud one at that. So to hear something, anything, after having no voice at all or being able to speak a word for several weeks, was very exciting for me!

I knew by the feel and sound of my voice that it would be a long time before I got my voice back to what it used to be. But, it was a start and I would not give up. I was told that my voice may never be the same again due to the length of time that the tubes were in. It was thought that there could have been some permanent damage done. I am happy to report though, that at the time of this writing, almost five years later, I am singing again! My voice is not quite the same as it once was and it has been a very long road, but I can SING!

The next step was to figure out if I would be able to swallow. Remember now, I have not had any nourishment for 3 days because I had pulled my feeding tube out before leaving Saint John. This next test was very important because I needed nourishment. I still had an IV in, but if I was to continue to heal my body needed nutrients. The concern at that point, was that if I swallowed something and it went into my lungs rather than in my stomach, I could aspirate. Which could lead to all kinds of potential problems. Pneumonia for instance, which nobody wanted. Especially me!

I was so excited! I could just imagine myself eating a big piece of prime rib steak, cooked to perfection, once I was on solid foods again. I really love steak and oh how I had missed it! For now, however, I would be happy just to have water and lots of it! Without having to suck, or chew it from a dampened face cloth. Lol.

The test was going to be done with a purple popsicle that had been melted, in a cup, in the microwave. It was thick and disgusting looking, but the thought was that if I could swallow some of this warm purple slop, without it going down the wrong pipe and choking on it, then I could start to have a liquid diet. Her thought with using this method was that if I coughed up any purple stuff then we would know that some of it had gone into my lungs. It made sense to me, it didn't look very appealing, but it made sense. I managed to swallow a couple of mouth fulls and didn't cough up any purple stuff, so the decision was made to start me on very soft foods and liquids, in small quantities. I was so excited!

Once the order was given that I could have liquids and soft foods again, it was time to start filling out the menus and get some grub up in here! I tried many different things but nothing seemed to taste right to me. It was as if my taste buds had taken a long vacation and were not interested in coming back.

Even water tasted weird to me. During my time in Saint John, well, the parts I can remember at least, all I could dream about was having a big tall glass of cool water and now, that day had finally come. My dream had become a reality. All of the build up, the waiting, the scheming, the hatching of elaborate plans, it was all about to become a reality. Pour me a big glass and watch me go. I got the cup up nice and close to me and I tried to hold onto it, as best I could at least. I got the straw in my mouth. I took nice big sip, and wait for it. All I could taste was ash! I was so disappointed!!

I think that the medications I was on were playing tricks on me and that my body was still adjusting to everything. Not to mention that I had not had anything by mouth, except for whatever face cloth drippings I could steal, or had my teeth brushed in weeks. No wonder my taste buds took a vacation! It was a very long time before anything really tasted good to me!

Derek brought in some popsicles for me and left them in the fridge freezer in the MSICU. This way I could have one whenever the mood struck me. The nurses were always so great about bringing me things and looking after me, when Derek wasn't there. Oh, and of course, he took out all of the purple ones. Yuck! The other flavours still tasted weird to me, but the cool frozen treat in my mouth was heaven and seemed to quench my thirst.

One night, after Derek had left, I was laying in my bed and thought to myself that a fruit cup might taste good. There had been a four pack of peaches sitting on my bedside table for a couple of days now. Yes, I thought, a fruit cup is just what I need. That would taste good! I had the bright idea that I could have one and do it by myself. This way I wouldn't have to bother the nurses to help me or ask them to get me a popsicle.

It was great thought and I was proud of myself for coming up with it! However, there's more to the story. I was still very weak. My right hand and arm still were not working well, at all. My left hand was all that I could use, somewhat effectively. So, I tried and tried to hold the fruit cup with my right hand and arm. I clutched it between my arm and my body while trying to use my left hand to open the sealed tinfoil covering on the top. I'm sure that I worked on trying to get that damn cup open for a half hour. Now patients, you see, is not my strong suit and after getting extremely frustrated. I lifted the cup up to my mouth and just bit through the sealed foil covering. Finally, I broke through the seal and of course when I did half of the juice spilled all over me. But, I got the other half into me and I managed to swallow it down. Which made it much easier to get to the fruit! Ahh the yummy sweet goodness! What a sight it must have been.

Eventually, I did have to call my nurse in. I was all wet and sticky, from the syrup and could not possibly rest in such a state. When she arrived in the room, her first words were, "Oh my, what have you been up to?". Looking back now, I have to laugh although at the time I was seeing red! It was a battle of wills between me and the fruit cup. I mean I had to win! After all, *I* was the one with the brain. I told Derek about my big adventure the next day and we both had a good laugh over it.

I discovered that learning to hold utensils again was something that took a lot of practice. Some days, I must have looked like some kind of cave woman, with no manners at all. Derek was great at helping me but I had to learn how to do it myself. I had lost all control of my motor skills and had to learn how to hold and use them all over again. It proved to be quite a challenge. I had to learn to use them again and actually get food in my mouth, that is. Instead of on the table, the floor or on the wall! It took weeks before I was able to actually use the utensils effectively, and months before I was able to master them again. Some days, I just gave up on eating because it was so tiring. I must admit though, hunger is a great motivator. Each morning's hunger brought with it a whole new round of inspiration and motivation.

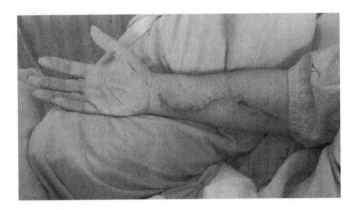

Initially, I just picked at my food. I ate when I had too, but my desire was not for how things were tasting to me. It was for how I remembered them tasting! The nurses were concerned that I wasn't getting enough nourishment and nutrients. They would always look at my tray and ask me how much I ate, to which I would always say that I had enough. There is no need to worry, however. I am happy to report that food now tastes as good as it used to. Maybe too good, in fact! I have to watch myself closely. I have managed to keep my weight at a healthy level which is something that I am happy with. Maintaining a healthy weight is something that has been a real challenge for me, my whole life. Please don't use food to comfort or console your young children. It can really create challenges for them later on in life. After a lot of hard work and discipline, I have been able to overcome those damaging patterns and food associations. It seems that my palate has developed some and I have cravings for foods that I did not even care for, before my heart attack. It just took some time and adjustment.

My hair

The first couple of days in the MSICU were full days of tests, questions, assessments and evaluations. I was exhausted all the time, but I knew that I would have to keep fighting hard to continue to improve and be able to go home again. There was one thing that I thought could help me feel a little better as I fought on, however. At the time of my heart attack, I had very long hair. While I was in Saint John, however, my hair was the least of my medical team's concerns. They were concerned with keeping me alive not making sure my hair was well groomed. As a result, my hair knotted up into a big ball on the back of my head. I wasn't even able to rest my head comfortably on the pillow because of this knotted mess. The nurses in Saint John tried to brush it out a couple of times but were not successful. In fact, I think it just made it worse. Blood had drained into it and it had not been washed in about six weeks. It just seemed to get more and more tangled, knotted and tight, as each day progressed. It was to the point where something now had to be done. Derek made a call to one of our friends, who is a hair dresser. He asked her if she would consider coming to the hospital to cut my hair for me. As there was absolutely no hope of saving it. She agreed to come in and do whatever she could with it.

Upon her arrival, Derek and a nurse held me in a sitting position so that she could cut the enormous knotted ball from the back of my head. She worked as fast as she could the whole time. I think she could tell that it was taking every bit of energy I had, just to stay in that position. I can still recall her apologizing, repeatedly, for how much she had to cut off. Honestly, I truly didn't care at that point. I just needed to have the knotted mess removed, so that a nurse could wash my hair. I just knew that I would feel so much better afterwards. I'm sure that it only took a few short minutes for her cut it all out. But, it seemed like hours to me, being held up in that position in my weakened sate. My friend was able to get the mess cut out and everyone agreed that, even if it wasn't perfect, it was good enough. It was a hell of a lot better than it had been. That's for sure! At least now, I could get it washed and would be able to rest much better, as a result. My friend offered to come back and fix it up when I was feeling a little stronger, which I thought was so very kind of her. I will never forget her kindness. Derek walked her out and tried to pay her for her time and trouble, but she would not even discuss it. Thank you my beautiful friend, you helped me so very much and made me feel human again!

So instead of long haired Tanya, I was now short and sassy Tanya. A character that I play quite well, if I do say so myself. It felt and looked great! It reminded me of how much the small things in life are to be appreciated and not taken for granted! Little things like being able to brush my own hair and rest my head comfortably on a pillow before falling to sleep at night. I felt a greater appreciation for absolutely every good feeling I had.

So, after I had a little time to rest, the nurse washed my hair and it felt amazing. It felt like it was the first time I had ever had this done. The feeling of a soft touch to the back of my head was wonderful. I slept very well that night!

Two days later, I started to feel sores forming on the crown and back of my head. These sores started to drain liquid and form scabs. With this new development, I was sent to one of the dermatologists in the hospital and after seeing her, it was decided that there should be a couple of biopsies done. I had not had my hair washed in weeks and with the knotted mess on the back of my head, the skin had not been able to breath. So, who knew what type or amount of bacteria had gathered under the knotted mess. As it turned out, the biopsies did not show much, so we kept the sores clean and they eventually healed up. The hair never grew back, however. I now have two large bald spots on the back of my head. As long as I don't cut my hair too short, they are always covered though. Sometimes, if the wind comes up they can become exposed, but that's okay. These two little bald spots, were then and still are, the least of my worries. They are just a couple more reminders of what can happen when you let your life become too far out of balance.

Little by little, I was starting to feel like maybe life could become enjoyable again. It had been years, if ever, in fact, since I had really taken the time to truly be present. Present, in the moments of my own life. I was always just going through the motions of each day and was not truly feeling each one of them. I was not really feeling the value of it all. This experience had reminded me of the true importance of being present in one's life. These circumstances had forced me to do so, whether I really thought I wanted to or not. The fact was, that I was not going home until I was truly present. Until I was present and well. Both physically and mentally. I had to truly become present in my situation because it was all I had left. I had to hold onto the fact that I was alive and that I now had a second chance. I had a second chance to really live a well balanced and present life. This time, I would get it right!

A counsellor came into the hospital to talk to me shortly after I was admitted to the MSICU in Moncton. I believe it was her job to check in on patients who had gone through traumatic, life altering medical events such as mine. She was very kind and soft in her approach. She was amazed at my story and wanted to know how I thought I was coping, mentally. At the time, I thought I was doing quite well. That was until I started to try to talk to her. I quickly realized that I felt like I had done this to myself. When I told her this, her response was "now you are free!". To this day, I still think about that when I start feeling down. I think about those words and the way she said them to me. What does it really mean to be "free"? How does that feel? What is that like? I guess it must be different for everyone. I don't think that I have ever felt it. Well, at least not up until that point in my story.

I feel that I have struggled mentally with the feeling of not being enough, no matter how much I did or gave, my entire life. I have never felt like I was enough. Enough to be a good daughter, or sister or friend, and certainly never felt like I was enough to myself. What is enough? When will I get it right? Will I ever be enough? Have you ever thought about it?

The constant messages of condemnation and disapproval that I received through being ignored, shamed and devalued had a real impact on my well being. Being compared to others, not being smart enough, or not standing straight enough were all messages that I very much took to heart and punished myself for. Repeatedly! For the longest time, I believed that not valuing myself, and my contribution to the world, with more regard, was a fault of my own. I believed that it was just another thing that I wasn't doing right. I believed that it was a flaw, or something that I did to myself. I now know the difference and I struggle every day to change those thought patterns. The ones that have plagued me my whole life. Humans are the only species that can take an infant, raise them to believe that they are irreparably flawed, give them no guidance or suggestion for correction and then convince them that it is their own fault. Please be kind to children!

I now know that bad habits can be broken. Old patterns can be changed. It can be done! It does however, take time, discipline and patience. Most of all, it takes self-love. This is something that I have always had great difficulty with. How can I love me? I'm so flawed. I can never do anything right. Nothing I do is ever good enough. No one else really seems to truly love and accept me for me. How can I be worthy of my own love, when I can't make others happy? I mean, that is what life is all about isn't it? Those were my very first life lessons, after all. You must always put wants and needs of others, ahead of your own Tanya! Overcoming this and moving beyond these thought patterns is something, that I now know, I will have to continue to work on, daily, for the rest of my life.

So I was going through the motions and fighting as hard as I could. But, I found myself struggling with the question of, who am I now? Who or what would I be now? After this, another huge and traumatic life altering event?

Before I knew it, New Year's Eve was upon us. The nurses in the MSICU told Derek that he could stay to ring in the new year with me, if he wanted. I think they knew it would brighten my spirits to have him there at midnight. I reflected back to all those New Year's Eve gigs that he had played with his bands, early on in our life together. I thought about how I would always be dancing and enjoying having fun with friends and then when the clock struck midnight, I would run up on stage to give him a big kiss and wish him a happy year. Wait, run? I used to run! Will I ever run again? I'm not so sure. Will I ever dance again? Because, at this point all I know is that I can't move my legs. Well actually, I can't move them, or feel them. How is this going to work? What is this year going to bring?

As the night went on, we talked and watched some television specials covering New Year's celebrations around the world. We were just enjoying every moment together, alone. Alone at last, well except for the nurse, but she made herself scarce that evening. We were together. We were back in our home town and that was all that I could have hoped for in that moment.

Instead of clinking our drinks together at the strike of midnight, we clinked our popsicles together and kissed. It meant more than words can express. My heart was full! It was filled with my love and appreciation for him! Once our popsicles were gone, I suggested that he go home to get some rest as I knew he would be back bright and early the next morning. I didn't really want him to leave but I was concerned that he wasn't getting enough rest. He agreed that tomorrow was another day and that he would be back.

## Neurologist

As the holiday season wound down for another year, the next step was to have my legs evaluated by a neurologist. The swelling in my legs had been a huge issue and I hadn't been out of bed more than a couple of times, for about an hour each time, since my heart attack. My legs and feet were numb and I was unable to move them. This was very troublesome for both me and the doctors. Derek was in my room bright and early that day because we knew I was seeing the neurologist and he did not want to miss the appointment. My communication skills were still not the best and he wanted to hear what the doctor had to say. Two sets of ears were a good idea, as there was still a lot of information coming at us everyday. In addition, he could help me to communicate with the doctor as he got really good at reading my lips and interpreting the sounds that I made. In addition, because I was still on a lot of pain medication, it was good to have him there to hear and retain everything that was being said. I was thankful he was with me!

The doctor's assistant came in and performed some tests on me. During which, I was connected to a machine that monitored my nerves as they were being stimulated with electrical pulses. Basically, my nerves had a small amount of electrical current put to them and the machine recorded the reactions to this current at different levels of intensity. Once she completed her portion of the testing, the doctor came in and introduced himself. He was a very pleasant man with a great bedside manner. He also had a fantastic sense of humour. I really liked him! He then conducted some tests involving the same machine with more electrical current put to my nerves. He then stuck little tiny needles into my legs and turned on a sound option, so that he could hear the sounds that were being created when my nerves reacted.

As he turned the volume up he looked at me with a most serious and puzzled look and asked me what those sounds were. With an equally puzzled look on my face, and after looking at Derek, I turned to him and said "I don't know you are the doctor?" He laughed a big hearty laugh and as he did, I quickly realized that he was teasing me. We all had a good chuckle over it. I think it was his way of trying to lighten the mood. I think he could sense that both Derek and I were a little nervous about the potential outcome of these tests, as I had been in bed so long and had so much swelling. The outcome of which had put a great deal of pressure on the branches of my sciatic nerves. He explained that it was as if my legs had fallen asleep for a month and a half. Usually when this happens to someone, they would feel it and adjust their position in order to relieve the pressure. In my case, however, I had been laying on these nerves for a very long time and there had been no movement to relieve the pressure for a little over six weeks. Therefore, the continuous pressure actually killed some of the nerve endings in my legs and feet.

Because so much time had passed, we were now in unfamiliar territory when it came to this, he said. In most cases, people are not immobilized for that length of time and as a result typically do not experience the same level of damage. So, when you watch a show on television that shows someone who has been in a coma for a long time, and then all of a sudden, they wake up and start walking around, that is crap! It doesn't work that way. After that amount of time, muscle mass is lost and mobility does not just come back like that. The doctor said that he thought it would take a very long time for the numbness to go away, if it went away at all. He said that it could take years. I then asked about my ability to walk and told him that I wanted to know his honest opinion. His response was that, IF I ever walked again it would be a long hard road. What was left of my working heart jumped right into my throat! I was devastated! All I could focus on was him saying, *IF*! I did not ask anymore questions, in fact, I think Derek and the doctor were still talking but I was in my own little world. There were all kinds of thoughts racing through my mind and I was really fighting hard to hold back the tears.

Once he was done with his evaluation, I was wheeled back to my room in the MSICU, while Derek followed silently. After we arrived and I was settled in, Derek spoke. He said there had been a lot of damage done to my legs and feet. I could barely speak. I went to a very dark place in my mind. How could I have let this happen, I thought? I started to cry and I cried all day and night. I was totally beside myself.

Then my mother came in, which made my mood worse. I told her what the doctor said and her response was that I should just be thankful that I was alive. It was like it didn't phase or upset her a bit. I think that she was, all the while, thinking that it would be a way for her to be around more, as I would now need her. At that time, I truly believed that she would have been just as happy if I had never walked again. That way, I would become dependent on her. Little did she know that I would never let that happen! I would die trying or go into a home before letting her become my caregiver. It would have been great for her however. She would be able to play the sympathy/attention card. Oh look at me and how wonderful I am, looking after my poor disabled daughter. This news almost seemed to make her happy. I could just tell. I know her, better than anyone! She did not stay as long that day. Which was good because I was in no mood for company and especially her foolishness and nonsense. The nurses did not even come around unless they absolutely had to. I could see on their faces that they felt sorry for me. Even Derek wasn't sure what to do or say. All I could think about was, how would I ever cope with this and find a way to go on. It was a rough night! I could tell Derek was exhausted but didn't want to leave me in such a state. I assured him that I would be fine, hoping that he would give in and go home to get some rest. I really did just need to be alone with my thoughts for awhile. It was one of the longest days and nights that I spent in the hospital. I wallowed deep in self pity.

The next day, I asked one of the male nurses if he would get me up to sit a chair. That was it! I had decided that I would do my very best to prove to myself, and everyone else, that I would walk again and it was going to start by getting in and out of a chair. I was told that it was already a miracle that I survived and had made to this point. No problem then, I will just make another miracle happen. I will walk again!

At that point, there was still the possibility that the nerves could slowly grow back and that I would regain some level of normal movement with my feet and toes. I will talk more about this part of my journey a little later on. For now, just know that the end result of all of this was that I would eventually walk again, with a condition known as foot drop. Foot drop is the inability to lift your foot and toes up, as you walk. With this condition, one is unable to lift one's toes up from the ground, while having one's heel remain firmly planted. In order to lift my toes high enough to clear the ground or floor, I have to lift my legs. I have to lift them high enough so that the dangling part of my foot will clear the ground and allow for forward movement without getting caught and causing me to trip and fall.

I spent almost two weeks in the MSICU before the doctors felt confident that I was strong enough to be sent to another floor. The goal was to get me on the fourth floor and into the rehabilitation unit. The problem was that in order to qualify for admittance into this unit, I had to spend two whole days and nights in a non ICU room, in another part of the hospital. I was sent to two different floors before getting settled into my somewhat permanent room in the rehab unit.

The first room they put me in was a little scary. When my family doctor came in, she told me they were moving me to another room, as soon as possible. Apparently, there had been some sort of outbreak in the same ward, on that floor and it just wasn't safe for me to be there. They were going to lock the ward down and she didn't want me to be stuck there with the risk of becoming more ill. I didn't even spend a whole night in that room before I was rushed to another floor. I was moved in the middle of the night and it was a little unsettling because Derek didn't know where I was. I was glad to be in a different section of the hospital, however.

The next room I was put in already had an older lady staying in the bed beside me. She wasn't very friendly and she kept peaking around the privacy curtain at me. I asked the nurse to speak to her as she was hard of hearing and trying to communicate with her with my whispering voice was pointless. The nurse politely asked her to stop invading my privacy. It didn't seem to matter to her though. She continued to do this and not only did it creep me out, but after awhile, it started to make me somewhat angry. I was trying to rest and she would just stare and glare at me. That is of course, until I would look over, then she would quickly let go of the curtain. She wasn't very good at hiding the fact she was being nosy. I really don't think she was even trying. Finally, I decided that I would fix this problem once and for all. I stared at the curtain with a mean look for almost an hour and sure enough, eventually she pulled the curtain back to see what I was doing. My mean, icy stare startled her and she almost fell out of her bed when she jumped back from the curtain. There we go, problem solved! The next time the nurse came in I told her what I had done. She laughed and then gave my roommate a piece of her mind. Then I laughed! It was a good day!

I think I recall being in that room for two nights before being moved to the fourth floor rehab unit. As I mentioned earlier, the fecal management system that had been used on me in Saint John created some very painful sores from the leaking waste. My skin was raw and very damaged in the entire area. The constant pain that it caused made it very hard for me to sleep. One particular night, after Derek had gone home, I was feeling very down and very uncomfortable. It was very late and I was feeling extreme pain and home sickness. I was crying when the nurse on duty came in to check on me. She was so sweet! She asked me what was wrong and I told her as I sobbed. I just wanted the pain to go away and most of all I wanted to go home! The nurse left the room and a few minutes later came back in with some cream and some warm water to wash me up. Even though she had the most gentle touch, it was so very painful and I flinched when she touched me. It really hurt, but there was something about the way she cleaned and dressed my wounds that was comforting to me. She reminded me of a young version of my grandmother. She was very caring and gentle, just like her. My Grammy was a nurse who had worked at the same hospital for many years.

As I lay there crying, she tried to sooth and talk to me. She was doing her best to help calm me down. She took some time after she was done, to just sit and talk with me. I think she did all she could to make me feel better. I will be forever grateful for the kindness she showed me on that very dark and lonely night. I know she had a lot of people to look after but she took the time for me, knowing I needed a little extra attention. The next day, I was moved to the fourth floor rehabilitation unit and I never saw her again.

My new space in the rehab unit was a bed in a large room with two other roommates. My bed was in the largest section of the room. I had a sink, a cabinet unit, room for a couple of chairs and a wheelchair. The room was located very close to the nurse's station because the doctor in charge of the unit was still a little nervous to have me there, at that point. He told me that he didn't think I was stable enough to be there yet and that they were going to have to keep a very close eye on me. The reason why I had such a large portion of the room was because I needed a wheel chair and space to learn how to work with it, in case I wasn't able to walk again. The room did have a shared bathroom, not that I was able to use it yet. I still had the catheter in and was still bed ridden. I was set up with a team of physio and occupational therapists who would come in to work with me at least twice a day.

The occupational therapist (OT) set me up with the wheel chair and some temporary braces for my legs and feet, to help keep them in the proper positions. She would visit with me at least once a day to work on every day maintenance and personal hygiene tasks. I would not be able to go home until the doctors knew that I could look after myself, even if I did have to use a wheelchair or some other type of mobility aid, like a walker for instance.

My days were very full and I made the most of every bit of help that was offered to me. Derek was asked to bring my sneakers in so that I would have them for my physio therapy. I recall that it was quite a chore to get them on my feet. I had not had anything on my feet except for socks for weeks and my feet were still very, very swollen. Every time my foot was put into the sneaker my toes would curl up under my foot because I had no control over them and could not keep them straight. Derek was the only one who seemed to have the knack for getting my feet into them. He would come early every morning to make sure I had them on my feet and I was ready to go. I think the nurses were thankful for his attention to me as they were very busy and it would free them up for other patients who were also in need of help. He wanted to be there to help me through every hurdle. He was my rock and it made me work all that much harder to get some mobility back so that I wouldn't be a burden or let him down. We have always been a team and I would not have gotten through this without him.

The OT fitted me for a wheel chair, which I did not think I would care for. But, it soon became a good thing. I was mobile again! With it, Derek could take me for walks around the hospital, when there was time. The wheel chair gave me independence again and a kind of mobility that I had missed. Other than porters and nurses taking me places on beds, I hadn't been mobile in weeks. I can recall the first time Derek took me outside of the unit in the wheel chair, I couldn't wipe the smile off my face. It was so nice to get out on a little tour.

Once I was settled on the fourth floor, I had a lot of friends and family who inquired about coming to visit. We decided that it was better to limit the number of visitors I had. I was either in rehab or resting and needed to spend my time getting better. Visits tired me out and there really was no time for socializing. I really didn't want people to see me like that anyway. It was a time when I felt like I had hit rock bottom.

The other thing that I did not want, was the "flying monkeys" coming in to spy on me, for my father. I still wasn't talking to him and I didn't want to be concerned about what they were telling him. If he wanted to know so bad he should have flown home from Switzerland and cut his visit with his step daughter short. If I truly had been of concern, he would have come to see me himself. Besides, my brother was keeping him somewhat informed, I guess. My brother said that he was willing to come home but that if I wouldn't see him there was no point. He didn't want to waist the money on the air fare. I guess maybe that says it all. My brother talked to Derek about it when I had my heart attack and Derek told my brother to tell my father to call him, if he wanted to know something about my condition. He never called.

My mother tried to come in every day, but I discouraged it

because she used to upset me so much. I was to avoid all stressful situations, considering my condition. One day, my mother came in and told me she heard that the community where we live had held a fund raiser for me at the church. She had first brought this up when I was still in the MSICU. I explained the situation to her, as I understood it, but that wasn't good enough. She was furious at me because she didn't know anything about it. I told her they didn't have a fundraiser. The people in the community just put some money in a card and gave it to Derek and I to try and help us out. It was a sweet gesture and it did help. I had already told her about this, weeks ago. But, she kept insisting that it was a fundraiser and she was upset because she didn't know about it. She was angry and just kept repeating it over and over again. I think the reason why she was so upset was because, in her mind, it somehow made her look bad. Her mind is a twisted place to visit and I never want to go there.

Once I was on the fourth floor, she came in one day and brought it up again. I lost it! She upset me so much that the nurse came in to see what all of the commotion was about. I think the nurse was ready to throw her out of the hospital. In fact, I almost asked her to do just that but didn't want to cause any more of a scene. Even my roommates couldn't believe the way she went on like that, about such a kind gesture. My mother accused me of lying to her and just would not let it go. Then, I had finally had enough! It was ridiculous, so I did all I could to discourage her from coming for any more visits. My whole life, she has either smothered me or ignored me. I sure was wishing for some ignoring, at that point. Good riddance already! I didn't need the extra stress of trying to keep her away from me. I mean really? So, with doing my best to keep her and her antics away, I then tried to focus on working hard on my rehabilitation. For which, I think my efforts were rewarded.

It was a long and very painful, hard road, but Derek was there when I took my first step. The smile on his face was priceless and one I will never forget. I was beyond happy to be upright and standing never mind taking a step toward my husband. I was assisted with a person on either side of me helping to hold me steady. But regardless, I took the step! Nothing was going to stop me now!

Day after day, I worked as hard as I could. I knew that if I could show the doctors and everyone on my medical team that I could look after myself, there was a good chance they would let me go home. I was determined to go home, even if it was in a wheelchair. Everyone kept saying it would be a long hard road and it was, but I wasn't giving up! I was going to do whatever it took to get home to Derek and my kitties. I kept thinking that the longer I was away, the more chance there was that my kitties wouldn't remember me. Jam was the oldest, at the time of my heart attack. She was four years old. Our bond was very strong and I figured she would probably remember me but she would likely be upset at that the fact I had been gone so long. Berry and Jelly were still kittens and only about eight months old when I up and disappeared. They were so young and had been left alone for so long, I wondered how would they react? I was fearful about it all but did my best not to over think it.

I had to just focus on what was right in front of me. My main goal was to get strong and mobile enough so that I could go home and be with them again. Absolutely as soon as possible!

# CHAPTER 13

## *The Long Road Home*

requently, in the early hours of the morning, during our
time in Saint John, when Derek was not sleeping. He
would communicate with one of his cousins who lives
in western Canada, in the beautiful province of Alberta. They
mostly talked via text message and with the time difference,
they were both awake. Initially, I met them all when they came
down for a family vacation in the late nineteen- nineties. A
couple of the cousins and I really seemed to hit it off and have
stayed in touch over the years. In addition, Derek and I went
out to visit them a couple of times. One of his cousins has a
fair bit of medical terminology back ground and had worked
in the field for some time. He found it very helpful to share the
things that were going on and the information he was getting
from my medical team, with her. She seemed to understand
the terminology and was able to help clarify some points. Also,
she was willing to discuss the ongoing strategy that was in the
works for me. She helped the process of determining which
questions to ask next and how best to guide the flow of my
care, in terms of the next steps required, which suggestions to
make and when and so on. Which seemed to help centre and
ground Derek, somewhat. Then, the next morning he had a
strategy for how to approach the things that were happening
and needed to be looked at or questioned that day.

Once I was back in Moncton, these two cousins decided to book flights and come to see me. They were hoping to maybe help out, in what we all hoped would be, the early days of me returning home. As it turned out, my release date would be much further along my journey than any of us had hoped, or anticipated. That didn't matter to them however, they still came to offer help and support where they could.

Upon their arrival, I was starting to get a little more comfortable in my rehab unit quarters and my busy daily schedule. My rehabilitation was a very long process and took a lot of my energy, so I felt quite tired most of the time. Regardless, their visit was just what I needed to lift my spirits. They came to the hospital every day to visit with me, in between my appointments, which were plentiful. That didn't seem to matter to them though. They came in with smiling faces and warm hearts. They would hang out in the common room or go to the cafeteria during the times when I was attending my therapy sessions and appointments. Then, as soon as I was finished, they would come back in and we would visit a little more. It was a sense of normal in a time when nothing else in my life was, or seemed like it would ever be again.

I have truly been blessed in having found sister like relationships on both sides of Derek's family. Though I felt that I tried, I was never able to develop any close relationships with any of my biological cousins or my sibling. But, that's okay because I have found great amounts of love and support with Derek and his family and friends.

The cousins from out west were extremely thoughtful in their preparations for the trip to see me. They told me that since I missed having a Christmas at home, they wanted to give me one while they were here visiting. They came bearing gifts and I got to have a Christmas celebration with them for the very first time. Their thoughtfulness and efforts touched me deeply! It wasn't the gifts you see. It was the thought and the fact that they travelled all that way to see Derek and I in person. It is a memory that I will always cherish and be thankful for. I hope that someday I can return the kindness they have shown us both!

While they were visiting, I started to develop some discomfort and redness in the middle of my back. It was like the skin had been irritated in some way. It was the type of irritation and redness that looked like chaffing or maybe a burn of some sort. I thought maybe it was from the soaker pads that were placed on my bed, underneath me. A soaker pad, as I call them, is large piece of very absorbent fabric that is sometimes placed between a patient and the mattress, in order to absorb moisture and liquids that may become present. Sometimes the edges of this pad would feel very rough on my skin, which of course was extremely dry at the time. This, in combination with mostly wearing hospital gowns that were always open in the back, seemed to be a possible logical explanation for what was this irritation. Or, so I thought at the time. In a matter of just a couple of days, it had turned into a large and angry looking red, square shaped patch. It felt like my back was on fire and was getting more painful by the day.

All of the nurses in the rehab unit and several of the doctors had a look at it. But, nobody really seemed to have an answer or possible explanation. It was like nothing they had ever seen before and they had little to no idea what it was or what could be causing it. The redness then started to break the skin down, and soon after, it started to form blisters. Which formed and then broke, and then formed and broke again. It was so painful that eventually, or should I say quickly, it got to a point where I could no longer lay on my back, because the pain was so intense.

As the days turned to weeks, the outline of the affected area seemed to be taking more of a square like shape. The doctors still seemed unsure of what this was or why it was presenting itself in the way that it was. There were some questions asked and some discussions had about whether or not it could be from the defibrillator pads, in particular when the pads were doubled, during resuscitation. Initially, this theory was met with some resistance and it was not thought by the doctors, that it could be a reasonable explanation for what was happening. So, at that point, it seemed that I would just have to continue to see the dermatologist and wait to see how things progressed.

After a bit more discussion, the decision was made to apply some different creams while changing the bandage and dressing on a daily basis. The hope was that this would help to start the healing process and keep it clean, as an infection in my back was the last thing I needed, at that time. I already had enough to deal with and adding another infection to my already heavily burdened immune system, in its compromised state, would have definitely slowed my overall healing progress. The scenario with my back was ongoing during my stay in the hospital and eventually got much, much worse. In fact, eventually, it put me back in the hospital again. I will talk more about the gory details of this situation in the chapters to come. But for now, let's get back to getting out of the hospital, for the first time.

Eventually, I was told that if I could get to the washroom and back unassisted, wash myself and look after getting my own meals, that I could have a weekend pass to go home. Wait, "you mean I could go home?". It was news that I had been dreaming of for weeks. Weeks that were starting to lead into months. As soon as I was told that I could possibly get a pass to go home, even if was just for the weekend, I worked even harder at achieving the criteria for this goal. I was not going to let anything stop me from getting a weekend pass. I really needed to go home! Even if it was only for a short visit and I would have to return after the weekend. It was enough to keep me focused and motivated.

The thought of Derek taking me home filled me with pure joy and excitement! It was almost more than I could stand. I caught myself wiggling in my seat with excitement, when I would think about it. I would lay awake at night dreaming of what it was going to feel like to *walk* through the doors of our home and greet my kitties. The three little fur balls that I had left behind months earlier. "How good that is going to feel!", I would dream, as I lay awake at night. Which was a regular, and in fact, daily occurrence for me then. I could only sleep for a couple of hours at a time and would then wake up crying in pain. It was accumulative pain. It was the pain from my liver healing, the terrible sore on my back, my arm and hand ached constantly and the pain in my back side from the damage done by the fecal management system. It was all so very painful that I felt defeated. I felt completely defeated and at times, I didn't know if I had the strength to go on.

But that news, the news that there was a chance for me to go home! The news that I was about to have the catheter removed and I was going to start working towards going home, was the only thought that kept me fighting. Crying was my only release and I could only do so in private, at night. I did not want Derek or the medical staff to see or hear me. There were times, however, when a tear would form and fall in front of them. But I tried to keep it brief. I thought I needed to make everyone think that I was okay. I thought I needed to give the *appearance* that I was okay and that everything was fine. But, in reality, it was not! Emotionally, I was just barely holding it together. How damaging keeping up *appearances* can be to one's self.

The rehabilitation unit program provided me with an opportunity to see a mental health professional. She was helpful in some ways, but I chose to share and reveal very little about me and my true state, to her. I was scared that if I did, it would slow the progress of my home visit. So, I did and said what was necessary to keep things moving forward. Some of our sessions were helpful. But, deep down inside, I knew that the issues, the scars and the stressful situations that had put me in this position, could not be resolved from a few talks with a psychologist. Come to think of it, we wouldn't even have gotten the file drawer unlocked with a few sessions. Let alone resolve anything?

The state of my mental health was and is still an ongoing and daily battle for me. Even after years of therapy and a lot of hard work. I mean, a lot of really hard work. My wounds run very deep, to the core of my soul! It feels like the damage can or will never be undone. I am just now *starting* to learn how to keep all of my demons at bay. There are still times when I have great difficulty staying focused on the right direction and the best approach for my mental health and well being. I find this especially difficult in situations where others want to tell me of their troubles and perhaps unload their burdens a little. On the one hand, I want to try to help and show them empathy. On the other hand, however, I want to scream and tell them that they have very little to be upset about. It feels like sometimes people forget, or maybe even "block out" what I have been through. In some cases, it seems like they are looking to be coddled or maybe validated. I don't know what it is. But, I do know that there are times when it makes me see red! There are days when I only talk to my animals. There are days when I just cannot sit through someone else showing me a bruise or telling me about their doctor's appointment or how someone hurt their feelings. Really? I mean come on people, pull yourselves together! After what I have lived through? I just cannot deal with the trivial issues that others have or are just so eager to share, some days.

I will say that I understand that not every human on this

earth tolerates hardships in the same way and there are some individuals, or personality types, who just don't deal with anything well. But, whatever happened to common sense? Where did that get off too? Are some people really just that insecure? Do they need to cry out for acknowledgement or constant attention for every little boo boo? I guess for many individuals in today's world that seems to be the case. This is why now, I choose to surround myself with a small group of people who seem to somewhat get it, or as well as anyone could at least, and have distanced myself from others. I am doing well just to keep my own head above water. Now, I find it best to reserve anything that I do have left to give, for those who do not take advantage of the situation. My fellow empaths are the only ones who I can truly relate to, at times.

The day they took the catheter out was a happy day. It meant I could use the bed pan at night and go to the bathroom, with some assistance, during the day. I slowly worked my way back to having some sense of independence. One very small, wobbly step at a time.

I can still remember the first time that I managed to go to the bathroom unassisted. I was able to pull myself up off of the toilet seat and into a standing position by using the pole that was right next to the toilet, in our rehab unit washroom. What a day to be celebrated! I HAD THE STRENGTH TO PULL MYSELF UP OFF OF THE TOILET AND INTO A STANDING POSITION! THIS WAS HUGE! Imagine, just for a second, how it would feel if you were at a point in your life where *that* was a monumental accomplishment. Where it was something that you had striving to achieve for weeks, or months. You had the strength to pull yourself up off of the toilet seat. Think about it.

As I came out of the washroom with my nurse, who was grinning from ear to ear, I could hardly wait to tell Derek. I was going to be able to go home yet, I told him. One small step at a time, I conquered every obstacle. All of those little things that

I used to take for granted, I now had to learn how to do all over again. I soon started to go to the bathroom at night, instead of using the bed pan. I still needed some assistance at first, of course. But then eventually, as I persisted, I worked up from that to being able to wash and feed myself. Which was all with a right hand and arm that had been sliced open and left that way for weeks. Soon after, I was able to go to the washroom by myself and then, finally, I took my first shower. I will never forget how good that felt. I had to sit on a seat but just the feeling of the water running all over my body filled my heart and soul with pure joy.

Even now, my shower is sacred to me. Every time I take a shower, I think back and recall what it was like to have lost that ability and to have to fight with all of my might to regain it. I stay very present washing myself and rejoicing in such a blessed act. Do you ever think about what it would be like to not be able to wash yourself? Do you ever think about what it would be like, to not have enough strength to keep yourself upright and standing long enough to take a shower? How important would the latest social media post be then, if that ability was suddenly gone? Have you ever thought about it? The next time you find yourself in a hurry and rushing through your shower, take a breath and be thankful that you can.

When I started to eat solid food again the act of using utensils was something that my muscles had to learn to do all over again. I had to hold one utensil, sometimes with both hands, and try ever so hard to pick up a small piece of food and get it to my mouth without dropping it. It was as hard as any of the other tasks that I had to learn to do all over again. My hands would get tired before my stomach was satisfied with the amount of food that I had consumed. At the time, I thought it was okay though because it would help me to keep my weight down. I was terrified that I would regain all of the weight that I had lost. Besides, the food still tasted like ash in my mouth for the most part anyway.

My heart attack and the complications that followed were not going to be the end of me. One by one, I overcame all of the challenges that were between me and my ticket home for a weekend. Finally, the day came when I got the go ahead and I had a pass. I was going home for a whole weekend! I recall being nervous of leaving the security of the hospital and the staff that had been supporting me. But, at the same time, I couldn't wait to sleep in my own bed! It had been months since I had been able to do that.

I was scared, though. I was scared that I wouldn't want to go back to the hospital after having a taste of being home for a whole weekend. I was also scared that the cats wouldn't know me. Would they have forgotten who I was? I mean after all, I wouldn't smell the same. I certainly did not look the same. My hair was all cut off and was very short. I weighed eighty pounds less and last but not least my voice was not the same. I sounded very different. I was having to learn to speak again and stretch my vocal chords, after having a trach in for such a long time.

The night before I was scheduled to go home for the weekend, I laid in bed thinking about being home in just a few hours. I thought about how wonderful it was going to be to just sit and watch the birds feed from the window while I was curled up with my little Jam. But then all of a sudden, the doubts and fears started. What if she was mad or didn't want to have anything to do with me? What if she didn't like this stranger that Derek had brought home? To say that I had mixed feelings that night would be a bit of an understatement! But then, as the hours passed, it was finally morning and Derek was punctual, as usual, and arrived right on time.

Once I saw his smiling face I was filled with pure joy. My fears subsided as he helped me into my wheelchair. I could hardly sit still as he wheeled me out to the van. Once I was in my seat and buckled in, our journey home began. The twenty something minute drive home, on the exact same route that I had last taken *to* the hospital, ten or eleven weeks ago, was relatively quiet. I think that maybe Derek was as nervous as I was. This was the first time that I had left the safety of the hospital and my medical team. How would I fair at home? The doubts and fears were very loud in both of our heads. But, as we do, we persevered and carried on. The last time I had been in the van, I was dying. It felt very strange to be sitting at that same seat again. So much had changed for me, with all that had happened and the time that I had spent in the hospital.

As we drove, I asked Derek about the remnants of a building that we had passed. "When did that burn?", I asked with surprise. It was like time had stood still for me. It was then, that I truly realized that the rest of the world had just kept on moving. It was a very strange feeling as we drove along and I saw all of the changes that had taken place in just a short time. Then we drove by some friends houses which was comforting and familiar. The closer we got to home the more excited I became! I could hardly sit still!

As we pulled in and drove up our long driveway, my eyes filled with happy tears, as I knew this was my first step in moving back home. I knew then that I could do it with Derek's help. He parked the van and then brought my walker to me. Once I was home, I was able to use the walker instead of my wheelchair. Our home is an open concept and all on one level so using the walker seemed to be easier. He helped me out of the van and assisted me and my walker, to the door. I had butterflies in my stomach as we walked into the porch and opened the door to the house. As I looked inside and pushed my walker through the door, Jam met me right there at the door. She looked at me was as if she was saying "Where have you been?". She came right to me and I cried like a baby. I could feel her happiness and she could feel mine.

The other two kittens were a little unsure of the whole situation at first. But, then within a half hour or so, they were all over me. I was overjoyed! I was finally home with my family!

This trial weekend home was a bit of test, to see how I would manage in looking after myself. Derek was very attentive and had done some minor renovations, to make my introduction and adjustment to a new way of life a little easier. He installed handles around the toilet so that I could use them to help pull or push myself up. They also helped me to steady myself as I lowered down onto the toilet seat. He had picked up a special chair to put in the shower, because I was unable to stand long enough to completely wash and rinse myself. Not to mention that my balance still was not great at that point.

There had to be a step placed on my side of the bed to make it easier for me to get in and out. Our bed has storage drawers underneath it, which makes it higher than a regular bed. The other thing that he installed was a step in the bathroom. Because our home was built on a concrete slab, part of the bathroom floor had to be elevated to allow for plumbing, which made for a larger than normal step up. It was too large a step for me, so he split the difference to make it two shorter steps, which made navigating much easier.

Just the act of taking a shower was a huge event. An all day event in fact, at first. It would take all the energy I had just to shower, that day. It was well worth the heavenly feeling it gave me though. Especially in my own bathroom, without a nurse watching me. I left the door unlocked and Derek would check on me and help me with the areas that I could not reach. After finishing and getting out of the shower, Derek would come in and help me to dry off and get fresh clean clothes on. It was amazing how good it felt to crawl into our bed after taking that first shower at home. The first night home was a dream come true! Finally, I got to sleep in my own bed with Derek and the kitties!

The excitement of the day had worn on me, but it was a good kind of tired. Derek helped me into bed, made us some food and we just enjoyed being alone together, for the first time in months. I had almost forgotten how comfortable our bed was. I will never take that feeling for granted, ever again. I reflected on the day and how quickly it all went by. I didn't want it to end, but I was so exhausted that I had to sleep and tomorrow would be another day.

I want to say that Derek has cared for me and helped me in ways that a spouse should never have to, in my opinion. He did anything and everything he could in the most loving and caring manner. He never made me feel awkward or made me feel like it was a negative obligation. He is and always will be my hero.

It seemed that the next day came and went so quickly. I sat next to the window with a cup of tea and watched the birds feed, with Jam on my lap. Just like I had dreamed of doing all of those long and lonely nights in the MSICU. I did not want to go back to the hospital, but I knew that I had to finish my therapy and check in with my doctors. They needed to know how well I had managed. Even though I was anxious about returning to the hospital at that point, I felt it would be short lived and I would soon be returning home to stay.

Derek drove me back to the hospital around supper time. We could have waited until a little later on in the day, but I felt that if I didn't go then, I might not want to go at all. I had to go back and get settled in my room and the hard hospital bed, something I had become all too familiar with. I could tell that Derek was tired as the excitement of the weekend had drained him. I think that it was mostly our uncertainty with how things would go, maybe a little anxiety about returning home together and the things that could potentially go wrong, that tired us both out. But, everything went extremely well and we managed just fine.

All of the nurses came in one by one, after I was settled, to see how my weekend went. They all seemed to be excited for me and glad to have me back with them to hear all about how it went. They had all become like a second family to me. Believe it or not, I really missed them and their companionship, when I finally did go home to stay.

I had to go through a lot of testing before the doctors were comfortable enough to release me from the hospital permanently. They tested my brain function twice and my motor skills were constantly being evaluated. All of this testing was very nerve racking and somewhat stressful for me. But, it was all worth it in the end. During my time in the hospital, my drivers license had been suspended and in order to get it back, I had to first complete the rehab program's own strict testing. Then, once I passed that test, I would get a letter from the province, saying that I could now make an appointment to take the driver's road test with a driver examiner, before I could get my driver's license back. The whole process took months. But eventually, I took my test and I passed. I was free and I had wheels again.

I was discharged one week after my visit home but had to continue to go back for therapy sessions, once and sometimes twice a week, for several months. It proved to be very challenging and they were long and tiring days. But, we managed with some help from a close friend who was very helpful in providing me with drives, when I needed them.

I was discharged on the first day of February 2018 and Derek went back to work on the seventh. He stayed home for a week with me and then returned to work. Neither of us wanted him to go back, but we had to face our fears and start our journey back to some sense of normality eventually and we both felt that sooner rather than later was the best approach. It was not the first time that we had to claw our way back to some sense of normal living after a traumatic, life changing event. We both knew that the longer we put it off, the harder it would become. He was worried, but my friend lived just up the road and we have wonderful neighbours. All of whom knew that I was finally back home. I had many, many offers for help, should I need it.

One of the hardest things I had to do when I moved back home was figuring out my pill schedule. I had always just relied on the nurses to bring me what I needed, when I needed it. Now, it was up to me to figure it out and keep it all straight. The first thing I did after the nurses gave me my medication schedule, was get myself a pill organizer. I like to be organized and wanted to set myself up to follow the schedule, to the letter. At first it was a lot for my damaged brain to sort out and keep straight. But it was good therapy. I caught on quickly and was able to keep myself organized and on track.

I had been appointed an extra mural nurse who come to our home three times a week to change the bandages and dressing on my back and monitor the healing progress of the open sore that had formed. After about two months, the sore seemed to heal up and as a result, the nurses discontinued their visits. That was in April of 2018. The nurse said that my wound was dry looking but she thought it would continue to heal up, if we just kept it moisturized with some vitamin E cream.

The days I would have to go back to the hospital for therapy were long days for me. Derek would drop me off before he went to work at six o'clock in the morning and my appointments would usually start around nine o'clock. I would have a break for lunch and then be back at it in the afternoon. Sometimes,

I would wait for Derek to pick me up after he finished work for the day, at four-thirty. Other times, I would be done early and my friend would pick me up and drive me home. I was thankful for the days when I had an early drive, as I was truly exhausted and just wanted to lay down and rest.

On the days when I stayed home, I would work on my own therapy by using a stationary peddle bike that could be placed in front of my chair. It was small and compact and was a very good tool for me to use. It helped strengthen my legs and got my heart rate up. I made sure I used it at least five mornings a week, for at least a half an hour. But, usually I would try to push myself to get forty five minutes in. Another thing that helped me to regain my strength was performing simple tasks around our home. For instance, changing the bed sheets was extremely difficult for me and at first would take me hours to complete. But, even if I had to take a break in the middle, I would finish it in the same day. Yes, that's right, I said the same day. How many of you can imagine it taking you a whole day to change the bed sheets or take a shower?

Loading and unloading the dishwasher was another great therapy exercise for me. It helped to strengthen my arms, my back and legs. I started by lifting one dish at a time up into the cupboard. Then, slowly and gradually, I increased the amount of dishes that I lifted at one time and eventually I built up and regained strength. I still can't lift what I used too, but I'm no slouch either. I can lift six large plates up to the cupboard at once now. Which may not sound like much to you, but it is quite an accomplishment for me. It is okay, you can clap. I know you want to. I do all the time!

I had been through and had to work through so many challenges, that even though I remained hopeful, it had become clear that I would never be able to return to my grooming career. There are days when I still miss it, very much! It was a huge part of my identity for over twenty-five years. All of that said however, after that much time in the business and a massive heart attack, it was time to move on. I did last a lot longer than the average individual in the business, though. It can take a toll on both one's physical and mental well being. But while I was in it, I loved it and I was good. I was really good! I am proud to say that, because I worked hard and earned the right to do so.

Part of my rehabilitation therapy included a program known as the Cardiac Rehab Program, at the Moncton Hospital. It is a wonderful program, run by highly qualified medical professionals at one of the clinics in our hospital. It was this program, along with all of the therapy that I received while being in the rehab unit, that helped me to learn how to live life the best way I could. Especially after experiencing such a life changing event. I had not only lost my mobility but I had also lost confidence in myself, as well. The support I received in those programs made a world of difference and I will be forever grateful to the team and the staff for all their encouragement, help and guidance.

I was thankful for the social aspect of the program, too. I was thankful for the people I met and the friends I made during our time together. I looked forward to seeing them all, each time we were together. We really encouraged and supported each other. Not to mention the physical component of the program, which helped me to regain my strength and independence. When I started this program, I could not walk from the door of the hospital to the clinic without stopping several times and sitting on my walker to rest. I was very independent, however. Just ask Derek. He would help me get out of the truck and get the walker set up and loaded and then that was it. He was to be hands off after that point! "I can do it!", was my only response, to offers for additional help.

The ladies at Cardiac Rehab were very nervous of me getting on the exercise machines. They assisted and monitored me and my withered, frail looking body very closely to make sure I didn't overdo it. I was a pitiful looking creature with the loose, hanging skin that did not bounce, or should I say tighten, back up after all the inflammation and swelling. I had lost most of my hair. I had bald spots on the back of my head. But, I was there each day, pushing my walker into the gym. I didn't let it get me down. The key thing, even though I had to remind myself of it many times, was that I was walking. I was alive and I was walking. Two things that a great number of medical professionals thought I would never be or do again, at times. I had a second chance and I was determined to make the most it!

The twelve week cardiac rehab program had classroom information sessions, as well as an exercise component, in the gym. I really enjoyed the information and the new knowledge that I gained in the classroom sessions and the gym helped me to build strength and improve my heart function. I made sure to inform the staff that I had been using the new step machine and stationary bike when I was in the fourth floor rehab unit, and that I would be sticking with those machines. That was, until I felt more comfortable and was able to move on to something a little more challenging. I also made sure to tell them that I got tired easily. But, looking back I'm sure I did not have to tell them that. I'm sure they could tell.

I took full advantage of all the help and information that was provided in the program. After having my heart attack, I did a lot of reading and thought that I knew most of what there was to know about recovery. What I should and shouldn't do. Well, there is always more to learn and I had not covered everything in my self-study. I learned *a lot* more in working through this program. They even taught us how to read the labels on food products, so that we could make informed decisions when buying and consuming processed or prepared foods. I have learned that whole foods are by far the best way to go, when fuelling your body. I made a lot of friends in the program, even though I was by far the youngest patient who attended that round. We all encouraged and challenged one another and it was a great experience! The twelve weeks seemed to go by very quickly.

Once I had completed the program, I was asked to be a guest speaker for new patients who were completing the program. The attendees were people who had experienced heart attacks, had major or minor surgeries, had diabetes or were high risk patients for having any type of heart issues. The staff asked me to tell my story because few people had lived through or even heard of an ordeal such as mine. The thought was that it would give these attendees some hope. Because, if I could survive all that I had, and be there talking to them, sharing my story, they too could survive and resume and healthy and active life. A lot of the attendees would approach me after my talks and thank me. Sometimes they would hug me. Sometimes they would share their own story. They all seemed to have the same thing in common after listening to me speak, and that was hope. They had hope! If I could survive my situation, they could do the same in theirs. I would pass by the gym and look in to see them working even harder on the exercise equipment, afterwards. They also talked among themselves, recanting my story. It gave me a sense of giving back to a program that had helped me, so very much. I shared my story with classes for a year after I graduated. That was until the pandemic changed the design and delivery of the classes.

The program was designed to teach individuals how to become more heart healthy and encourage them to set goals, no matter how small or how large. My goal was to wear the wheels off my walker and then never have to use it again and well, get my license back. I can still remember my class mates encouraging me in the days before my road test and cheering for me with all of their might on the morning I went in, after I had passed my road test.

I wish this program was available to everyone. Not just the people who have had issues with their heart. I think that sharing this information with more people could change a lot in the ways that they choose to live and for the better. It certainly has changed my way of life and I wish I would have had the information and knowledge, before my event. I think I would have made some very different choices.

I felt my confidence growing everyday, with the encouragement of the staff and my class mates. I could feel my mind, my body and my spirit getting stronger with every class. By the time graduation came, I was able to walk thirty minutes, non-stop, on the treadmill. What an accomplishment! What a feeling!

Unfortunately, before I graduated from the program my world would be turned upside down again. I was discharged from the hospital on February 1, 2018. The following month, Derek's father was admitted because he had become increasingly ill. He had fought and survived cancer twice but it was back, with a vengeance. He ended up with a rare blood disorder and the cancer came back. I'm sorry to say that he passed in April of 2018, with all of us by his side.

Derek's Dad had been a big part of our lives. We lived right next door to one another for the last fifteen years, since we had moved back home from Nova Scotia. We all spent a lot of time together and weren't just family but close friends. I felt crushed. How much more are we going to have to go through, I thought? In addition, I felt a great amount guilt in being the one who had survived, at first. I had just gotten out of the hospital and he went in. We never got to enjoy the new camp that we had started to build together, on the back part of the homestead property. Although, he was able to help with the biggest part of the construction of it. I know that he would have spent most of his upcoming retirement years back there, with a dog by his side. We were crushed! He was 68 years of age.

I spent most of the days that followed just waiting for something else bad to happen. With continued therapy and help from the staff at the cardiac rehab unit, I was able to get my head right and get back on track with focusing on what was right in front of me. I was able to resume the practice of being present in my life. The practice of living in the moment. I will say however, that there is not a day goes by that I don't shed a tear at the fact that he is no longer with us. I miss him so very much! He does come to me at times though. By sending me little messages in a dream or in a vision as I'm walking the trails of the property we shared. His presence is still here. He is still here and this comforts me.

At the time of graduation from the rehab program, I had taken my driving road test and I had passed. I was so excited that I had gotten my license back. Not only did I achieve this goal but I also stopped using my walker and I was able to walk through the hospital without stopping. I was slow, but I had far more mobility than anyone ever thought I would.

It has been almost 5 years since my heart attack, at the time of this writing, and I still have foot drop, with numbness that remains in my legs and feet. I still have days when I get tired and need my walker but they are fewer and farther between now. I certainly have come along way thanks to all of the help that I have received.

In June of 2019, it was once again time for the annual fundraiser for the cardiac rehab program. It was a walk-a-thon event that was held at one of the parks here in our city. I participated and managed to walk the entire one kilometre course, while holding Derek's hand. Oh, what a HAPPY DAY!!!

I have spent a great deal of my recovery trying to discover who I am. I believe that I have spent most of my life being what everyone else wanted, or what I thought everyone else wanted me to be. As a result, I have felt lost my entire life and just now, at 53 years of age have decided that it is now time for me to be what I want me to be. It is time for me to find myself.

In the process of writing this book, I have learned many, many things about myself. But, I know that I have only just scratched the surface. I still have a very long, long way to go. But, *I'm* doing the work. *Me, I'm* doing the work that *needs* to done, and I'm doing it for *me*.

I want to thank Derek and the ladies at the cardiac rehab for encouraging me to write this book and take this journey into the unknown.

There is one note worthy thing I have learned so far in this process and that is that I can accomplish *anything* I set my mind to, and so can you!

# CHAPTER 14

*My first steps*

After being discharged from the hospital in February and doing fairly well. That summer seemed like the perfect time for Derek and I to take a week and go on a little trip to one of our favourite places. We have always loved touring around Cape Breton Island in Nova Scotia. I was a little nervous about going too far away from the hospital and the medical staff in Moncton, who I had very much come to rely on. But, it was time to test the limits of my anxious feelings.

Once we decided we were going to take off for some well deserved time away, I just focused on the adventure. We had no real plan, we just decided to fly by the seat of our pants and go. We would just see where things took us and stay wherever we decided, along the way. It was late June of 2018, and I couldn't believe we were going on a road trip. It seemed amazing to me considering the events of the last few months. I had my trusty walker and we decided that if I got tired we would just stop at the first cabin, hotel or motel that was available. Then we would get up the next day, once I was rested, and move on to another part of the Island.

I felt like I was seeing it all for the very first time. It's was like I had been given a new set of lenses. It was like I was seeing some things for the very first time in my life and it was absolutely amazing! Everything seemed so new and so fresh. The colours were more vibrant than anything I had ever seen. The natural beauty that surrounded us was absolutely breath taking. My appreciation for having the ability to go on such a trip was tremendous. I could hardly believe it was real! Just a few months ago, I was told that I may never walk again. Not to mention the fact that my doctors didn't think I would survive, on multiple occasions. Now, all of a sudden here I was taking a trip to one of the most beautiful places in the world and the best part was that I was doing so with the love of my life. My soul mate.

Life simply could not have gotten any better for me, at that point. We stayed in places where I was able to use my walker and Derek was always by my side, helping me every step of the way. My heart felt whole again. We started our visit to the Island in the central Bra's D'or Lakes region and then slowly worked our way around the Cabot Trail from East to West. We just took our time and really enjoyed ourselves. We stopped whenever we saw something that looked interesting. We ate when we were hungry and we slept when we were tired. It was just the way a vacation should be. As we made our way around to the West side of the trail, we decided that we would see if we could get a cabin, for a couple of nights, at one of our all time favourite places on the Island. It's a place called Inverness Beach Village, located just outside of the town of Inverness. It is an absolutely beautiful spot located right on the water. We had stayed there a couple of times before during previous vacations, but had always tented, as they have both a campground and cabins for rent. On this trip, we thought it would be better to rent a cabin for a couple of nights and as luck would have it, we were able to get one of the two cabins that were closest to the beach and water. Which I thought was amazing considering we didn't have a reservation. We could see the beach, right there in front of us, from every window in the cabin and the view from the deck was breathtakingly beautiful!

It was there, on the beach in Inverness, where I walked on the sand and out into the water, for what felt like the very first time in my life. I have absolutely loved anything to do with or in the water, my entire life. I love to swim, tube, boat, float, and fish. I am a huge fan of it all! This particular day felt like the first time however, because I was truly *feeling* it, for the first time. I was truly *feeling* the healing power and the energy of it. I was like a new born baby discovering that I could make my feet move anytime I want them to. I'm not sure that my words can truly describe the emotions I felt as Derek helped me walk on the sand and out into the water. It was something that I never thought I would ever do again, just a couple of months earlier. Tears formed and ran down my cheeks, and yet I couldn't stop smiling. Derek made it all possible and it was the best trip of my life!

That afternoon as we were visiting the local shops and stores in the town, we decided to purchase a small portable charcoal barbecue and some steaks for that night's supper. Remember earlier when I was telling you about how I would dream of having a nice steak, cooked to perfection when I was in the SICU? When we returned to our cabin paradise on the beach, we set our steaks to marinate and prepared our veggies for our evening feast. Oh, and our bottle of red wine of course. Can't forget about the red wine. I love a nice glass of a dark, dry red with a steak. So, as evening approached, Derek lit the charcoal, corked our beautiful bottle of red and we began to cook and feast on the deck in front of our cabin on the beach. The entire meal and the company were completely divine. After our meal, Derek made a fire in the fire pit and I wheeled myself over to the fire where Derek played his guitar and we drank wine while we watched the sun go down. It was like a fairy tale! It is a memory that will forever be etched in my mind and in my heart. It was without a doubt the best day of our whole trip!

Over the years, Derek and I have been on many adventures. We spent many years travelling with the bands he was in, as well as travelling together for business events and a variety of vacation trips. We have had many wonderful trips but this trip, for me, had far more meaning and was at the top of the list. I felt that I was truly alive and had a new and very profound appreciation for everything that I saw and experienced. It was like it was all for the very first time. A relaxed sense of independence was the theme and energy for the entire trip. We felt so free!

As we travelled around the Cabot trail, I started to feel an irritation on my back. It was right in the middle, right where my bra strap was. My first thought was that maybe I did not get all the soap rinsed off in the shower that day. But, with each passing day, it felt a little more irritated. Then I started to think that maybe my bra strap was rubbing on the newly healed, sensitive skin. After a little discussion, we thought that maybe putting a bandage over the area to cushion it from any the bra strap might help. At this point, we were nearing the end of our beautiful trip and had started working our way toward home.

After arriving back home, it did not seem that the irritation was going away. In fact, it was getting worse. Much worse. With that, I made an appointment to see my family doctor and she prescribed a medicated cream to be applied regularly. Because we did not really understand what it was or what was happening at that point, the cream she prescribed actually made it worse. By mid July, what was once a spot on my back had turned into a very angry, very red and very hot and heated mess. It was inflamed and infected, and a very large open sore had formed. So back to the doctor we go. "We have to figure this out.", I pleaded. "I just don't know how much more I can take!". So, we discontinued the cream and antibiotics that were prescribed. But, even with that, it just kept getting worse with each passing day. It was growing larger and the redness was spreading. It was so painful that I was no longer able to wear a bra or lay on my back and as a result, was unable to get any rest. Which was a real problem for me because after my heart attack and all of the other complications, I needed to be able to rest in order to maintain my strength and heal. It was very concerning and very stressful! I could not understand what was happening to me.

We went back to our family doctor and after one look, she said that she thought the antibiotics needed to be stronger. Right away, she ordered antibiotics to be given to me intravenously (IV). After two doses, my back was getting more and more angry by the hour. Finally, the decision was made to admit me back into the hospital, so I could be monitored more closely.

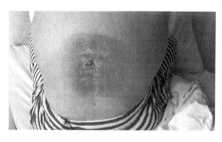

My immune system was still very compromised and at that point the doctor was getting quite concerned. Specialists were called in to evaluate the situation and I was given more IV antibiotics to try to get the infection under control. An infectious disease doctor was called in to look at my back and even he was perplexed by what he was seeing. It was a mysterious, very angry square patch and hole in my back. With this, several other doctors were consulted and many discussions were had about my particular case and situation. Still, they could not come to any reasonable or agreed upon cause or conclusion for what they were seeing and what I was trying to live through.

Finally, after a week or so of being back in the hospital, the doctors realized that the antibiotics were not working and that my body was building up a tolerance to them. With that, the best infectious disease doctor in New Brunswick was called in to look at my wound. My case had been a topic for conversation and discussion among many doctors and they wanted his opinion. He came to the conclusion that whatever was going on with my back was not an infectious disease. He said that something had caused this wound, but it was not in his realm of expertise. I was discharged from the hospital and was referred back to the original dermatologist, to continue consultations. Personally, I think that this situation was a little outside of her area of expertise, too. However, she thought that we should do a biopsy, which was in the form of a very painful debriding procedure. Derek watched as they peeled and cut away layers from my back, in order to get the samples they needed for the biopsies. They did this with only 2 milligrams of dilaudid, in pill form, for pain some twenty minutes before. He held my hand and wiped the tears from my face, as she cut and peeled pieces away from me. It was excruciating! But, I was willing to do anything to get this massive hole in my back to heal. I had already been through so very much.

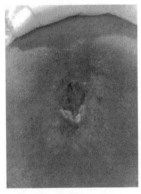

Eventually, the dermatologist and one of the infectious disease doctors teamed up to try and decide, together, what the best approach was and which steps should be taken next. There were several collaborative appointments and a lot of sitting and waiting on our part. It sort of felt like they were just grasping at straws and hoping that something, anything, would work, so that I would be able to get on with my life.

It got to the point where the amount of pain killers I needed to take were starting to make me feel like a Zombie. I was taking gabapentin twice a day and over 64 mg of hydromorphone, in a twenty four hour period, just to get through the day without wanting to end my own suffering. Believe me, I thought about it! Several times. I just needed it to stop! When I look back, I am surprised that I didn't overdose. There were days when I wondered why I came back from the dead, to then have to try to live through such pain and sorrow. The only thing, and I really mean that *the only thing*, that kept me going was my love for my husband and our animals!

It was a constant schedule of back and forth, to and from appointments. Sitting and waiting and waiting and sitting. It was an ongoing ordeal, several times and week, for a year. They took biopsies and tried different creams and nothing seemed to work. It was a complete mystery and it was wearing me down. Not one of the doctors involved could figure it out. I was starting to feel like a lab rat and I hated it.

It was only after Derek started to do some more digging and found a collection of different medical articles that contained some very interesting information, that we started to get somewhere. He had found a study that sited two other individuals who had also received multiple defibrillation attempts during a cardiac event and they too, had similar reactions and patterns on their skin. One man had only shown the burn some 5 years after having his event, but the other was within a much shorter time period. This information was key in finding out what needed to be done next, in my opinion. These two examples were both case studies in trying to determine the true cause of why these burns present themselves, sometimes only years after prolonged defibrillation events. The root cause of which is still unknown. It is puzzling why a burn will or can lie dormant, under the skin, for years in some and not others. I guess, well actually, we now know that I am one of those rare cases. It is even more puzzling that, in my case at least, the burn presented and then healed a couple of months after my heart attack. Then reappeared, a few months later and the second time, came back with a vengeance. It was angry! It just would not heal.

Derek printed copies of the articles and gave them to both of the doctors who were overseeing my case. They quickly flipped through them and commented that they found them to be interesting, but neither of them did anything with the information. Finally, we decided to go back to our family doctor to see if maybe she could make another referral or offer some other kind of help. Her first question was, "What is their plan B?". For which, we had no answer. It was then that she referred me to a plastic surgeon.

This particular plastic surgeon, as most do, had a very long waiting list. Especially if one was going through the Medicare system, which we were. No millionaire family members offering to help here! Not that I would have accepted it anyway. Or, would I?

I mean if you were looking for a new pair of perky boobs and you had cash, straight to the front of the line... But, unfortunately, he was the only surgeon that we knew of at the time, who would do any type of procedure covered by the medicare system. Derek and I were doing well just to make ends meet on his salary, alone. I was denied any financial help from the provincial or federal government and to this day have not received a penny. They claim that the rules are the rules and that because for one year in the last six that I worked, I did not make enough money to pay into the Canada pension plan, they could not help me. In order to qualify for any benefits or any type of help at all, I had to have paid into Canada pension for four consecutive years, in the last six. I appealed their ruling and they simply told me that their hands were tied and they wished me the best, but there was nothing that could be done.

I had been working since I was fourteen years old. I spent several years working for myself and had employed others and yet I was not eligible for the Canadian disability pension, in any way. Even though the doctor said that, due to the extent of my complications and the damage that had been done as a result of my heart attack, I would not be able to ever work again. That being said, we could not afford to pay for plastic surgery. So, I waited for an appointment so it could be determine what he could or would do to help me. In the end, it was determined that because there were so many attempts at defibrillation, I had basically been cooked to the spine and there was tissue inside me that was dead. As a result, it would have to be removed, in order for me to heal.

Initially, the plastic surgeon gave me hope that I would not have to live with this big gaping hole in my back for the rest of my life. He said that he could do a butterfly incision and get me healed up. At the time, I thought I could just look it up on the internet and find a detailed explanation for the procedure he had suggested. He was always very busy and did not show any interest in, or seem to want to explain what was involved with the procedure, at the time. Even though we asked several times. Considering how long I had been living in pain, I honestly didn't care, I just wanted to have it fixed and be able to move forward with whatever my life would be. I tried to find some information but wasn't able to find anything that offered a sufficient explanation. The information I did find on plastic surgery was very gruesome and scared me and so I decided that maybe it was best not to dig any deeper. I thought that perhaps if I did, maybe I would change my mind. So, I decided to trust that he had my best interest in mind. After all, he acted very confident that he was going to be able to fix my back and that it wouldn't be a big deal. I should have pushed him for details. I should have pushed much, much harder. Now, after the whole experience, I really just want to *push* him!

From the time of my initial meeting and consultation with him, I had to wait a whole year before I got a date for surgery.

It was finally scheduled for August 3, 2019. I believe the only reason why I received a date when I did was because I ended up back in the hospital again in July of 2019. My back had become infected, again and I believe that someone with some pull took pity on me and pushed to have the surgery done right away. Anyone who is waiting for a surgery, that is considered to be non-urgent, is put on a long waiting list. Which is mostly because our medical system is so very overloaded, in my opinion. I was relieved to know that finally, after such a long time of living with this painful, open hole in my back and taking pain medication like it was candy, that it was finally going to be fixed. It would finally be fixed and I could move on to the next chapter in my life. What ever that would look like. After all, it had to be better than what I had been living with for so long.

## The Day of Surgery

I arrived to admitting early that day, as is required for patients having surgery, and was very nervous. This was going to be the first time that I had been put under again, since my heart attack. At the same time, I was glad to think that this would be the answer. I was glad to think that this was going to put an end to the pain and suffering that I had endured for over a year. I was admitted and was waiting in a temporary room for the surgeon to come in and see me. Finally, it was time for Derek to leave my room and the nurses came in to finish prepping me. I was scared of the possibility that it would be the last time I would see my husband, again. Fear started to settle in and I made sure I told him how much I loved him and said good bye for now with tears in my eyes.

As usual, when the surgeon entered, he did not have much to say. I thought that perhaps he was just very eccentric and maybe that was just his way. He asked to look at my back and as he did, he started to draw lines on my back with a black marker. I thought that it was odd that the lines he was drawing were large and covering my whole back. But, I guess I just thought it was part of the procedure. He drew a large butterfly like figure on my back. The hole was in the middle of my back so I guess what entered my mind was that he would have to nip and tuck here and there to get the hole covered considering he was not going to do any skin grafts. I had heard that skin grafts were very painful and was glad that he was going to take an alternate approach. I guess I thought, or hoped, that this approach would be less painful. I trusted that it would all work out in the end, so I didn't ask any questions and he offered no information.

Quite soon after that, they wheeled me into the operating room. Once, inside the team was upbeat and friendly. They all did their best to put me at ease and I felt somewhat comforted by their energy. The next thing I remember, was waking up in the recovery room in the worst pain I had ever felt. Believe me when I tell you, that is saying something! I couldn't understand what was happening and then finally, I realized that they had positioned me so that I was laying on my back. My first words to them were to get me the hell off my back. Now, instead of just the middle of my back hurting, my whole back was screaming in absolute torturous pain! I was so confused. How could this be? Am I just having a nightmare? Will someone please help me?

The nurses gave me some pain meds but it didn't seem to be helping me at all. I thought I was going to pass out from the pain. Now remember, for the last year or so, I had been taking two doses gabapentin and some 64 mg of hydromorphone every day, just to be able to live with the pain that I was in.

Finally, I managed to get a nurse to help me to get partly on my side. But, the steady stream of tears just kept coming. She felt so bad for me that I could see my pain reflecting back to me, in her eyes. She quickly said, "I will go get your husband!". I said thank you and she ran off and it was but a moment and I saw Derek come rushing in and straight to my bedside. One of the other nurses was not happy that he was in the recovery room with me, but I was glad that he was. I needed him with me! The look on Derek's face said it all. It told me that he understood just what kind of pain I was in and that he felt great sadness for me. Not only was I in pain from whatever had just happened to my back, but I was also having chest pains. I could not understand it. Did something go wrong during surgery? Why am I hurting so very badly?

Finally, the cranky nurse asked Derek to leave. I'm sure that her discomfort in having him there, must certainly have been far greater than the comfort he was bringing me. Yes, that was sarcasm! As he left, the other nurse, who had brought him in, apologized for her behaviour and said she would be done her shift soon and that he would then be able to come back in.

Once Derek came back in, I told him that I didn't think I would be able to stand the pain much longer. He talked to the nurse and she couldn't understand why the pain meds weren't working. Then they figured out that the surgeon had ordered morphine for pain. I had been on a lot of hydromorphone, for a very long time, and morphine couldn't touch anything that I was feeling. I'm not a surgeon, but I knew that! They quickly got me some hydromorphone and it did help a little. But the pain was still almost more than I could bear. I told Derek of the pain in my chest and he immediately told the nurse. Considering my history he wasn't taking any chances.

In very quick order, some tests were run and the doctors were convinced it was probably anxiety from the pain. The surgeon had originally told me that I would be staying in the hospital for one or two days after my procedure. As the doctor who was taking over in the recovery room consulted with the surgeon on the telephone about my condition and the results from the testing for my chest pains, the surgeon said he referred everything to the doctor taking over and saw no reason why I couldn't be sent home that evening. I was somewhat shocked by this, considering that I was having chest pain as well. You see, it was a Friday before a long weekend and I think they wanted to send me home instead of admitting me and having to check on me over the weekend.

What he did to my back was excessive in my opinion. Basically, he cut and peeled two big flaps of skin off of my back and put them on a table. Then, he removed all of the dead tissue down to and around my spine, of which there was a lot, as I was told later. He also told me that he moved some tissue around and tried to fill in the empty hole. Then, he put the skin back on my back and with stitching and staples sewed me up and put me back together.

When evening arrived, and I was the only one left in the recovery room. The surgeon, as I said earlier, had been long gone since the afternoon and the only ones left were the anesthesiologist and the cardiologist, along with a couple of nurses. By around 8:00 pm, that had all decided that it was time to send me home. The nurses got me some of the clothing from my overnight bag and managed to get a couple of the loose fitting items that I had brought, on me. It was excruciating! The whole time, I was in complete disbelief of what was happening to me. How could this be? "What have I ever done to deserve this?", I thought?

One of the nurses helped to get me into a wheel chair and then helped Derek wheel me down to the truck. They tried to help me get in the truck, but I was in so much pain that I could barely move. I could not lean against the seat, so I sat forward trying to hold myself in such a way that my back did not touch anything. The clothing and bandages that were touching were almost more than I could bear.

The drive home was slow and painful, as I could feel every bump and dip in our old country road. The pain went straight to the overactive and functioning nerve endings that remained. I recall thinking that this was all just a horrible dream and that I would wake up at some point and that everything would be just fine.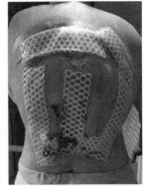

Derek drove as slow and cautiously as he possibly could in an effort to ease my suffering and when we finally arrived at home, he helped me get into the house. As he was helping me into bed, I asked for the pain meds I had been taking. At this point, I did not care if I overdosed, I was just in that much pain! We decided that I should write down when and how much I took, just in case of an emergency. After doing so, I tried to somehow get comfortable on my side. I was completely exhausted and as the pain meds started to take effect, I was grateful that I could feel sleep coming on. As I drifted off, I remember thinking that I was hoping that tomorrow would be a better day. If I made it through the night, that was. At least now, the surgery was over. Somehow, I got through it and now I could start to heal and move forward with my life. Finally.. Again!

Looking back, I was glad to have been sent home. I took what pain meds I needed, when I needed them  in order to get through the excruciating ordeal. I was able to govern myself without the nurses or doctors telling me that I could only have a certain amount at a certain time. After all, I had been self-medicating through all of this torture and pain for well over a year now. I knew when and what I needed in order to rest and I took it. I would worry about weaning myself off of it after this was over and I was healed. Right now however, I was going to focus on rest because I knew that I would heal much quicker if my body was at rest. Now, as I am writing this, if I had known then what I would have to go through in order to heal, I would not have had the surgery. I would have found a way to live with the hole in my back.

I was told that four days after the surgery, I could to take part of the blood soaked dressing off. It looked like a new butcher in training had miscut the piece of meat that he was working on. It truly looked like I had come straight from a horror film set.

They also told me that I could shower at that point, and so I did. I was nervous to let the water run down my back and was scared that it would hurt, so I made sure I took a little extra pain medication before hand, just in case. Any contact or pressure to my back was extremely uncomfortable. I got into the shower and let the warm water run over my shoulders and down my back. As it gently rolled down the length of my back, I watched as the old blood ran down my legs and into the drain. I knew that it was important to get as much of the old dried blood off of my back as I could stand. Keeping it clean and dry would definitely help in the healing process and I would then be able to get a better look at what the medicare butcher had actually done to me.

In the days that followed, my back started to look like someone had inserted balloons under the re-attached flaps of skin and blown them up. This swelling caused pressure which was becoming increasingly more uncomfortable, which was on top of the pain that I was already feeling. I had no experience with this type of surgery and did not know what to expect. Therefore, I figured everything I was feeling must have been somewhat normal, considering what had been done. Looking back, I should have known that what I was experiencing was far from normal. Eleven days after my surgery, I developed significant pressure and redness in my back. I couldn't do anything other than take pain meds and try to sleep. It was the only thing that kept me from loosing my mind, as my ability to move was very limited. One morning, I decided to lay back down in bed for a rest, after getting my morning cup of tea. Which was an event all on its own. After about and hour or so, I woke up to find that the bed beneath me was completely soaked. My first thought was that maybe I slept so soundly that I had wet the bed.

I had wet the bed alright! The difference was that instead of urine, it was a tremendous amount of fluid, mixed with blood, that had drained out from underneath the flaps of skin on my back, while I was sleeping. Fearful of what had just happened, I took pictures and sent them to Derek, at work. My next step was to call the surgeon's office and explained what had happened to the nice lady who answered the phone. Her response was that it was normal and so I was able to relax a little after our conversation. Besides, it did release some of the pressure that I had been feeling. However, there was still a fair amount of fluid that remained under my wings, as they are now called. It continued to drain for another couple of days.

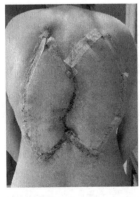

Two weeks after the surgery I went in to see the surgeon to have the staples removed. Of which, there were at least twenty four in the middle part of my back. There were a few that had come out on their own before my visit. I tried to keep track of how many there were but between the pain and the meds, I can't be sure of the actual amount. The process of getting the staples out was no walk in the park but I was happy to be moving forward in my life and this was one more step in doing so. Five days after having the staples removed from the middle of my back the hole that was supposed to be fixed, opened back up. Wtf? Needless to say,

I was beyond upset. I was devastated! It was a Sunday and so of course there was no way of getting in touch with the surgeon or his office. The wound had started to drain again and you could see right into my back. It was clear that this hole was not going to close over anytime soon. This gruesome sight almost made me sick to my stomach. I could not believe that after everything I had been through, there was an open hole in my back, again. The tears flowed down my face as I showed Derek. We decided to be waiting at the surgeon's office door when they opened the next morning. They opened the door to the office and we went straight to the desk to explain what had happened the day before. The receptionist asked us to take a seat in the waiting room  and after a few minutes, we were escorted into one of the examination rooms. A few minutes later, the surgeon came in. He was just as nice as pie, as Grammy used to say, acting like it was no big deal. It seemed that it was not concerning for him at all.

Later, I did some reading and based on my findings, I think that if he had drained the fluid at the first sign of it, all of this may have been avoided. All my research led to information that stated that when fluid appears after a surgery of this type, it most definitely should be drained right away. He then proceeded to tell me to go to one of the clinics at the hospital, with a note that he had given us to get a vacuum 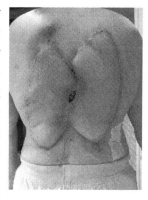 pump put on my back. He said that this would help draw the fluid out and help to close the hole over by healing it from the inside out. I guess the thought was that the fluid that had built up in the void left behind from cutting all of the dead tissue out, had put pressure on the healing incision, which led to it opening back up. I understood that he had filled in the void by moving tissue and muscle around, so there really should not have been a void. But, regardless of what I had understood, I now had a hole in my back again. "How much more am I going to have to go through?", I thought. Is this vacuum pump going to hurt my back even more and cause me more pain and suffering?

As it turned out, the pump put a constant vacuum, or pulling pressure on the hole in my back. There was a type of medical packing sponge that was inserted into the hole and then the vacuum attachment was well sealed to my back so as to prevent any draw of outside air. Then there was a hose connected to the attachment on my back, at one end, and to a battery powered pump, at the other end. The pump was equipped with a holding container for the blood and fluid that was to be extracted. I had to wear/carry this pump with me twenty four hours a day. I had to learn how to sleep with it on and was not able to shower, only sponge bath while having it attached to me. It was like it was part of me now. It was awkward and painful and I hated it!

At this point, for me, the surgery was a failure. I was once again travelling to the hospital three times a week, at my own expense, to have this pump dressing changed. The process lasted for six long months. Then somewhere along the way, one of the nurses said that I should have had tried the pump before having surgery. She said that it might have saved me a lot of pain and grief. Really? Now someone suggests this? I guess we will never know, now.

Every time I would go for a dressing change, I would ask the nurses if they thought it was getting any better. I still had to get someone to drive me for dressing changes for a few months, until I got my license back. Derek would take time off work or I had friends who were willing to take me, when I asked. In addition, the stress and pain of having the dressings changed, tired me out. It was probably best that I was not driving any way, considering the pain meds I was taking had a definite effect on my motor skills. I really don't think it would have been safe for me to drive even if I would have had my license.

I was quite a sight, I had lost most of my hair, I was using a walker, I walked like I had soiled my pants and now, I had this pump device hanging on me. It is amazing that I didn't get more stares and comments than I did. It was truly a living nightmare! In every way possible. Or, should I say another nightmare? You've all been reading and paying attention up to this point right?

The nurses at the clinic were all so very nice to me. There was one nurse in particular that I liked the best. He was very gentle and patient with me. If you are reading this I want to thank you and tell you that you are an amazing individual and in my opinion, you have found your true calling.

I usually got the same individuals when I went in. This way they could keep an eye on my progress and perhaps notice any subtle changes that were occurring, from week to week. I was a frequent flyer at our hospital for sure and to this day when I walk through the halls I still see and talk to several of the many wonderful people who have helped me over the years.

After a while, I had a lot of trouble with the skin around my wound breaking down and getting raw and irritated from having the dressing changed so often. Sometimes when they would remove the tape, they would peel off a layer or two of skin with it. Even after the hole got to a point where they thought I didn't need the pump anymore, I still needed to keep a bandage on it, in order to keep it clean. This went on for months and during the same period I would go in to see the surgeon every couple of months. This doctor was so arrogant that he would book all of the patients that needed to see him that day for 9:00 am. Then at times, he would not even show up to the hospital until after 10:00 am, which meant that we would all have to wait, for however long it took to see him, one by one. I never got out of the hospital before noon on the days I was supposed to see him and it was always the same thing. It was a short two minute visit with him just poking at me and saying very little.

The last straw with him, for me, was the last time I had an appointment to see him. My appointment with him had been booked for 9:00 am and I had a separate appointment with my family doctor the same day at 11:00 am. Her office is not located in the hospital, which meant that I had to travel between appointments. As usual, I waited and as it got closer to the time that I needed to leave in order to get to my other appointment, I told the nurses that I would need to leave soon. They informed me that he was usually late and that today was no different. It was 10:30 am and he wasn't even in the hospital yet. In addition to making the patients wait, he was also late for a meeting with another doctor. I know this because I heard the other doctor angrily complaining in the hallway about the surgeon's tardiness. That was it! I had enough. I told the nurses that I was leaving and informed them that I wanted them to tell the surgeon that it would be a cold day in hell before I would ever let that so called doctor look at or touch me, ever again! I was very angry and upset. The nurse could tell from my actions and my tone. She felt bad and was very apologetic. I told her that I did not feel it was her fault, but that I still wanted her to tell him just how angry I was. Not that it was really going to make any difference to him. But in some small way, I think it made me feel a little better.

I just made it to my family doctor in time and when I saw her, I told her of the recent events. She told me that I would not have to go back to see him and that, if necessary, she would refer me to someone else. That said however, she felt that she could monitor my progress and healing from that point on. She also apologized which I found to be comforting. But the thing that really bugged me, was that all these nice and courteous people were apologizing for the same arrogant surgeon who thought his time was more valuable than everyone else. He is the only doctor out of all of the ones that I have seen throughout my journey (almost forty different individuals) that I would never endorse. In my opinion he is in the wrong profession.

It was ten months after my surgery when the hole in my back finally closed over. Even to this day, I believe that there is still tissue growing underneath the scar, trying to fill in the void. For over two years, it has looked like I have a belly button on my back. At one point, I thought I was going to have accept and learn to live with that too. But slowly, little by little, it is starting to fill in. The surgery has left me with permanent nerve damage all over my back, along with large scars that looks like lop sided wings. The nurses call them my angel wings. I guess I feel like I have earned them after what I have been through.

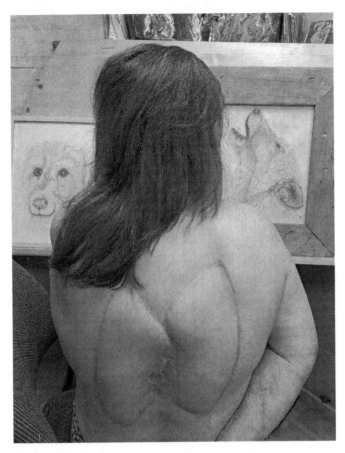

I still have regular pain. But, I am no longer taking the pain medications. Slowly and with focused determination, I was able to wean myself off of them.

I am glad that the hole has healed over and I do wish that I had been better informed before authorizing such a procedure. I have learned a great deal and many valuable lessons. My wish for any of you out there who are thinking of having reconstructive surgery is that you make sure to ask a lot of questions and always get a second opinion. Especially, if your situation is as unusual as mine was.

It's your right to ask questions. Don't let yourself be butchered.

# CHAPTER 15

*The Volleyball*

After I had my heart attack, the doctors in Saint John found a cyst on one of my ovaries that was very large. At that time, and considering everything else that was going on with me medically, it was not a concern that was real high on the list of priorities. If I was to make it, the cyst would have to be looked at and dealt with at a later date. There was no way that I would have survived having a surgery of that type then. Besides, at the time, it wasn't the biggest threat there was to my life.

Once I got back to Moncton and started to get back on my feet so to speak, I saw my OBGYN and she said that once I was feeling up to it, she would remove the cyst. I agreed and we set a time when I thought I might be ready. Otherwise, we would continue to monitor it and any progression until then. Shortly after my back issues started, we had another conversation and decided it was more important to get my back fixed first. We had no idea it would take two years for the whole process to play out. By that time, the cyst had grown to almost the size of a volleyball and was becoming uncomfortable, to say the least.

During the same time, she had gotten pregnant and was on maternity leave, so another very qualified and well educated doctor was filling in for her. After it seemed that my back issues were finally coming to a close, we scheduled a date for surgery. We then had a preparations consult in my doctor's office leading up to the date. She was very kind and thorough and, though I would have preferred to have my own doctor perform the surgery, I felt good about her stepping in. We had also discussed removing the ovaries and tubes at the same time. I agreed that it would be a good idea, as I would not be having kids at this late stage in my life and especially now with my heart condition. I always felt that my reproductive system had never really worked the way it was supposed to anyway, or we would have had children. So, with that said, it made sense to remove them and any other funky looking parts at the same time.

Years ago, I had some troubles with some cancerous cells in my reproductive system and it was unknown if that would have affected my ability to get pregnant or give birth. I think that deep down, a part of me always knew I would never have children. I accepted it and lived with the thought that if it did happen, I would be thankful and if it didn't, there was a reason and I would accept whatever fate had brought my way. Regardless, I do not feel that I had any less of a life because we did not have children. I feel that my life has been full and complete with Derek and our animal family.

By removing both ovaries, it would eliminate the possibility of having to do another surgery in case another cyst were to appear. There was a concern that once she got into the surgery she may find scar tissue from all of the bleeding that had taken place during my heart attack and the damage that had been done to my liver. We discussed it and I gave her my permission to remove any other parts that she felt should be removed, at the time. The last thing I wanted was to have to go through yet another surgery. So, if she felt that it was in my best interest, I told her that I would prefer that she perform a full hysterectomy. This way, I would be done with it all. I had already been having menopause symptoms for years, so I figured there was no chance of having children now any way. Much to my mother's, regularly verbalized disappointment. It's just a fact. I am no stranger to disappointing her though. In fact, I have spent a half a century trying to perfect my technique for ignoring it.

It ended up being a full two years after my heart attack before I could have the volleyball sized cyst removed. It had become very uncomfortable by the time July 2020 rolled around, which was the second date that had been scheduled. The first date had to be postponed due to the chaos of the pandemic. I was extremely nervous to have the surgery done, when the time finally did come, because Derek was not able to be with me, due to all of the restrictions that had been put into place. However, the good news was that my regular OBGYN was back from maternity leave and she was going to be performing my surgery herself. Knowing this made me feel much more comfortable. The original plan was that I would stay over night in the hospital, after the surgery, so that I could be monitored due to my heart issues.

I was really nervous! All I could think about was the last horrible situation I gotten into with my previous surgery, and this time Derek would not be able to be with me. I kept thinking that I may never see him again. Then I tried to keep reminding myself that I know this doctor and I trust her. Not to mention that this is a routine procedure. Even though it seems that I am not a routine patient, she knows what she is doing and I trust her. I had to go through with this because it could just keep getting bigger and eventually burst and I did not need that scenario added to my already arm's length list of complications.

The morning of the surgery Derek drove me to the hospital and dropped me off at the front door. He told me that he might not be in the hospital with me but that he would be close by, sending me good vibes, positive energy and love through the walls of the hospital. He said that the only thing that would be separating us would be some bricks and mortar. He actually stood and sat right next to the outside walls of the hospital, where the operating room was located. Waiting for a call from my doctor, who called him personally, as soon as the surgery was done. She told him that everything went well and that I was fine. She then told him that he could come in to visit me at 2 pm, that afternoon.

I was able to keep my uterus and she was able to do laparoscopic surgery. Which was less invasive and offered a much faster recovery and healing time, than if she had opened me up. In addition, there would be less scaring, which I already have plenty of. When I woke up from the surgery, I was pleasantly surprised. It felt like I had surgery done, but I was not in a great deal of pain. In fact, compared to what I had just previously experienced, this was nothing at all to be concerned about. They told me that I still had my uterus, that everything had gone well and the doctor would be in to see me a little later on.

I was admitted to a room and Derek came in to visit when 2 pm rolled around. Shortly after, the doctor came in and told me that seeing as everything went so well and because I was feeling good that I could go home, if I wanted to. She also said that the only reason she was allowing me to go was because she knew that I was in good hands and she thought I may do better resting at home, in my own bed. We all agreed that home was the best place for me to be and I got packed up and left the hospital with a smile on my face. I did heal very quickly and I felt better as each day passed.

It has been about a year since my last surgery, at the time of this writing, and I have been feeling the best I have in many years. I have been writing this book and working on re-doing a quilt that Derek's grandmother and mother made decades ago.

Now he will have a quilt that all three of us have worked on.

The changes in the way that things were done at the beginning of the pandemic gave me time to heal without any pressure or expectation from others. Albeit, Derek and I had no idea what the world was coming to, our little oasis was then and continues to be a healing refuge filled with positive energy. We have had our ups and downs, without a doubt. But, the one constant is that we have a special bond and a love for the life we have created together.

At the very beginning of the pandemic, we decided to get some laying hens. They are much more intelligent and entertaining than I thought they would be. They are social creatures and I have really enjoyed having and looking after them. We also have a new resident in the form of a beautiful, all black cat with yellow eyes, who has decided that she wanted to make our barn her home. I later found out that she came from the farm across the road from our place. Our neighbours decided to take in some male cats from a local rescue organization, to help look after the rodent population on their large hobby farm. The problem with getting the male cats was that they then started to bully the smaller cats and they eventually pushed this soft and friendly, beautiful little female out. So, in her search for a new place to call home, she started to hang around our barn and has never left.

We tried to introduce her to our cats, but it did not go very well. The new little female is so soft that our cats just tried to run her off. So, we built a big beautiful catio run and pen for our house cats and now Missy, the new resident, has a cat door in the heated outbuilding we use for an art studio / leather workshop for Derek and I. It used to be my grooming shop but proves to make a nice little "Missy hut", as I like to call it. I named her Missy because I did not want to get attached to her in case she decided to move on, at some point. She likes it so well that she has chosen to live here for a little over two years now. She helps me with my chores in the morning and earns her keep by helping to control the rodent population. She is very loving and loves to cuddle. She always has a warm or cool place to sleep and has full bowls of dry food and clean water. I make sure she stays parasite and flea free and she also gets a couple of treats on a daily basis.

Our neighbours at the farm across the road know that she is here. They told me that she was spayed and that they were sad to see her go, but were happy that she found a good place to live out the rest of her days. We love her and are happy that she has chosen to be part of our lives and home.

## School and Lessons Learned

I believe that, we, as human beings are put here on this earth to learn. To learn how to be kind and to love. To be kind to plants and animals and to truly love one another and most importantly ourselves.

When I had my event I was very unhappy with myself and my life. I was on a quick moving, out of control, downward spiral that was starting to really show itself in my health. I had so much self-hatred that I could not see anything clearly. I hated how I looked, no matter how little I ate or how much I exercised, I just couldn't seem to change my appearance. I hated how I talked, I hated how I thought and in most cases I hated most people in general. All I could see was pain and suffering and because of this, I think that my judgment was clouded. I could not see the potential for what my life really and truly could be. I learned that this behaviour and these views were normal, as I think you probably got from reading the early chapters of this book. This is just the way that life was for me. For me and the people that I grew up with. The people that, at that time, I still spent a great deal of time with. Then, I had no idea that life could be any or, in fact, so much different. Maybe keeping me from knowing this, was their goal all along?

I'm really not sure.

Even after everything that I have lived through and experienced, there are still times when I have trouble focusing on the present moment and really being conscious and aware. Habitual thinking, about the past or the future distracts me and brings disruption to my true happiness. Achieving and mastering the fine art of obtaining and maintaining balance in one's life, is truly the key to it all I think. Once there, however, it's a feeling and a way of living like none other I have experienced.

All of this is easy to say but not so easy to do. It takes constant discipline and habit changing hours of practice and time. Huge amounts of time. But, once you get there, once you have had the pleasure of living life in this way, I believe one comes to realize the real reason that we were given a chance to learn these valuable life lessons.

My journey is now closer to the end than it once was to the beginning and I still have so much more to learn. I wonder sometimes if my brain still has the capacity to learn what my soul needs to teach me before my time in this life runs out. My time is limited and I don't want to leave this vessel until I have learned all of my lessons and gotten A's on all my exams, if you will.

If one was to believe that life is like a school and that when we stop learning, we stop living then my heart attack and my trip to the beyond was a huge test and thankfully I passed. Or, I would have had to repeat a grade by leaving this vessel and moving on to another, in another life. My event was like being sent to the principal's office because I was failing miserably and was in danger of expulsion. I had received a good talking to by the one who makes the decisions and it was decided that I could come back to work harder and eventually graduate from this school of life, as it were.

The doctors tell me that this is my last chance and so I am working extremely hard, every day to keep my life and my thoughts on the right track. It is so very hard to unlearn what had been drilled into my head for so many years. Let's just say that I did not have the best of teachers. I was not encouraged to follow the paths that would have or could have led me to an enlightened and fulfilled way of being. Instead, I was encouraged to stay close to the ones who convinced me that they needed me and that their needs and wants were far more important than my dreams and goals. These were their lessons to me, which I then excelled at accepting and learning. I am not a victim, nor do I wish to come across as one. I was a product of my conditioning, at that time. *I* have done the work and I have learned that this behaviour was my choice, at the time. I *now* choose differently, much differently. I choose to live in a way that is best for me and my life.

Every bit of what has happened to me in this life has been to teach me something. The good and the bad, alike. I guess at times, I was slow to learn. Well up until now, that is. Or, maybe I just wanted to get each lesson, in as thorough a manner as I could, so that I would get it completely and not have to repeat any of these difficult lessons. I am now figuring things out much more quickly and learning my lessons completely. I am doing my absolute best to make the most of whatever time I have left.

I am surrounded by love and positive energy. All I have to do is look around me, to be reminded of this. I look at my animal friends, my husband and the family I have gained through our marriage and my friends. I am truly blessed! I know people who do not have this kind of pure love in their lives nor will they ever. They simply cannot understand the life lessons they are being given and will reach graduation day with a failing grade, and consequently will be sent back to repeat the process.

The people in my past that I have had to let go of, for the betterment of my own well being are failing at their life lessons, in my opinion. They are destined to live there lives over and over again until the lessons are learned and they get it right. I truly feel bad for them and I hope that they will open their eyes and hearts, so that they may live a truly well balanced, happy and healthy life. I understand that they are miserable and simply cannot spread love, joy and encouragement in such a state. I wish them well and I wish them much peace. Simply put, I am just not strong enough to do it for us both, anymore. Those are their lessons to learn. I will continue to work on and learn mine.

So, what's next for me? It's a question I ask myself everyday and some times all day every day. I have good days and bad days, both mentally and physically. There are days when I am very happy, feel good and can see all of the opportunities and possibilities in front of me. Then, there are days when I am very sad, hurt all over and cry all day and night. My recovery from all of the things I have talked about in this book, has been, and continues to be a very long, hard and bumpy road. But, I am going to keep fighting, with everything I've got. I'm going to keep doing the work. I'm going to keep doing the work for me and for others like me.

For others who have experienced similar situations or circumstances in their lives and need a little support and encouragement to keep fighting for something better. Or, for others who are just starting their journey in life and need to know that there is a better way. Those who may need to know that they don't have to endure the same type of pain and suffering, at the hands of another.

For those who, like me, were also taught in the ways of the wolf, but never allowed into the den, I would like to create a den. I would like to continue to share my experiences, my story and my strategies for coping with it all.

If any of my efforts, in doing this work and sharing my story and experiences, can help just one child who feels as empty, lonely and terrified as I have felt, my entire life, then I will consider my efforts to be a fulfilling success. I would like to create a den that embodies the true spirit of the wolf.

A community where any and all who understand and appreciate the meaning and application of these principles are welcome.

Live a well balanced life and be well my friends!

Love Always,

Tanya Jean

For those of you who may be interested in following more of my story and my journey, or would like to help with my efforts, in any way that you can. Please visit any one of the following sites for more information on how to get involved.

From one Artist's heart to another,

Thank you!!

www.mypathasanempath.ca

www.tanyajeanart.com

www.williamshousepublishing.com

# ACKNOWLEDGEMENT

A special Thank you to my true love and soul mate! I could
not have done this  without your love and support.

You have saved me everyday since we met!

# ABOUT THE AUTHOR

## Tanya Jean Steeves

Born with an Artist's heart

Thank you very much for buying and reading my book! I hope that in sharing my story and experiences, I have been able to help you or someone close to you, in some small way.

Love always,

Tanya Jean

# AFTERWORD

For those of you who may be interested in following more of my story and my journey, or would like to help with my efforts, in any way that you can. Please visit any one of the following sites for more information on how to get involved.

From one Artist's heart to another,

Thank you!!

www.mypathasanempath.ca

www.tanyajeanart.com

www.williamshousepublishing.com

Printed in Great Britain
by Amazon

36433834R00178